The Mystical Maze

Pat Means

Cover and book design: Gale Younker; cover photograph: KD Lawson; photo credits: UPI, Time Life; illustrations: Kevin Davidson; typesetting: Pacesetting Services.

Printed in USA

To Sandi,
for her love and understanding
during this whole project.

ACKNOWLEDGMENTS

This book has definitely been a team effort. Of the many co-laborers God provided to help in one way or another, Bryan Pollock deserves the lion's share of the credit. Bryan is a writer with the Publications Department of Campus Crusade for Christ, and was my research coordinator for the project. In addition, he did in-depth research on the Nichiren Shoshu/Sōka Gakkai movement and wrote Chapter VIII on Buddhism. Humanly speaking, without Bryan's help this book would not be a reality today.

I'd like to give special thanks to several other members of the team: Bill Parker was research assistant on the Hare Krishna movement and the Martial Arts; Neil Buttermore did invaluable research on Sun Moon and the Unification Church.

In addition, my thanks goes to John Weldon for reading and critiquing the manuscripts; to Alan Scholes for his help in editing and in organizing the Supplementary Research Section; to the brothers of the Spiritual Counterfeits Project in Berkeley, California, and to Mick van Buskirk of CARIS, for supplying much helpful information on the cults; to my editor, Cathy Hustedt, who did a tremendous job in "de-mystifying" my writing; and lastly to my secretary, Nancy Wilson, for her hours of running down books and cheerfully typing the manuscript.

I wish to thank the following for permission to quote from copyrighted materials:

Koestler, Arthur, *The Lotus and the Robot* (MacMillan Publishing Co., Inc., NY, ©1960, 1966).

Hesse, Hermann, *Siddhartha*, translated by Hilda Rosner (New Directions Publishing Corp., ©1951).

Watts, Alan W., *Beat Zen, Square Zen and Zen* (City Lights Books, San Francisco, ©1959).

Walker, Benjamin, *The Hindu World: An Encyclopedic Survey of Hinduism* (Frederick A. Praeger, Inc., NY, ©1968).

Weil, Andrew, *The Natural Mind: A New Way of Looking at Drugs and the Higher Culture* (Houghton Mifflin, Boston, ©1972).

Ornstein, Robert, *The Psychology of Consciousness* (Viking Press, Inc., NY, ©1972).

Smith, Adam, *Powers of Mind* (Random House, Inc., NY, ©1975).

Chapman, Rick, *How to Choose a Guru* (Harper & Row, NY, ©1973).

Suzuki, D.T., *Mysticism, Christian and Buddhist* (Harper & Row, NY, ©1973).

Pitt, Malcolm, *Introducing Hinduism* (Friendship Press, NY, ©1955).

Smith, Huston, *The Religions of Man* (Harper & Row, NY, ©1958).

Aven, Gene, *My Search* (Life Messengers, Seattle, WA, ©1972).

Sire, James W., *The Universe Next Door* (Inter-Varsity Press, Downers Grove, IL, ©1976).

Guinness, Os, *The Dust of Death* (Inter-Varsity Press, Downers Grove, IL, ©1973).

Stott, John R.W., *Your Mind Matters* (Inter-Varsity Press, London, ©1972). Used by permission of Inter-Varsity Press, Downers Grove, IL.

Alpert, Richard, *Be Here Now* (The Lama Foundation, San Cristobal, NM).

Table of Contents

PART ONE
THE MYSTICAL MINDSET

PART TWO
THE CULTS: PSYCHIC SLAVERY
IN THE WEST

*Seek for Your Self ... Enlightenment on Parade
... Chanting for Change ... Forgetting You
Remember.*

*Missionary Buddhism ... Short-cut to
Enlightenment ... Conversion by Force ... The
Chanting Meeting ... Chanting to Cheerleading
... Mystical Materialism ... Physical Equals
Spiritual ... Buddhist Monism ... Nirvana, Not
Heaven ... The Biblical Perspective.*

*Communing with Jesus? ... Innocent Victims ...
Divine Men ... Two Falls ... Serpent Blood ...
The "Third Adam" ... The Deity of Jesus ... The
Mission of Jesus ... Jesus' Miraculous Birth ... A
Female Holy Spirit.*

THE REFERENCE SECTION

FOREWORD

A recent Gallup Poll of college freshmen shows that 93% believe in God or some "universal spirit." This upsurge in religious faith is closely related to the influx of religious thought from the East.

As I have traveled throughout North America and Europe, I have observed this explosive growth of interest in the East. One can hardly pass through a major airport without being approached by the Hare Krishna. One can hardly walk across a university campus and not see the advertising of the TM movement.

Far from being a passing fad, this trend has major implications for the Christian. A subjective experience is becoming a substitute for objective evidence and for Scripture as people search for truth. Rational communication of the gospel is being muddied as mysticism redefines the meaning of almost all key biblical words and concepts.

After many of my lectures in universities, I am confronted by people influenced by eastern mysticism. There is a constant barrage of, "God is in everyone"; "Meditation is giving me all the peace that I need—I don't need Christ"; or "Jesus is just another manifestation of God like Krishna or Buddha."

Pat Means has given us the answers to these and many other questions in The Mystical Maze. Such a practical approach to understanding and communicating the gospel to the mystic cults is long overdue.

In addition, many Christians will find this to be a valuable resource for further study into the mystical movement. It is well documented and will be useful as a "mini-encyclopedia" on the eastern cults.

The Bible commands a Christian to be equipped to converse with others concerning his faith. I Peter 3:15 says the Christian is always to be "ready to make a defense to everyone who asks you to give an account for the hope that is in you."

As we get more involved in this spiritual battle against eastern mysticism, we had better have in our possession the best tools available. The Mystical Maze is definitely such a tool.

Josh McDowell
Traveling lecturer

INTRODUCTION

Today's Christian often looks with bewilderment on the proliferation of gurus, yogis and assorted swamis dotting the western landscape. What's behind the shift toward eastern religion? What's the secret of its appeal? And is there any way to effectively communicate the gospel of Jesus Christ to those who have adopted the eastern mindset?

This book is dedicated to giving some thoughtful answers to those questions. It is born out of nine years of evangelistic ministry on the college campus, and three years of intensive research and ministry within the eastern mystical subculture. The approach is intended to be very practical, rather than strictly philosophical. There are a number of excellent books available that cover the philosophical aspect of the new mysticism in more depth (e.g., Os Guinness' *Dust of Death*). There are virtually none available, however, that give the Christian the practical "tools" he needs to communicate effectively with those who are participating in one form or another of eastern religion.

To better equip the reader, each chapter is followed by either a summary of the key points, some practical "how-to's" in the area of communicating the Christian message or suggestions for further reading.

Because I'm not assuming any prior knowledge of eastern philosophy on the part of the reader, a glossary of eastern mystical terms, groups and personalities is included in the back. In addition, for those who desire to go into more depth, or to use this material to prepare lectures or articles, I have included a Supplementary Research Section in the back.

Just one final warning. As powerful as this material has proven to be, it has two limitations. It is not to become a substitute for the simple gospel, and it is not to become a substitute for love. No one is ever argued into the kingdom. Great sensitivity is called for to know *how much* of the facts to share with someone. There are many sincere spiritual seekers in the eastern subculture, but there are also many there who are merely turning away from a God who holds them accountable. In *either* case, a loving presentation of the simple gospel is the most powerful approach initially. Then one should share only as much of this material as he perceives a willingness to receive it.

This book is one part of a larger training package available from Campus Crusade for Christ to equip Christians in effective outreach into the world of eastern mysticism. Other materials include a Teacher's Guide for use in conjunction with this book, evangelistic literature and an evangelistic film on eastern mysticism.

The apostle Paul's warning to the Colossians in the first century is a theme that needs to be sounded again in the 20th: "See to it that no one takes you captive through hollow and deceptive philosophy, which depends on human tradition and the basic principles of this world rather than on Christ" (Colossians 2:8, NIV).

PART ONE

THE MYSTICAL MINDSET

"I don't know what you mean by 'glory,'"
Alice said.

Humpty Dumpty smiled contemptuously. "Of
course you don't — till I tell you . . . When I use a
word, it means just what I choose it to mean —
neither more nor less."

"The question is," said Alice, "whether you
can make words mean so many different things."

"The question is," said Humpty Dumpty,
"which is to be master — that's all."

—from *Through the Looking
Glass* by Lewis Carroll[1]

Mining the Eastern Mind

Mystic missionaries in the West? Political endorsements for Hindu religious movements? Yoga and meditation classes sponsored by local churches?

As improbable as these phenomena would have seemed even a generation ago, their presence in western society today denotes one of the most remarkable shifts toward the metaphysical in the history of western civilization.

Not that the gods of the East have been total strangers to the West, however. Even though western leaning has been predominantly Judeo-Christian through the centuries, western philosophers have, on occasion, been strongly influenced by thought from the Eastern World.

As early as the late 1600's the Dutch philosopher Spinoza was teaching Europeans a specialized form of pantheism, the dominant philosophy of India which stresses the divinity of all things.

In America, Hindu philosophy surfaced in the mid-1800's as New England transcendentalists such as Emerson and Thoreau preached their own specialized versions of pantheism. To Emerson, the "highest revelation" was that God existed in every person. "I am divine," he declared accordingly.[2]

As for Thoreau, who was in many ways a prototype of the 20th century mystic, he meditated, read the Hindu scriptures and practiced yoga faithfully at his famous Walden Pond. He described himself as "a mystic, a transcendentalist, and a natural philosopher to boot."[3]

It remained, however, for a Hindu swami named Vivekenanda to first bring *missionary* Hinduism to the West. A disciple of the revered Indian sage Ramakrishna, Vivekenanda turned up in 1893 at the Parliament of World Religions in Chicago where he astounded the Western World with his wisdom. Six years later, Vivekenanda founded the Vedanta Society in New York City.

At about the same time, another mystic sect, the Theosophy movement, was also founded in New York. These two sects have had a significant influence on a number of intellectuals in this century, including *Brave New World* author, British novelist Aldous Huxley.

The Psychologist's Search

Another 20th century student of eastern religion, especially of Zen Buddhism, was Swiss psychiatrist Carl Jung. Jung's particular sympathy for mysticism stemmed largely from his research into the irrational realm of the human mind. His psychologically-based defense of irrational mystical experience — a key ingredient in eastern religion — set the stage for much of the current interest in wedding western psychology to eastern spiritual practices.

Despite the interest of individuals such as these, eastern mysticism remained during most of this century the pursuit of a small minority of the intellectual elite. The base of eastern students was broadened, however, when a watered-down version of Zen Buddhism became the credo of the Greenwich Village beatniks in the early fifties. It was Alan Watts who ultimately emerged as the leading figure of that movement, remaining until his recent death the chief spokesman for the East in America.

By the early sixties, the Western World, and particularly its youth, was prepared *philosophically* for the rise of eastern mysticism. It remained only for the drug culture to prepare it *experientially*.

The parallels between the drug experience and its mystical counterpart make it understandable that the one should lead to the other. Both emphasize the attainment of states of altered consciousness, both are often described in religious terms (albeit pantheistic ones), and both look primarily to the traditions of the Orient for support.

A Realm Beyond Reason

Among other results, the drug experience gave many western youth a vision of a realm within themselves which was beyond reason and beyond the five senses. For many, the step from a drug-induced experience to the drugless enlightenment and "God-consciousness" promised by the eastern sects was a short one.

In 1967, the Beatles made their now-famous link-up with a then-unknown guru, Maharishi Mahesh Yogi and his occult-sounding product, Transcendental Meditation. In that same year Paul McCartney and John Lennon wrote "I Am the Walrus" which opened with the pantheistic declaration: "I am he as you are he as you are me and we are all together." "Instant Karma" followed in 1970 and the next year saw the release of George Harrison's "My Sweet Lord" with its alternating chorus of "Hallelujah" and "Hare Krishna."

The Beatle's songs were widely popular. Not only did their success help pave the way for a growing litany of eastern lyrics in rock music, but it did much to foster a general interest in all things eastern, from mysticism to the martial arts, from Vedanta to vegetarianism.

While the West was being prepared both philosophically and experientially for eastern mysticism, a number of self-appointed eastern messiahs began to head west to develop followings. These included Swami Prabhupada who brought the Hare Krishna movement in 1965, and, more recently, young Guru Maharaj Ji and Sun Moon who introduced the Divine Light Mission and the Unification Church respectively.

Packaged in western terminology and stripped of many of the strict disciplines associated with their mother religions in the East, these new cults have attracted hundreds of thousands of young people throughout the West in the last few years.

A Meditator's Market

The result has been the emergence of an eastern mystical subculture of vast proportions. The Transcendental Meditation movement (TM) has already initiated more than one million Americans into its ranks with 30,000 more joining each month. Another 100,000 Americans have completed the sixty hours of Erhard Seminars Training (est), which is a high-powered mixture of Zen, Scientology, and Dale Carnegie. The Buddhist sect known as Nichiren Shoshu/Sōka Gakkai currently claims 250,000 followers in the United States, the majority of whom are young Anglo-Saxons. Sun Moon's aggressive Unification Church has collected an additional 30,000 members, the Hare Krishna movement another 10,000. And there are virtually thousands involved in the Sufi cult, Zen Buddhism, Guru Maharaj Ji's Divine Light Mission and a dozen other cults.

All in all, more than two million people in the U.S. alone are actively involved in some eastern cult or discipline!

These statistics, however, represent just the tip of the iceberg, for the eastern subculture goes much deeper than mere statistics can reveal. In fact, there are actually three levels of eastern religious involvement in western society today.

At the center of this involvement are the hard-core members of various mystical cults; many of the two million just listed are

part of this core group. A larger group is comprised of the "dabblers" in eastern mysticism — the weekend meditators and others who may have read an occasional book on the subject, such as Hermann Hesse's *Siddhartha*, or who attend an occasional meeting of their local yoga group.

But the great majority who have fallen under the influence of eastern thought today is comprised of those who have never been to a cult meeting, have never read a book on mysticism, and who do not think of themselves as "mystics" or "pantheists" at all. This majority *has* nevertheless adopted a view of the universe that is saturated with eastern thought. And it is the widespread adoption of an eastern mindset — partial or otherwise — that is presenting the greatest challenge to the communication of the gospel in the West today.

The New Western Mystic

Why does this trend toward eastern thought present such a challenge to the would-be communicator of the gospel? Let's examine the mindset of the new western mystics at close range and find out.

Whatever their level of involvement, all of the new mystics share three distinctives: a pantheistic view of God, a subjective approach to truth and an emphasis on experience rather than reason. This is true whether the mystic is a fairly straight college student or a thoroughly Hindu yogi.

Pantheistic View of God

To understand the pantheistic view of God, let's contrast it briefly with the two other world views that have been predominant in 20th century thought.

Atheistic World View

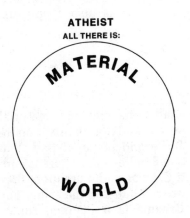

ATHEIST
ALL THERE IS:
MATERIAL WORLD

The atheist, or materialist, claims basically: "The only thing that exists is the material world — that which I can detect with my five senses. There is no supernatural, no 'spiritual reality' or God existing somewhere beyond the material universe."

Pantheistic World View

The pantheistic world view is the one which prevails in the East. The pantheist would agree with the materialist that there is just one level of reality. There is indeed no "spiritual reality" or God who is apart from the

PANTHEIST
ALL THERE IS:

THEIST
TWO LEVELS OF REALITY:
NATURAL & SUPERNATURAL

CREATOR

MATERIAL

CREATION

WORLD

material world. "Rather," says the pantheist, "God and the material world are one and the same. God is the sum total of all there is. He is not a separate being somewhere beyond the world; rather, all of the material world, everyone and everything in it is part of the Divine."

Theistic World View

Standing in sharp contrast to the materialistic and the pantheistic world views is that of the theist. The theist's reply to his two counterparts would go something like this: "I agree with the materialist that there *is* a material world that we detect with our five senses. But there is also a spiritual reality beyond the material world, and that reality is an infinite and personal God. You see, I believe that there is both a Creator *and* a creation; they are *not* one and the same. The Creator is a distinct, supernatural Being, and He has the ability to relate personally to His creation." (A relationship like that isn't possible for the pantheist, because it takes two separate identities to have a relationship.)

Over the last hundred years, the theistic, or biblical, world view has been steadily eroding from its position of dominance in the Western World. In a recent survey of 9,000 college students in the United States, only 33% still identified with the theistic view of a personal God. By comparison, 34% identified with the classical pantheistic notion: "God is in everyone; we're all part of God."[4]

The Cosmic Identity Crisis

The modern mystic holds to the pantheistic world view and thus believes that God, man and nature all share the same divine essence. There is no God "out there" to relate to; there is only one's own inner divinity to discover.

The process of realizing one's own divinity is described in mystic circles in various ways — "self-realization," "god-realization," "development of God-consciousness" — but all the terms really refer to the same self-deifying process. Each group, too, has a recommended technique for achieving the goal. Maharishi Mahesh Yogi, for example, claims, "He who practices Transcendental Meditation becomes acquainted with the inner divine consciousness."[5] Other groups might promote chanting or some other eastern discipline as the key.

Subjective Approach to Truth

The second major element in the eastern mindset today is a totally subjective approach to determining truth.

Have you ever talked to someone about Christ only to have him respond: "Well, that may be 'truth' for you. But what's true for you isn't necessarily true for me"?

This kind of subjectivism typifies the thinking of the new western mystic. Surveys indicate that such an initial response to the gospel will be given at least half the time on the college campus today. In the same nationwide survey cited earlier, only 37% were able to affirm, "There are certain absolute truths . . . certain beliefs are ultimately and universally true and others false." By contrast, 51% now believe, "Truth is basically relative; what is right or true for you may not be right or true for me."

For the majority today, a thing is "true" only if one *feels* it is. Truth has thus become subjective and relative instead of objective and absolute.

To Each, His Own

I remember a conversation I had with a student on a southern California campus whose response to the gospel was typically subjective:

"Well, that's fine for you," he said. "But it's not 'truth' to me. Whatever path helps you the most is fine for *you*, though."

"Yes," I said, "but there are certain absolutes. What about *after* this life? God's the one who created the ground rules for life. And we'll ultimately answer to *Him* in terms of where we spend eternity."

I'll never forget his response.

"I'm not going to the Christian heaven," he said vehemently. "And I'm not going to the Buddhist heaven or the Hindu heaven. *I'm going to my own heaven!*"

For this student there was no ultimate authority and no absolutes in the universe. Therefore, whatever he wanted to believe became, in his mind, "reality" and "truth."

The Experience Seekers

The subjective approach to determining truth is closely related to the third characteristic of the eastern mindset: an emphasis on experience rather than reason. The shift away from absolutes has resulted in a dethroning of the *mind* as the ultimate guide to reality and the elevation of intuition and feeling in its place. Personal *experience* has become the key to determining truth.

Perhaps the primary attraction of eastern mysticism lies in the promise of self-realization or God-consciousness through a mystical experience.

The rise of eastern mysticism in the West has presented many challenges to the Christian witness.

Anti-apologetics Bias

The swing away from the rational-analytical method of determining truth in favor of the experiential method creates a special challenge to the Christian witness: the mystical student does not tend to be as receptive to the traditional forms of evidence for the Christian faith.

Although a solid 48% of the 9,000 college students surveyed still indicated they would be "strongly influenced to believe that Christ was God" by rational, historical or testimonial evidence, a significant minority claimed they put no stock at all in that kind of objective evidence. A significant 15% indicated they would be unconvinced until Christ "appeared to them personally" and "demonstrated his miraculous power" — that is to say, until they had an overwhelming personal experience of their own.

Empty Cans

Another great challenge to the Christian witness is the current revolution in religious semantics. Because of the shift in world views from theism to pantheism, words like "God," "sin," "salvation" and "Savior" no longer convey the same meaning they did even ten years ago. To use Clark Pinnock's phrase, they have become "empty tin cans" to be filled with one's own meaning. Without understanding the shift in such terms, communication of the gospel to a mystic can be quite difficult. (A sample conversation with a hard-core mystic is included at the end of this chapter with suggestions on how to break through the semantic fog and clarify the issues of the gospel.)

Avoid the Extremes

There are two extremes to be avoided when sharing the gospel in the midst of the philosophical anarchy on campus. One extreme denies the need to understand current thought at all. Experience indicates, however, that a basic understanding of the secular mindset, and especially of the paradoxes of eastern thought, does help a lot of Christian students relate the gospel to the exact mental locus of their non-Christian counterparts.

On the other end of the spectrum are those campus witnesses who tend to give a lecture on comparative religion. This method has not proven wildly effective either.

Share the Simple Gospel

I'm often asked, "What do you share with someone who's into eastern mysticism?" My answer sometimes surprises them. I usually just share a simple presentation of the gospel, answering as best I can any legitimate questions that might come up in the course of conversation. The apostle Paul in I Corinthians 1:18 addresses himself directly to this issue:

"For the word of the cross is to those who are perishing

foolishness, but to us who are being saved *it is the power of God. . . ."*

And in I Corinthians 2:1, 2:

"And when I came to you, brethren, I did not come with superiority of speech or wisdom, proclaiming to you the testimony of God. For I determined to know nothing among you except Jesus Christ, and Him crucified."

During a recent trip to the midwestern United States, I had an encounter with a teacher of Transcendental Meditation. He had requested an appointment in order to see just what I was going to say in my campus lecture on TM. Before we met, I prayed that God would give me an opportunity to share the gospel; I certainly did not want to spend all of our time together arguing about whether or not TM is a religion.

After a time of getting acquainted, one of the teacher's first statements was, "I don't think there's any conflict between what we emphasize in the TM movement and what is taught in Christianity."

Sensing the opportunity I had prayed for, I replied, "Okay, let's check that out. I have here a brief presentation of what Christians believe. It's contained in this booklet called the Four Spiritual Laws. Why don't we go through it a point at a time, and you can tell me if there's any conflict with what you teach in TM."

The result was a tremendous hour-long discussion focused on his personal need for the Savior. What could have been a purely philosophical argument about extraneous issues turned into a discussion centered on Christ.

Clarify Three Key Issues

It's important to remember that except for the hard-core mystic, the mindset of the average college student today is really still a mixture of eastern philosophy and of more traditional beliefs, many of which are still based on a biblical world view. There are relatively few thoroughly indoctrinated mystics on campus who require some kind of totally unique approach.

But a definite shift in the general mindset *is* taking place. And with many western students today, there *will* be a need to clarify certain aspects of the Christian message. In particular, there are fundamental differences between the eastern and the Christian interpretations of three key issues: the issue of truth and how it's determined, the issue of sin and how it's dealt with, and the issue of Jesus and His identity. The next three chapters will cover each of these issues in depth in order to more fully equip the reader to be an effective communicator of the Good News in the midst of a changing campus scene.

For further reading on the subject of the eastern mindset please turn to page 219 *in the Supplementary Research Section.*

SOME PRACTICAL HELPS

I. Sharing Christ with the Mystic

The following is a sample evangelistic conversation with a hard-core mystic. Our purpose here is to give you a glimpse inside the mind of someone who is heavily into eastern thought and to present some clues as to how to deal with him. The mystic's semantic filter will be redefining the key words — yet all the while he will be inferring that the two of you are saying the same things!

Following each mystically-oriented response is a statement of its inherent weakness from a biblical point of view. (For a full presentation of the gospel as contained in the Four Spiritual Laws, see page 265.)

A. *God's love.*
   1. Christian: "God loves you and offers a wonderful plan for your life."
   2. Mystic: "Yes, I'll buy that. The God who is in everyone *is* all-loving and all-kind. There is no negativeness or condemnation emanating from Him who is an impersonal Absolute flowing through us all."
   3. Weakness: Only a distinct Being with a will and a personality can be "all-loving" and "all-kind." An impersonal Force, even a *positive* impersonal Force, cannot have the same capacities for loving and showing kindness as does a personal God. Explain God's love as seen in John 3:16. Also, share that God is clearly distinct from His creation: Psalms 102:25-27.

B. *Man's sin.*

1. Christian: "Man is sinful and separated from God. Thus he cannot know and experience God's love and plan for his life."

2. Mystic: "Well, man does sin in a sense. By that I mean he tends to hurt himself and his fellow man by being too attached to his own desires, his own opinions and his own identity.

   "What he needs is to get beyond all distinctions of good and evil, and to get rid of the illusion that he's a separate entity. You see, man's basic problem is his ignorance of his true identity; he just needs to realize his essential oneness with the Absolute."

3. Weakness: No concept of the vertical dimension of sin, i.e., that sin is a transgression against a holy God who is a separate and distinct Person. David's prayer after he sinned with Bathsheba was, "O God . . . against Thee, Thee only, I have sinned. . . ." See Psalms 51:1-4. For a complete discussion of the sin issue, see Chapter III.

C. *Jesus Christ.*

1. Christian: "Jesus Christ is God's only provision for man's sin. Through Him you can know and experience God's love and plan for your life."

2. Mystic: "Jesus Christ was indeed a manifestation of God. He realized His inner divinity, and He encouraged us to do the same. His teachings and His lifestyle were a magnificent example to us."

3. Weakness: First, a misunderstanding of Christ's claims to a *uniquely* divine identity. (See Chapter IV.) Second, a misunderstanding of the centrality of the cross in Christ's mission. Explain Ephesians 1:7.

D. *Receive Christ as Savior and Lord.*

1. Christian: "We must individually receive Jesus Christ as Savior and Lord. Then we can know and experience God's love and plan for our lives."

2. Mystic: "Each of us needs to find truth in his own way. Finding it through accepting Jesus is fine as long as you don't try to exclude other paths to God as being valid."

3. Weakness: Basically goes back to the misunderstand-

ing of the personal nature of God. If there is no personal God, then there is no accountability and, likewise, no ultimate truth. Any decision made is then a right decision. But the Bible teaches ultimate accountability. See John 3:16, John 5:25-29, Hebrews 9:27.

II. Summary of Key Points

A. *Characteristics of the new western mystic.*
1. Pantheistic view of God.
God, man and nature are all one.
All men are divine.
2. Subjective approach to truth.
All truth is relative.
There is no absolute truth.
3. Emphasis on experience. (Dealt with more fully in Chapter II.)
Experience and intuition are more valid than reason in determining truth.

B. *Challenges of eastern mysticism to the Christian witness.*
1. Anti-apologetics bias.
Hard-core mystics not as receptive to historical evidences for Christianity.
2. Semantics problem.
Key words like "God," "sin," "salvation " have been redefined by the mystics.

C. *The best approach.*
1. Share the simple gospel.
2. Be prepared to clarify three key issues:
a. Truth — how it's determined.
b. Sin — how it's dealt with.
c. Jesus — His unique identity.

III. Suggestions for Further Reading

1. James Sire, *The Universe Next Door*, (Inter-Varsity Press, 1976).
2. Os Guinness, *The East, No Exit*, (Inter-Varsity Press, 1974).
3. R. D. Clements, *God and the Gurus*, (Inter-Varsity Press, 1975).

Bibliography

1. Carroll, Lewis, *Through the Looking Glass*, (Random House, NY, 1971), p. 247.
2. Quoted in Paul F. Boller, Jr., *American Transcendentalism, 1830-1860*, (G. P. Putnam's Sons, NY, 1974), p. 78.
3. Quoted in Boller, p. 83.
4. See "National Religious Beliefs Survey" summary; Supplementary Research Section, pp. 220-222
5. Maharishi Mahesh Yogi, *On the Bhagavad-Gita: A New Translation and Commentary*, p. 141.

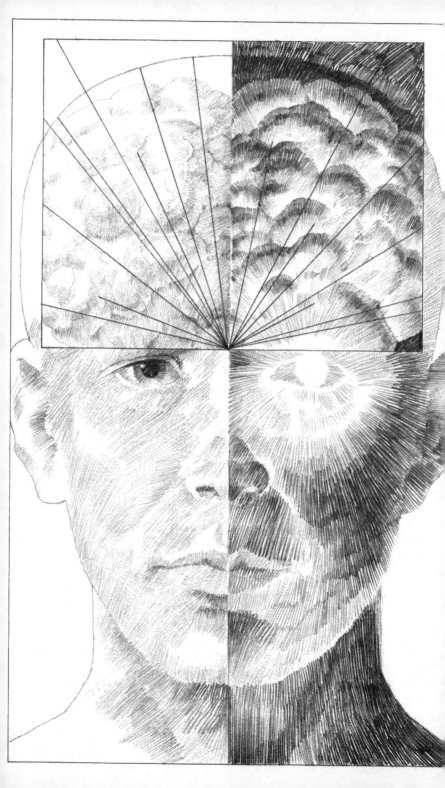

"Do not seek after truth, merely cease to hold opinions."

—Zen saying

"Ignorance is only created by the mind, and the mind keeps the secret that you are something Divine away from you. That is why you have to tame the mind first. The mind is a snake and the treasure is behind it. The snake lives over the treasure, so if you want that treasure, you will have to kill the snake. And killing the snake is not an easy job."

—Guru Maharaj Ji[1]

The Battle for the Brain

A pantheistic view of God, the deification of man, the loss of absolutes ... The effect of the new eastern mysticism on western thought has been profound. But none of the battles accompanying the invasion of eastern thought is destined to have as much impact on 20th century thinking as the battle surrounding the human brain. At stake is nothing less than the role of the mind in determining truth.

For centuries, western man has subscribed to rationalism — the belief that all knowledge can be determined through the intellect — and has relied on his mental faculties to perceive reality. In the West today, however, more and more often the questions are being asked: "*Is* truth in fact determined rationally as a function of the brain, or is it perhaps determined intuitively through some other element of perception? Is the mind a friend or a *foe* in the search for truth?" That such questions are even being raised illustrates the weakened grip of the rationalist viewpoint on the western mind.

Western rationalism received its first attack in the 20th century at the hands of post-war existentialists such as Albert Camus and Jean-Paul Sartre. Man, they told the world, is incapable of determining ultimate truth or finding meaning in life by using his mind because such things as "truth" and "meaning" do not *exist* in an irrational universe. The solution they propose is that each individual make up some sort of meaning of his own and live accordingly in order to escape the lonely meaninglessness of life.

A few years later, rationalism received further blows by theater-of-the-absurd playwrights Samuel Beckett and Eugene Ionesco, among others. According to their philosophy, life is utterly irrational, even absurd, and man cannot hope to infuse it with any kind of meaning — even that of his own devising. Their plays are written in nonsense language which forces the audience to abandon its reason altogether and begin to experience the absurdity being depicted onstage.

The Anti-mind Movement

But the strongest attack on the rational mind to date has come more recently from the eastern mystical subculture. In Zen Buddhism, for instance, one's intuition ("prajna") is pitted against one's reason ("vijnana") in an attempt to neutralize the mind, the idea being to "stop conceptualizing while remaining fully awake."[2] The Hindus refer to the mind as a "drunken monkey,"[3] the Hare Krishnas talk about the "garbage-pail mind."[4] And one chic new eastern cult called Arica has a song with a contemporary beat called "My Dear Mind, You Don't Exist"![5]

By the late '60s, the distrust of the rational mind was widespread among western youth. Reflecting the spirit of the age, the Mothers of Invention rock group sang out:

"What's the ugliest part of your body?
Some say your nose,
Some say your toes,
But I think it's your mind . . . ."

So why the wholesale sellout of the mind?

Rigidity of Rationalism

Perhaps it is partially a reaction against the rigidity of the rationalist philosophy that has held sway in the West for so long. To determine just why the rationalist viewpoint has become so unattractive to many, let's take a closer look at the philosophy.

According to the traditional rationalist, man is basically a machine, and his mind is just one of its many organs or parts. As

19th century rationalist Pierre Cabanis put it, "The brain secretes thought as the liver secretes bile."[6]

In his search for knowledge, the rationalist presupposes that his reason, which is the function of his brain-organ, is a completely reliable guide to truth. He also presupposes that all truth falls within the realm of the natural world, for, he believes, there is no supernatural or spiritual dimension to reality. For any conclusion to be considered valid by the mind, it must be based squarely on these two presuppositions.

In response to a survey question concerning the deity of Christ, one University of Michigan graduate student provided a clear example of the rationalist mindset:

> "Nothing would influence me to believe in supernatural persons or events. If such evidence were presented to me (for example, Christ appearing before me and demonstrating his supernatural powers), I would arrive at one of two conclusions: 1) some kind of trickery was involved, (or) if it were apparent to me that no trickery were involved, I would conclude, 2) I am insane."[7]

Perhaps another reason behind the popular abandonment of rationalism in the West is its inability to provide spiritual satisfaction. As Zen master D. T. Suzuki explains, "Zen has come to the definite conclusion that the ordinary logical process of reasoning is powerless to give final satisfaction to our deepest spiritual needs."[8]

So, whether we like it or not, the situation remains: offended by rationalistic rigidity and lured by the promises of the mystic, western youth have flocked to eastern mysticism by the thousands.

At this point, let's turn to the *eastern* mindset and see for ourselves just what it is that so many have found there.

The Eastern Mystical Viewpoint

Whereas the rationalist believes that all truth resides in the natural world, the eastern mystic believes that true reality is *spiritual* in nature. The mystic rejects also the rationalist view that truth is determined through one's mind. According to sometime mystic Aldous Huxley, author of *Brave New World*, the brain is *not* designed to perceive reality, but merely serves "to protect us from being overwhelmed by this mass of largely useless and irrelevant knowledge."[9] In Huxley's view, the brain acts as a screen against all data that is not absolutely useful for the physical survival of the body and is able to grasp only the mundane and the practical. In other words, the mind does a fair job of enabling you to ask, "Pass the butter, please," but when it comes to perceiving reality, one's mental faculties are useless.

The eastern mystic gives two primary reasons for his distrust of the brain when it comes to determining truth: First, the mind's dependence on language, with its pre-conceived categories of thought, necessarily conditions its perception of reality. In other words, the mind colors everything that goes through it and thus passes on a false view of reality to its owner. As Zen master Suzuki expresses it, "All our theorization fails to touch reality."[10]

Secondly, people tend to substitute words for experience, say the mystics. They become satisfied with intellectual concepts, instead of pushing on to first-hand experience which is more valid.

The Altar to Ignorance

According to the eastern viewpoint, then, the brain is not only useless in the determination of truth, it is a downright handicap. As a result, ignorance becomes a virtue in mystical circles. Zen spokesman Alan Watts tells us that the very core of Zen is a "sacred ignorance."

If the mind is an inadequate truth-perceptor, then how does the mystic perceive reality?

A New Organ of Perception

In virtually all the mystic sects there is talk of "a new organ of perception" in man, another way of "knowing." Yoga refers to the development of a "third eye" which gives spiritual sight to the advanced yogi. Other sects refer to the "intuition," the "psychic self" or the "unconscious mind" as the means of perception.

The first step toward spiritual growth, then, is to train oneself to ignore all the messages from the mind. Next comes attuning one's "second organ of perception" to the Universal

Mind, or the impersonal "god" of mysticism. Once attuned, the "psychic self" can bypass the mind and can thus perceive reality "directly."

The growing popularity of the *I Ching* (pronounced "E-Ching") is an example of the new reliance on intuition in the search for truth. Estimates of young people in America alone who look to it for guidance run as high as 600,000.[11] Literally translated "Book of Changes," *I Ching* is the Chinese Book of Divination.

I Ching Hexagram

The basic idea is that by randomly tossing coins (or Chinese yarrow stalks — either will do), a person will eventually be led to one of 64 pictographs, or hexagrams, in the *I Ching*. Accompanying each hexagram is a cryptic message such as:

"Return. Success.
Going out and coming in without error.
Friends come without blame.
To and fro goes the way.
On the seventh day come return.
It furthers one to have somewhere to go."[12]

As an individual meditates on this message and on any accompanying notes in the chapter, his intuition will eventually impress him with a course of action. The philosophical assumption is that the *I Ching* will help him bring his unconscious, *non-rational*, feelings to the surface — and that these feelings are more reliable to guide you than your conscious, rational ones!

But how do you know? How do you *know*, for instance, whether the impressions you receive from the *I Ching* are valid? How can you be *certain* that your "psyche" is really putting you in touch with God? Or, to pinpoint specific claims made by various eastern cults, how can you be sure that ultimate reality is in *fact* a "blue-skinned flute player with 16,108 wives" as the Hare Krishna devotees would tell you? Can you know without a doubt that the perfect manifestation of God in this age is a high-living teenager from India with a penchant for squirt guns and horror movies, as the Divine Light Mission claimed for so long?

Experience Is the Proof

The eastern mystics have an answer to this problem, and it is a simple one: the way to know whether or not a certain path is the "truth" is to experience it. As Meher Baba, one recently departed "messiah" put it:

> "In the spiritual life it is not necessary to have a complete map of the Path in order to begin traveling. On the contrary, insistence upon such complete knowledge may actually hinder rather than help the onward march . . . . He who speculates from the shore about the ocean shall know only its surface, but *he who would know the depths of the ocean must be willing to plunge into it.*"[13]

Ex-Beatle and current Krishna follower George Harrison points to the mystical experience induced by chanting the Hare Krishna *mantra* as proof for the validity of Krishna. In an introduction to some of the Hare Krishna literature, Harrison says that it's pointless to believe in something without "proof." He further states that the proof of the pudding is in the *eating.*[14]

A follower of teenage Guru Maharaj Ji once led me through this line of non-reasoning. George was explaining to me that the Guru claimed to be the "Lord of the Universe" and a divine incarnation.

"How do you know the Guru's claims are true?" I asked.

"You close your eyes," George replied, illustrating. "You close your ears. You look within yourself. And then you know." He opened his eyes again.

"So you're saying that the *experience* the Guru gives you proves his claims?"

"That's right."

"But," I persisted, "how do you know what you had an experience *with*?"

George shrugged. "You just know," he said.

At this point the non-mystic might well interject the argument that no experience can prove anything to anybody except that one has, in fact, *had* an experience. Does the fact that Guru Maharaj Ji can teach you a "high"-producing technique prove his claim to be "Lord of the Universe?" No — it merely proves that you can experience a "high" through his technique. Even more basically, does the fact that someone feels "enlightened" during meditation prove that he has had an experience with the Divine? No — it merely proves that someone feels "enlightened" during meditation.

Even pro-mystic psychologist Carl Jung admits as much in his foreword to Suzuki's *An Introduction to Zen Buddhism.* Observes Jung:

> "We can of course never decide definitely whether a person is *really* 'enlightened' . . . or whether he merely imagines it. We have no criteria for this."[15]

Does It Work?

But there's a more important point to understand here. In his book, *Your Mind Matters*, John Stott has observed that we have become a generation of "pragmatists." For the majority, mystically oriented or otherwise, the question no longer is, "Is it the truth?" but, "Does it work?" The inference of eastern philosophy is that if a religion produces an experience in an individual, then it does work and that is all that's necessary.

In eastern mysticism it *doesn't matter* whether a person is really "enlightened" or whether he's deluding himself in a fantasy world of his own making. All that matters is that he have some sort of satisfying mystical experience. As Andrew Weil expresses it, "It would seem obvious that the only meaningful criterion for the genuineness of any spiritual experience . . . is the effect it has on a person's life."[16] Whether or not he's in touch with reality is apparently irrelevant.

Fact and Fantasy

People who blur the lines between fact and fantasy and make reality what they want it to be based on how they feel are generally classified by society as psychotic. "But," says the mystic, "maybe it's society that's wrong and the mental patients who are right!" To quote again from Mr. Weil:

> "I am almost tempted to call the psychotics the evolutionary vanguard of our species. They possess the secret of changing reality by changing the mind; if they can use that talent for positive ends, there are no limits to what they can accomplish."[17]

British psychiatrist R. D. Laing would concur with Mr. Weil. Schizophrenia, he asserts, is just one way of seeing reality, normality another. "But who is to say which is the madness, especially considering the results of normality have been so disastrous in the West?"[18]

What do you say to a generation that considers ignorance a virtue and whose hero is the psychotic? What kind of warning is sufficient to communicate the dangers inherent in such a mindset?

For those who have already programmed their minds to reject the rational and who respond only to the experiential, no verbal warning will ever be sufficient. Tragically, many will have to enter the ranks of the eastern mystical casualties before they'll listen.

Obeying the Impulse

Just recently, my pastor asked me to accompany him on a call to a young man who was heavily into mysticism, psychic healings and a number of other related trips. I wasn't able to go, but when I called later to hear the outcome, I learned that the young man never made it to the appointment. It seemed that the night before, he had entered a deep mystical trance during which he continued to get a strong intuitive impulse to jump out his second-floor window. The message seemed to say that if he did this, he would be able to fly. As the session wore on and his impulse grew stronger, the young man became convinced that he was experiencing a valid psychic impression from God. His rational mind argued for awhile, but he eventually obeyed the impulse and jumped.

Two broken legs and a fractured skull later, the young man in question committed his life to Jesus Christ from a hospital bed. It had taken a near-tragedy to make him realize the deception inherent in the psychic/intuitive realm.

The Dangers of Defenselessness

There are really several practical dangers involved in relying on one's psyche or intuition to determine truth. Let's turn now to two of the major ones.

Eastern mysticism makes a deliberate attempt to break down the defenses of the rational mind. As Sufi mystic George Gurdjieff expressed it:

"We must destroy our buffers; children have none; therefore we must become like little children."[19]

The assumption here is that man has no enemies from which to protect himself apart from his own mind and its delusions. Some mystics will even use Christ's words to support this practice: "Unless you are converted and become like little children, you shall not enter the kingdom of heaven."[20]

The mystic here, of course, is taking Christ's words out of context, for He goes on to say in the next verse: "Whoever humbles himself as a child, he is the greatest in the kingdom of heaven." It is the *humility* of a child that Jesus wants from us, not the *defenselessness* of a child.

On a practical level, can you imagine the results of emptying a busload of two-year-olds in downtown New York City? And yet the eastern mystic would have us practice the same kind of irresponsibility in the spiritual realm.

Danger # 1: Human Deception

The first danger involved in relying on one's intuition to determine truth concerns human deception.

The history of western fascination with eastern messiahs is littered with examples of holy hypocrisy. (Although hypocrisy is by no means limited to the mystical subculture!) Guru Maharaj Ji's extravagant lifestyle at the expense of his disciples and his ultimate dethronement from the position of "Perfect Master" by his mother illustrates the potential for fraud among supposed spiritual masters.

The problem is so acute that there is even a book out called *How To Choose a Guru*. In this volume, author Rick Chapman states, "Because of the myriad 'masters' and teachers who have flooded the market since the recent interest in mysticism, the real task before the spiritual seeker today is not to find a guru but to sort out an authentic one."[21]

So how does the mystic separate fraudulent spirituality from the real thing? One way is to give himself over mindlessly to each "master" in turn in a kind of psychic Russian roulette. Former war activist Rennie Davis, apparently believing in the validity of such a technique, turned first to Guru Maharaj Ji. He had been leery of the master at first, but then:

> "I just surrendered my mind completely to Guru Maharaj Ji and said, 'No more — from now on out you do the thinking and I'll do the listening.' "[22]

This type of mindless approach has resulted in thousands of disillusioned ex-devotees of the Guru. They join a whole host of western youth who have become victims of human deception within various of the other mystical cults.

But there is an even greater danger involved in relying on one's intuition than that of human deception.

Danger # 2: Spiritual Deception

A very real phenomenon which has remained unacknowledged in mystical circles is the ability of the demonic world to counterfeit spiritual experience. In his second letter to the Corinthians, the apostle Paul warned of false prophets, calling them "counterfeits of the real thing, dishonest practitioners." He goes on to say, "Nor do their tactics surprise me when I consider how Satan himself masquerades as an angel of light."[23]

Much of the mystic's reluctance to consider the possibility of evil deception stems from his "monistic" viewpoint of life. In monism, God is considered the sum total of all there is; everything in the universe is really one and the same. As a follower of Sri Chinmoy once explained to me, "God is both personal and impersonal, finite and infinite, good and evil." If God is indeed everything, then the possibility of a distinct demonic world must be ruled out.

Mass murderer Charles Manson saw the logical extension of this reasoning: "If God is One," he said, "then what is bad?"[24] And, indeed, there is no "bad" in the monistic viewpoint as we shall see in the next chapter.

This may be an attractive world view for some, but in fact it lays a person who is relying on "psychic insights" and "intuitional impulses" wide open to the worst sorts of spiritual deception. The greatest danger regarding "psychic insights" and "intuitional impulses" is that they are not subject to any kind of rational analysis as to their source.

Christianity is not down on spiritual experience. But it is down on false spiritual experience, the type that gives a certain satisfaction in the short-run but ultimately brings great harm to the practitioner. One of the major weaknesses in the whole mystical approach to truth, it seems, is its short-sightedness. It never encourages the evaluation of possible repercussions or results, but, like Meher Baba, just exhorts us to "plunge in!"

Where is the balance in the search for truth? Has anyone ever charted a course that avoids both the extreme of arid intellectualism and that of mindless mysticism?

The Living Logos

Someone has. And the very titles by which He is known reflect that balance. Jesus Christ is referred to as "the Truth" (an intellectually-based title), but He is also known as "the Life"[25] (an experientially-based title). The apostle John describes the mysteries of experiential union with Christ,[26] but he also refers to Him as the "Logos."[27] "Logos," translated "Word," is a descriptive Greek title associated with the wisdom of God and the ordering principle of the cosmos.

Jesus offers a very real experience, but He always encourages man to investigate Him rationally before experiencing Him. Ultimately, He calls for a commitment of faith, but it is a faith to be based on facts and not a mindless faith.

The fifth chapter of the Gospel of John illustrates Jesus' desire that we base our belief in Him on facts. In John 5:18-47, a confrontation takes place between Jesus and the Jewish leaders of the day. The confrontation is sparked by Jesus' claim to be equal with God (vs. 18).

Instead of backing down when the leaders arrive, Jesus adds more fuel to the fire by interjecting several additional claims, namely that:

    (1) He alone has the power to give eternal life to the individual (vss. 21, 24).

(2) He alone will ultimately judge all men on the basis of their belief in Him (vss. 22, 25-27).

(3) All men should honor Him equally with the Father (vs. 23).

In a monotheistic Jewish culture, statements such as these were pure blasphemy, punishable by death. If ever there was a need to accurately and objectively validate a claim to truth, this was it.

If Jesus had taken the mystical approach to validation, He would have said something like this: "Men, I tell you what. You want proof, right? Well, I have this secret word I'd like to give you. If you meditate on it, it'll produce a very pleasant sensation. You may even develop a few powers that other people don't have. So how about trying it? I'm sure as soon as you begin to meditate, you'll have a real experience, and all your doubts about me will be cleared up."

In actuality, however, Jesus totally rejected that kind of subjective validation. "If I alone bear witness of Myself, My testimony is not true (vs. 31)," He said. Instead, Jesus points to two pieces of *objective* evidence to support His claims. These are perhaps the two main pillars in the case for the unique deity of Christ.

Pillar # 1 His Miraculous Works

"For the works which the Father has given me to accomplish, the very works that I do, bear witness of Me, that the Father has sent Me" (vs. 36).

Throughout His earthly ministry Jesus coupled His claims of deity with "attesting signs" or miracles. The "ultimate sign," He prophesied, would be His own physical resurrection from the dead. And, indeed, Jesus' empty tomb stands today as a silent testimony of the legitimacy of the God-man who dwelt among us. Jesus staked much of His credibility on the reality of that historical event.

I was speaking on "Evidences for the Resurrection" in a university religion class a couple of years ago when the professor interrupted, "Mr. Means, you're going to great lengths to prove that the resurrection really happened as an event in history. But wouldn't you agree that it doesn't really matter whether it happened or not; what counts is whether you *believe* it happened?"

As he was speaking, Paul's response to a similar question came to mind. Turning to I Corinthians 15, I read a passage that answered his question directly and succinctly:

"If Christ has not been raised, then your preaching is in vain, your faith also is in vain. Moreover, we are even found to be false witnesses of God . . . and if Christ has not been raised, your faith is worthless; you are still in your sins."[28]

One of the strongest biases of the monist is his bias against history. Because he believes only in the relative, not the ultimate reality of events in the space-time universe, the hard-core mystic cares little whether or not a certain thing actually happened. In Hinduism, for instance:

"It makes little difference to the worshipper whether the object of his devotion is a historical figure or a mythological one. History is relatively unimportant."[29]

But in Christianity, history is of ultimate importance! If Christ's death on a hill outside Jerusalem were only "maya" or "illusion," and God had not planned that event "before the foundation of the world"[30] as the means to man's salvation, then Christianity would be a hoax. Likewise, if Christ had remained in the tomb instead of rising as He prophesied, He would have clearly demonstrated that He was only mortal like the rest of us. His claim to be God's only Son and a sacrifice for our sins would have become meaningless. Christ asks us to weigh His claims with our intellect, and He points to his "miraculous works" culminating with His resurrection from the dead as the first objective piece of evidence for His validity.[31]

Pillar # 2 Fulfillment of Prophecy

"You search the Scriptures, because you think that in them you have eternal life; and *it is these that bear witness of Me* . . . . For if you believed Moses, you would believe Me; for he wrote of Me" (John 5:39, 46).

Christ is referring here to the more than 300 prophecies

made by the Hebrew prophets from Moses onward hundreds of years before His birth. Every one of those prophecies — including those relating to the town of His birth, the actual year of His coming, the exact amount to be paid for His betrayal, the manner of His death and so on — was fulfilled in minutest detail during the 33 years of Jesus' life.[31]

The contrast both in quantity and in accuracy between the prophecies concerning Christ and the "prophecies" floating around the Aquarian subculture is almost laughable.

Guru Maharaj Ji, for instance, claims that the prophecy in Matthew 24:30 concerning the second coming of Christ (". . . they will see the Son of Man coming on the clouds of the sky with power and great glory") was fulfilled in 1971 when he flew into Los Angeles from India on TWA Flight 761![33]

There is nothing in all of history comparable to the overwhelming evidence for the deity of Christ. And the fact that God has gone to such great lengths to objectively validate His Son's claims says much about the importance God places on man's mind.

Satan's Strategy

As we've seen in this chapter, Satan's strategy in the Age of Aquarius is to convince men to eliminate truth as being unworthy of consideration. His effectiveness in this endeavor has been stunning.

The next step in the satanic strategy is equally chilling. The systematic annihilation of the brain's reasoning powers through a sort of "mystical frontal lobotomy" is followed by the narcotic of the mystical state itself. The end product is an individual desensitized to truth and adrift in a sea of subjectivism.

H. L. Mencken, the anti-supernaturalist critic of Christianity, once said that "faith may be defined briefly as an illogical belief in the occurrence of the improbable."[34] But Mencken was wrong. True faith is the resting of the mind on the sufficiency of the evidence.

Christ said in John 8:32: ". . . you shall know the truth; and the truth shall make you free." We can offer nothing less to a generation that is rapidly losing touch with reality.

For further reading on the subject of the Battle for the Brain please turn to page 222 in the Supplementary Research Section.

SOME PRACTICAL HELPS

I. Three Approaches to Determining Truth

The following diagrams and explanations could be used in a discussion contrasting the biblical approach to truth with the rationalistic and the mystical approaches. Such a discussion could perhaps become a springboard into sharing the evidence for Christ's deity. In all three diagrams, "F" stands for "Finite" and "I" for "Infinite."

A. *Rationalist*

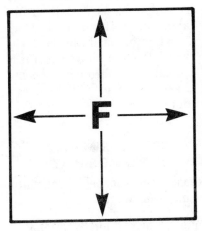

The rationalist lives totally within the boundaries of the finite world. For him, the infinite does not exist, and the finite, material world is all there is. Therefore, he believes, all the truth there is to know can be discovered through his five senses and the use of logic.

The rationalist's two key presuppositions are: (1) Reason is the only reliable guide to truth, and (2) The supernatural does not exist.

B. *Mystic*

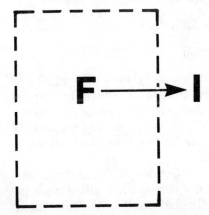

For the mystic, the finite world is "maya" or illusion. Ultimate reality is found only in the infinite realm.

There is no boundary between the finite and the infinite except in one's mind. So the key to finding reality is to mentally *erase* the boundary and *become* the Infinite oneself.

In this way one will know absolute truth *experientially*.

C. *Christian*

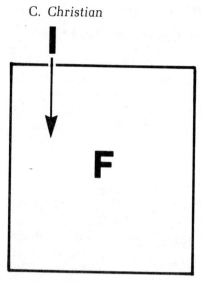

For the Christian, as for the rationalist, the finite world is real. It creates genuine boundaries around our ability to know first-hand what the Infinite is like, and what absolute truth is.

But the Infinite has invaded the finite world, has taken on a finite form Himself and has *revealed* to us certain truths about the Infinite, about God.

While on earth, Jesus Christ validated the source of these revelations through a significant body of objective evidence.

D. *Summary*

WORLD VIEW	TRUTH PRIMARILY DETERMINED BY:
RATIONALIST	Reason and sensory observation of material world.
MYSTIC	Intuition or psychic experience.
CHRISTIAN	Revelation, as evaluated by the rational mind.

II. A Mystic Objection

This may be one objection you'll encounter:

Mystic: "You can't approach God rationally! He's beyond all our attempts to fit Him in a logical little box. The *only* way to approach Him is spiritually." *One possible response:* "Well, it's true that our relationship to God *is* ultimately a spiritual one. And we're not saying that our finite minds can totally understand everything about God.

"But Jesus said in John 4:24 that 'God is spirit; and those who worship Him must worship Him in *spirit* and in *truth*.' He wants us to emphasize both: a spiritual relationship with Him that is more than an intellectual mind trip, but also a relationship that is based on the *truth* about God, and not based on falsehood. He's given us a mind to help in the search for truth and to keep us from being deceived."

Then you might ask, "Do you think it's possible to be spiritually deceived?"

Depending on his response, you might want to share about human deception (e.g., Guru Maharaj Ji) and spiritual deception (Satan masquerading as an angel of light).

III. General Suggestions

A. *Avoid over-emphasis on your testimony.*

Do not play up your testimony when sharing with mystics. Because of their experiential orientation, they can usually share a fairly dramatic testimony of their own. Your discussion would then be reduced to a subjective "battle of the testimonies"!

Instead, concentrate on coupling your personal experience with the objective evidences for the Christian faith.

By the way, you might want to examine your own walk with Christ. How much of your motivation is based on feelings? Many Christians have picked up the experience-orientation of the world and have imposed it on their Christian lives. Our walk with Christ is to be by *faith* in Him and in His promises, with the feelings coming as a result. See Hebrews 11:1, 6.

B. *How to use apologetics.*

Most of this chapter has focused on the need for apologetics, i.e., evidences for the Christian faith, in our witnessing. It's vitally important, then, that we understand how to use apologetics.

1. As you share, remember: Love is more important than knowledge. (See I Corinthians 13:2.) Often, an individual or an audience is looking more closely at how you're coming across than at what you're saying. Avoid contentious arguments at all costs!

2. Sometimes God will use a presentation of the objective evidences for Christ's deity to prepare an individual to receive Him as Savior. This was the case with the Jews

in Thessalonica who were "persuaded" by Paul's "giving evidence." (See Acts 17:1-4.) This should be our hope every time we share.

3. For many, the chief obstacle in coming to Christ is not an intellectual one (based on what they know or don't know), but is a moral and volitional one (based on their will). Romans 1:18-32 is a picture of the person who is "suppressing the truth," "knowing God but not honoring Him," etc.

Even with this type of individual, Christians have a responsibility to share, in love, the overwhelming evidence pointing to Christ as the Lord of Life. In a sense we are called to leave him "without excuse." (See Romans 1:20.) That is, our goal is to leave him with a clear understanding that his rejection of Christ is not based on the insufficiency of the evidence, but is simply a matter of his self-will. I usually review Law II of the Four Spiritual Laws with this type of person and explain that self-will is the heart of the sin problem described in the verses cited there.

IV. Suggestions for Further Reading

1. James Sire, The Universe Next Door, (Inter-Varsity Press, 1976).
2. Josh McDowell, Evidence that Demands a Verdict, (Campus Crusade for Christ, 1972).
3. John R. W. Stott, Your Mind Matters, (Inter-Varsity Press, 1972).

Bibliography

1. From Satguru Maharaj Ji, an uncopyrighted publication of the Divine Light Mission, Denver, CO.

2. Ornstein, Robert, The Psychology of Consciousness (Viking Press, NY, 1972), p. 156.
3. Quoted in "Oz in the Astrodome," New York Times, December 9, 1973; p. 88.
4. Quoted in Daniel Cohen, The New Believers: Young

Religion in America (M. Evans & Co.,NY, 1975), p. 112.

5. Smith, Adam, *Powers of Mind* (Random House, NY, 1975), p. 267.

6. Cabanis, Pierre Jean Georges (1757-1808), quoted in James W. Sire, *The Universe Next Door*, (Inter-Varsity Press, Downers Grove, IL, 1976), p. 65.

7. See "National Religious Beliefs Survey" summary in Supplementary Research Section.

8. Suzuki, D. T., *An Introduction to Zen Buddhism*, (Grove Press, NY, 1964), p. 59.

9. Huxley, Aldous, *The Doors of Perception*, quoted in Robert Ornstein, *The Psychology of Consciousness* (Viking Press, NY, 1972), p. 19.

10. Suzuki, op. cit., p. 41.

11. Petersen, William J., *Those Curious New Cults* (Keats Publishing, Inc., New Canaan, CT, 1973), p. 27.

12. *Book of Changes*, Number 24, "The Turning Point," quoted in Petersen, ibid., p. 30.

13. Baba, Meher, *Discourses, I, II, III* (Sufism Reoriented, San Francisco, 1967), p. 191, quoted in Charles T. Tart, ed., *Transpersonal Psychologies* (Harper & Row, NY, 1975), p. 230.

14. Harrison, George, *Preface to Krishna, the Supreme Personality of God-head*, Swami Prabhupada, (Bhaktivedanta Book Trust, Los Angeles, 1970), p. ix.

15. Jung, Dr. Carl, Foreword to D. T. Suzuki, op, cit., p. 15.

16. Weil, Andrew, *The Natural Mind: A New Way of Looking at Drugs and the Higher Consciousness* (Houghton Mifflin, Boston, 1972), p. 67, quoted in Sire, op. cit., p. 181.

17. Weil, ibid., p. 182, quoted in Sire, ibid., p. 232.

18. Quoted in Sire, ibid., p. 182.

19. Gurdjieff, George, quoted in Ornstein, op, cit., p. 132.

20. Matthew 18:3.

21. Chapman, Rick, *How To Choose A Guru* (Harper & Row, NY, 1973), pp. 45, 46.

22. Quoted in Ken Kelley, "The Guru Game," *Ramparts Magazine*, July, 1973; p. 50.

23. II Corinthians 11:13, 14 (Phillips).

24. Quoted in Os Guinness, *The Dust of Death* (Inter-Varsity Press, Downers Grove, IL, 1973), p. 197.

25. John 14:6.

26. John 15:1-11; 17:20-23.

27. John 1:1, 14.

28. I Corinthians 15:14-17.

29. Pitt, Malcolm, *Introducing Hinduism* (Friendship Press, NY, 1958), p. 34.

30. I Peter 1:19, 20.

31. For a summary of evidences for the resurrection of Jesus, see Supplementary Research Section, p. 224. For a more complete study, see *Evidence That Demands a Verdict* by Josh McDowell (Campus Crusade for Christ, 1972).

32. For a summary of these prophecies, see Supplementary Research Section, p. 228. For a more complete study, again see *Evidence That Demands a Verdict.*

33. From Divine Light Mission press release: "All brothers of love come to welcome Guru Maharaj Ji. He is coming in the clouds with great power and glory and his silver steed will drift down at 4 p.m. at Los Angeles International Airport, TWA Flight 761." Quoted in *Right On*, November, 1973, p. 1.

34. Quoted in *Your Mind Matters*, John R. W. Stott (Inter-Varsity Press, Downers Grove, IL, 1972), p. 34.

"The Hebrew-Christian universe is one in which moral urgency, the anxiety to be right, embraces and penetrates everything. . . . To be wrong therefore arouses a metaphysical anxiety and sense of guilt . . . . The appeal of Zen, as of other forms of Eastern philosophy, is that it unveils behind the urgent realm of good and evil a vast region of oneself about which there need be no guilt or recrimination, where at last the self is indistinguishable from God."

—Alan Watts, *This Is It*[1]

Diagnosing the Disease

"Ganga! Ganga!" swelled the cry in the railroad car around me. The Hindu pilgrims crowded to the windows to catch a glimpse of the moonlit river below. The serene face of the Ganges, India's most sacred waterway, slid by beneath us and silently accepted the coins being tossed into her depths and the fervent prayers being intoned by the pilgrims passing over her.

Our night train was headed north to the holy city of Hardwar and beyond toward the Himalayas. For most of the hundreds packed on board, this pilgrimage was a once-in-a-lifetime opportunity to bathe and be spiritually purified in India's sacred waters.

During my travels in India I had learned much to help me understand what it is that drives so many from the West to "journey" Eastward on spiritual pilgrimages of their own. But I also came away with a special awareness of the unbridgeable gulf that separates the eastern and the biblical views of man and the human dilemma.

Is man merely suffering from a metaphysical identity crisis, from a problem centered mainly in his mind? Or is there a deeper problem that the Bible calls "sin," a disease rooted in our very nature? The spiritual path of every individual will be directly determined by his answer to these questions.

Notice, for example, how the manner in which TM head Maharishi Mahesh Yogi views the human dilemma dictates his particular solution:

"Although we are all 100% Divine, consciously we do not know that we are Divine . . . and we suffer on the conscious level. On the level of the Transcendental Consciousness we are Divine already. So suffering on the conscious level has to be eradicated, because that is the main suffering. Meditation, just a few minutes morning and evening, and no suffering will be there."[2]

Meditation is certainly a painless solution, claims Maharishi, and "very easily a sinner comes out of the field of sin and becomes a virtuous man."[3]

Hundreds of thousands of westerners are buying the eastern solution today without ever realizing that the various systems of eastern meditation they are subscribing to are directly linked to a specific view of the human dilemma. At the heart of this view is the eastern belief in monism — the oneness of all things.

No Rights or Wrongs

Because God is considered the sum total of all there is, distinctions between right and wrong become meaningless. In fact, the whole thrust of eastern philosophy is to get you to quit *making* such distinctions. Zen master Yun-Men says:

"If you want to get the plain truth,
Be not concerned with right and wrong.
The conflict between right and wrong
Is the sickness of the mind."[4]

With a wave of a mystic wand, good and evil are both given the same divine glaze, and the world suddenly becomes perfect in every respect. In Hermann Hesse's novel *Siddhartha*, Siddhartha gives a spiritual seeker the following perspective:

"The world, Govinda, is not imperfect or slowly evolving along a long path to perfection. No, it is perfect at every moment. . . . Therefore, it seems to me that everything that exists is good — death as well as life, sin as well as holiness, wisdom as well as folly."[5]

Hitler and the Buddhists

There is, however, a price tag attached to a world without categories of good and evil. Journalist Arthur Koestler poignantly captures the ramifications of such a world view in his description of an interview with one of the greatest Japanese experts on Buddhism in the world today. Koestler asks: "You favor tolerance toward all religions and political systems. What about Hitler's gas chambers?" "That was very silly of him." "Just silly, not evil?" "Evil is a Christian concept. Good and evil exist only on a relative scale."[6]

If they believe the world's already perfect, you might ask, why do all the eastern sects feel it necessary to talk about "solutions"?

Werner Erhard, founder of Erhard Seminars Training (est), is perhaps the most consistent of the new mystics in his response to that question: "But don't get me wrong, I don't think the world needs est; I don't think the world needs anything; the world already is and that's perfect." "If nobody needs it, then why do you do it?" "I do it because I do it, because that's what I do."[7]

Less consistent, but hopefully more intelligible, would be the response of much of the rest of the eastern mystical movement. "Man does have a problem of sorts," they would grudgingly admit. "His problem is that he doesn't realize that he doesn't have any problems!"

The Root of All Evil Is . . .

In eastern thought, then, it is ignorance, not sin or self-will, that lies at the heart of the human dilemma. Zen master D.T. Suzuki explains it this way: "To think that there is the self is the start of all errors and evils. Ignorance is at the root of all things that go wrong."[8]

In Zen, the ignorance lying at the heart of our problems pertains to who we are not: we are not a separate self. In yoga, it involves who we are: we are divine, actually part of the One. And, according to Gopi Krishna, "This is the purpose for which you and I are here — to realize ourselves . . . to bring the soul to a clear realization of its own divine nature."[9]

Along with the deification of man in eastern thought comes the elimination of all concept of a personal God. There is thus no God with absolute standards to be sinned against. "Anything that has the semblance of an external authority is rejected by Zen,"[10] explains Suzuki. "Zen wants absolute freedom, even from God."[11]

The Price of Freedom

Ironically, while desiring to free itself from the yoke of a personal God, eastern mysticism merely exchanges one "external authority" for another. And the new authority, the law of *karma*, is a merciless master.

Karma is the iron-clad law of cause and effect that rules the universe. What a man sows, he also reaps — if not in this life, then perhaps in the next, or the next. For the handmaiden of the law of *karma* is the doctrine of reincarnation which holds that when a man dies, his soul passes into a new body and is reborn, complete with the good or bad *karma* accumulated up to that point.

Man thus lives out his existence in a virtually endless cycle of births and rebirths on a sort of treadmill referred to as the "wheel of samsara." Bad *karma* accumulated on the wheel must be worked out by performing deeds of righteousness (*dharma* in Sanskrit) and by spiritually purifying oneself through meditation.

This is not so easy as it might appear, however. According to the Hindu scriptures, such is the strictness of the law of *karma* that to obtain freedom from bondage to the *wheel of samsara* takes millions of years.[12] The burning desire of every yogi is "moksha," or liberation, and of every Buddhist, "Nirvana" (meaning literally "to extinguish").

In addition to its metaphysical implications, the doctrine of *karma* also has certain logical applications to practical, everyday living. For instance, the concept of *karma* is both creator and sustainer of the caste system in India, a phenomenon which is still very much alive today. If a person is born into a certain social position, no matter how underprivileged, he is thought to be merely reaping what he justly deserves as a result of former actions in past lives. As one western Buddhist leader puts it: "Evil is man-made, and is of his own choosing, and he who suffers suffers from his deliberate use of his own free will. Cripples, dwarfs, and those born deaf or blind are the products of their own past actions. . . ."[13]

The effect of these beliefs on Asian society has been tragic. Comments Arthur Koestler:

"The Oriental attitude toward the sick and the poor is notoriously indifferent because caste, rank, wealth, and health are preordained by the laws of karma. Welfare work in the slums and care of the poor in general was, and still is, a monopoly of the Christian missions in Asia."[14]

Jesus flatly rejected the concept of *karma*. When asked by his disciples about a man who was born blind, whether his affliction was a result of his own sin or that of his parents, Jesus replied, "It was neither that this man sinned, nor his parents. . . ."[15]

Die Only Once

Christ's view of the effect of sin is at once far less drastic and far more drastic than the eastern view. It is less drastic in that He repudiates the idea that a man has to suffer the consequences of accumulated sins over the course of a thousand incarnations. It is appointed to a man to die only once, the Bible affirms.[16]

But the effect of sin on man is far more devastating at the same time.

The Bible also points out that "the wages of sin is death."[17] The death the Bible is referring to here is the death of a man's *spirit*.

Every person is born with a body, a soul (i.e., his intellect, emotions and will), and a spirit (that part of the man which is sensitive to God and can commune with Him). The impact of a man's sin is not just on his body, inflicting it with sickness or deformities, as is thought in eastern religion. Nor does sin affect only the "soul" or psychological nature, as western psychology might emphasize. The effect of sin on man is much more devastating, for it destroys that part of his being which is capable of having a relationship with God. And because it

is nothing less than spiritual death that is at the heart of the human dilemma, Christ emphatically taught that the solution involves something far more profound than a few minutes of meditation every day.

In the third chapter of John's gospel, Jesus had a very revealing conversation with a Pharisee named Nicodemus. Now the Pharisees of first-century Palestine and the yogis and gurus of our own day have much in common. For one thing, both groups believe in attaining spirituality through various religious disciplines and acts of righteousness (dharma).

At any rate, Nicodemus approached Jesus with a compliment, saying he knew that He (Jesus) was a teacher who'd come from God because of the miracles He performed. Jesus' reply was rather abrupt and very much to the heart of the issue: "Truly, truly, I say to you, unless one is born again, he cannot see the kingdom of God ... that which is born of the flesh (physical birth) is flesh and that which is born of the Spirit (spiritual birth) is spirit."[18]

Recast of the Inner Nature

Jesus' point was clear. Nothing less than the birth of a new spiritual nature within us is necessary to resolve the dilemma of sin and make man acceptable before God.

The Buddhist Eightfold Path is both a careful analysis of the symptoms of man's problem and an attempt to treat those symptoms (e.g., through right speech, right behavior, right livelihood, etc.). But as sincere as such a plan might be, no human self-improvement projects go far enough in making man right before a holy and perfect God. No amount of dharma or spiritual discipline is enough to stave off the repercussions of sin. The implantation within us of a new nature is the only effective cure.

The first step toward spiritual rebirth, which is effected by God's Spirit, not through our own effort, is a repentance for our sins and a looking to God for forgiveness: "If we confess our sins, He is faithful and righteous to forgive us our sins and to cleanse us from all unrighteousness" (I John 1:9).

The self-humbling that's involved in asking forgiveness continues to be the biggest stumbling block to men coming to Christ. In a discussion I once had with a teacher of Transcendental

Meditation, the ultimate issue became whether or not a person has to ask Christ to forgive his sins. "God loves us anyway," was his response. "There's no need to ask for forgiveness. We just need to clear our *own* minds of all guilt through meditation."

It is ironic that while the eastern disciplines purport to eliminate the ego, it is just the opposite that actually occurs. Zen enthrones self as the highest authority, yoga preaches the essential divinity of one's own nature, and neither encourages its followers to ask anyone for forgiveness. James Sire has pointed out that although Siddhartha hurts many people along the path to enlightenment, "he never apologizes or confesses. *Neither have meaning in his system*"[19]

X-ray of the East

The apostle Paul's assessment of the Jewish religious establishment in the first century is equally applicable to the eastern religious system today: "For I bear them witness that they have a zeal for God, but not in accordance with knowledge." And how was their knowledge deficient? In three ways: "For not knowing about God's righteousness (inadequate understanding of the holiness of God), and seeking to establish their own (self-perfectionism), they did not subject themselves to the righteousness of God (refusal to submit to God's authority)."[20]

Beneath all the god-words and the pseudo-spiritual trappings, the message of eastern mysticism bears evidence of a much older authorship. Ever since the serpent tempted Eve with ". . . you will be like God, knowing good and evil,"[21] the satanic call to enthrone the creation in place of the Creator has been sounded in countless ways. So Zen today beseeches us to exalt "jiriki" or "self-help," and yoga encourages one's becoming "fully realized" or completely divine. But what these systems hold to be a virtue — the exaltation of self — the Bible identifies as the most basic of sins.

From Eden onward the issue has been one of authority. Is man the highest authority in the universe, or is God? Buddhism candidly claims the former. Hinduism, on the other hand, more deviously confesses God to be the highest power in the universe, but then adds in a loud stage whisper, "But man is really God, you know."

Zen spokesman Alan Watts accuses Christians of stirring up

"a metaphysical anxiety and sense of guilt" [22] by making a distinction between good and evil, and between God and man. Mysticism's answer for such guilt is to reduce God to the safe, controllable level of an impersonal force. In one fell swoop, God is stripped of authority and man relieved of accountability. And as long as the conscience can continue to be silenced through the denial of good and evil, a certain false peace is the experiential dividend.

The Great Divider

Ultimately, it is the cross that looms as the great divider between mysticism and Christianity. While in India, I spent some time talking about Christ and the significance of His death to an American disciple of Sai Baba. Joseph's response was one I'd heard before from those involved in eastern mysticism. "I don't like Christianity's emphasis on the cross," he said. "It's so morbid. I'd rather focus on singing and dancing and joy."

Truly, the cross of Christ does represent everything mysticism scorns. The mystical focus is *inward* and experiential. ("What is needed in Buddhism is enlightenment, neither crucifixion nor resurrection," says D.T. Suzuki.)[23] Christianity's focus is *outward* on an historical event that has eternal significance.

Besides running counter to the mystical bias against history and the physical realm, the cross stands as a reminder that sin — which is a very real commodity — must be dealt with, and that suffering is an inherent part of the solution.

Pleasure and Pain

Eastern mysticism does not know how to deal with the central position given the atoning death of Christ in the New Testament. In a ludicrous attempt to fit the crucifixion into the mystical world view, Maharishi Mahesh Yogi goes so far as to say that Christ never suffered on the cross, but went through it all in a kind of transcendental bliss![24] American guru Baba Ram Dass also de-emphasizes the suffering of the crucifixion: "Pleasure and pain, loss and gain, fame and shame, are all the same — they're all just happening."[25]

(As we'll see in the next chapter, the eastern mystic is ultimately backed into an ideological corner on this issue and is forced into the awkward position of paying Jesus lip service as an "avatar" of God while denying the significance of the climactic event of his earthly ministry.)

In an interesting parallel cited in the eighth chapter of Mark's gospel, Jesus asks the disciples who they think He is. They're quick to affirm Him as the Messiah. But then Jesus goes on to talk about the necessity of His coming death: "And He began to teach them that the Son of Man must suffer many things and be rejected by the elders and the chief priests and the scribes, and be killed, and after three days rise again."[26]

At this point, Peter foreshadows the modern mystic's reaction by breaking in with an objection; the idea of a messiah who had to suffer and die was repugnant to him. Christ's rebuke to Peter re-emphasizes the necessity of the cross and at the same time speaks directly to the "sweetness and light" theories of mysticism: "If anyone wishes to come after Me, let him deny himself, and take up his cross, and follow Me. For whoever wishes to save his life shall lose it; and whoever loses his life for My sake and the gospel's shall save it."[27]

No Bad Karma

In reality, Jesus' sacrifice in our place offers the only hope for those in bondage to the impersonal laws of karma. This was dramatically demonstrated to me again just last year. A student whose campus I had visited earlier wrote to say that the local TM teacher had just accepted Christ as his Savior. My student friend shared the gospel with him many times (as I had when I was there) but the understanding had just come during a recent late-night session. They had been talking about how Christ was uniquely qualified to be the mediator between God and man because He was the one perfect individual who had ever lived and thus had no sin of His own to pay for. The TM teacher's eyes lit up. "I see it!" he said. "Jesus didn't have any bad 'karma' of His own to pay for, so He took all of our 'karma' on Himself at the cross!" Perhaps those aren't the words the New Testament would use, but our friend had grasped the heart of the gospel.

As we've seen in this chapter, the second prong of Satan's strategy in the Age of Aquarius is in many ways more diabolical than the first. With the rational mind neutralized, the attack began to center on silencing the conscience. The distinctions between good and evil were erased, the concept of God as a just Judge was mysticized and sin became simply a matter of innocent ignorance rather than a question of self-will. Grace and mercy and the concept of forgiveness were replaced by the burdens of karmic debt payed for over countless reincarnations.

But the diabolical master-plan has a third prong. A direct attack on the unique identity of Jesus Himself completes the strategy. Chapter IV takes up this issue.

For further reading on the sin issue please turn to page 231 in the Supplementary Research Section.

SOME PRACTICAL HELPS

I. Sin Issue

As you share the gospel with someone who's into eastern thought, one or more of the following questions regarding the sin issue may need to be clarified. Several of the diagrams and key Scriptures used in this section come directly from the Four Spiritual Laws booklet. This should make it easier for you to use the material.

A. *Two approaches to sin.*
   There are basically *two* approaches to sin in the mystical subculture:

   1. The ascetic approach: Zen, Hare Krishna, "serious" yoga and certain other cults place a strong emphasis on discipline and self-denial as a way to eliminate ego and the sin problem. Individuals involved in these disciplines usually need to hear about God's grace and forgiveness.

   2. "Pop" yoga and meditation: TM, est, and other *westernized* mystical cults claim there's no need for discipline or a change in lifestyle. With a little meditation (or whatever) every day, "very easily a sinner comes out of the field of sin and becomes a virtuous man" (*Meditations of Maharishi*, p. 119). The seriousness of the sin problem and the issue of self on the throne of the life usually need to be clarified here.

B. *Cause of sin.*
   1. Eastern view: ignorance.
   2. Biblical view: self-will.
   3. Key Scriptures to share:
      a. Romans 1:18-21: Man's problem is *not* ignorance. He *does* know the truth about God, but in sheer self-will *suppresses* that truth.

      I John 1:8, 9 We need to be willing to admit we've sinned and claim Christ's forgiveness. The resistance to this self-humbling is the heart of the problem of self-will.
   4. Diagrams (from Law IV of Four Spiritual Laws):
      Self-directed life   Christ-directed life

   Contrast the life with self on the throne versus Christ on the throne. The key point to make is that no matter *how* much meditation is done in the name of eliminating ego, *self* is still directing that life, and not God. A person needs to admit his need for a Savior rather than continue trying to save himself.

   With a mystic, *don't stress the "abundant life," or the "inner peace versus frustration" comparison between the self-directed and Christ-directed lives. The mystical experience does produce a certain superficial peace in the life.*

C. *Results of sin.*
   1. Eastern view:
      a. "Bad *karma*" eventually results in sickness, deformities and other tragedies, as well as a slowing of one's "spiritual evolution."
   2. Biblical view: spiritual death and separation from God.
   3. Key Scriptures to share:
      a. Romans 3:23 — All have sinned.
      b. Romans 6:23 — Spiritual death.
      c. Isaiah 59:1, 2 — Our sins separate us from God.

4. Diagram:

Western psychology claims that sin affects only the psychological portion or the "soul" of man. (The Greek word for soul is *psuche* from which we get the modern word "psychology.")

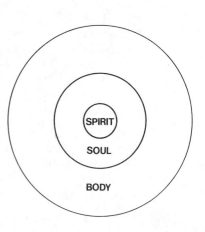

Eastern religion claims that sin retards your spiritual growth and also affects the body by causing it to be afflicted with sickness, accidents, deformities, etc.

The Bible, however, tells us that the result of sin is spiritual death — the death of that part of one's being which is sensitive to God and able to commune with Him. This is why it's impossible for us to achieve spiritual perfection through our own efforts. There's no spiritual "life" to work with until Christ's Spirit is born within us.

D. *Solution to sin.*

1. Eastern view: spiritual evolution through meditation over the course of many lifetimes (reincarnation).

2. Biblical view:

   a. Christ's death in our place satisfies God's justice, bridges the separation between God and man.

   b. Birth of a new spirit within us gives us the power to live a Christ-directed life.

3. Key Scripture to share:

   I Peter 2:24 — "And He Himself bore our sins (you might substitute the word *karma*) in His body on the cross, that we might die to sin and live to righteousness; for by His wounds you were healed."

4. Diagrams:

a. Eastern solution:

"Although we are all 100% Divine, consciously we do not know that we are Divine ... On the level of the Transcendental Consciousness we are Divine already. So suffering on the conscious level has to be eradicated .... Meditation, just a few minutes morning and evening, and no suffering will be there" (*Meditations of Maharishi*, p. 177).

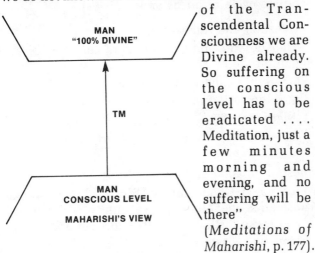

b. Problems with eastern solution:

1) Doesn't deal with problem of spiritual death. (You can't perfect a corpse.)

2) Has no conception of a holy God whose just nature demands a payment for sin.

c. Biblical solution:

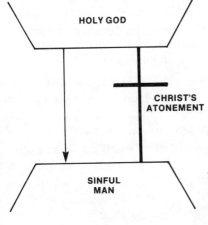

God reaches down to man by sending His Son to die on the cross, paying for all our "bad *karma*" in our place.

    d. Key contrast to make:
       God's love and forgiveness
             vs.
       Bondage to *karmic* debt and the *wheel of samsara* (endless cycle of births and rebirths).

5. Key question and follow-up:
    a. "What do you think is the significance of Christ's death on the cross?"
    b. Allow him to share his opinion.
    c. Share the scriptural view:
       1) Matthew 20:28 — A ransom for many.
       2) I Peter 2:24 — Bore our sins (*karma*).

E. *The question of good and evil.*
    1. Eastern view: Good and evil don't ultimately exist because all is one; all things are a unity. It's unhealthy to try to make distinctions between right and wrong.
    2. Problems with eastern view:
      a. Creates lack of compassion for those suffering, undergoing evil. Example: caste system in India.
      b. Creates indifference to actions of evil men. Example: the Buddhist view of Hitler.
      c. Leads to licence in an individual's life, dulls his conscience.
    3. Biblical view: Good and evil *are* realities, both in terms of the spiritual realm, and in terms of human actions.
    4. Key questions to ask if someone denies the ultimate reality of good and evil:
      a. "Is God both good and evil?"
      b. "If so, why should I worship Him in peaceful, loving ways? Why not 'worship' Him by murdering people or in other violent ways? (Example: Charles Manson said, 'If all is one, what is bad?')"
      c. "Would you agree that Hitler's actions were evil?"
      d. "If not, then human life is evidently completely meaningless. Would you object if I were to pull out a gun and shoot you right now? Why would you object if one action is as 'good' as another?"

Note: Our goal here is not to be crude, but to shock a person out of a philosophical mind-trip that really bears no relation to the way he lives his life. He needs to see his own inconsistency. Be careful not to leave him in a vacuum, but lead him on to an experience of God's love and acceptance.

II. Summary of Key Points

According to Romans 10:2, 3, there are basically three weaknesses in the eastern view of sin:

A. *Inadequate view of God and His holiness.*
   ("For not knowing about God's righteousness . . .") The god of mysticism is an impersonal force, without the characteristics of personality. If God cannot be described as "holy," then there's no ultimate basis for calling one thing "good" and another "evil."

B. *Attempt at self-perfectionism.*
   (". . . and seeking to establish their own . . .") The problem is, sin causes spiritual death, not just retardation. A corpse can't perfect himself; new life is needed. Christ brings that life as we invite Him into our hearts.

C. *Self-will: refusal to submit to God's authority.*
   (". . . they did not subject themselves to the righteousness of God.") The attempt to solve the sin problem independently has been the hallmark of man's religious systems since Cain offered a vegetable rather than a blood sacrifice. Eastern mysticism's refusal to bow before the cross of Christ is just one more example of this.

Bibliography

1. Watts, Alan, *This Is It* (Pantheon Books, NY, 1958), pp. 89, 90.
2. Maharishi Mahesh Yogi, *Meditations of Maharishi Mahesh Yogi* (Bantam Books, NY, 1968), pp. 177, 178.
3. Maharishi, ibid., p. 119.
4. Yun-Men quoted in Alan Watts, *Beat Zen, Square Zen and Zen* (City Lights, San Francisco, 1959), p. 10, who was then quoted in Os Guinness, *The East, No Exit,* p. 40.

5. Hesse, Hermann, *Siddhartha*, trans. Hilda Rosner (New Directions, NY, 1951), p. 116, quoted in Sire, p. 142.

6. Koestler, Arthur, *The Lotus and the Robot* (Harper & Row, NY, 1960), pp. 273, 274.

7. Quoted in Adam Smith, *Powers of Mind* (Random House, NY, 1975), p. 284.

8. Suzuki, D.T., *Mysticism, Christian and Buddhist* (Harper & Row, NY, 1957), p. 153.

9. Quoted in John White, *Everything You Wanted To Know About TM — Including How To Do It* (Pocket Books, NY, 1976), p. 103.

10. Suzuki, D.T., *An Introduction to Zen Buddhism* (Random House, NY, 1964), p. 44.

11. Ibid., p. 97.

12. *Mahabharata*, 12.281.31.

13. Humphreys, Christmas, *Karma and Rebirth* (Brown, Knight, and Truscott, London, 1943), p. 55.

14. Koestler, op. cit., p. 280.

15. John 9:1-3.

16. Hebrews 9:27.

17. Romans 6:23.

18. John 3:1-8.

19. Sire, James, *The Universe Next Door* (Inter-Varsity Press, Downers Grove, IL, 1975), p. 228.

20. Romans 10:2, 3.

21. Genesis 3:5.

22. Watts, Alan, *This Is It* (Pantheon Books, NY, 1958), p. 89.

23. Suzuki, D. T., *Mysticism, Christian and Buddhist*, op. cit., p. 149.

24. Maharishi, op. cit., p. 123.

25. Alpert, Richard, *Be Here Now* (Harmony, NY, 1971), p. 107.

26. Mark 8:31ff.

27. Mark 8:34.

"Therefore also God highly exalted Him and bestowed on Him the name which is above every name,

That at the name of Jesus every knee should bow, of those who are in heaven, and on earth, and under the earth,

And that every tongue should confess that Jesus Christ is Lord, to the glory of God the Father."

—Philippians 2:9-11.

Jesus: God or Guru?

"Lord Jesus is the son of the Supreme Absolute Truth. And Krishna is the Father. He is the source: Krishna says, 'I am the source of everything. From me the entire creation flows. Knowing this, the wise worship me with all their hearts.' So Krishna is the Supreme Father, and every other living entity is his part and parcel, or his son."[1]

—Hare Krishna devotee

"I don't think Christ ever suffered or Christ could suffer . . . . The message of Christ has been the message of Bliss."[2]

—Maharishi Mahesh Yogi

"Jesus, on earth, was a man no different from us except for the fact that he was without original sin[3]. . . . He can by no means be God Himself."[4]

—Sun Myung Moon

"So Jesus is living, right! Jesus is living, Ram is living now, Krishna is living now, Buddha is living now, but they have all been united into one very powerful power.

And when this power spreads its hand . . . all the things that are going on wrong in this world are going to be abolished."[5]

—Guru Maharaj Ji

The yellow-robed figure bobbed up out of nowhere. "Would you like a free magazine about Krishna?" Big smile.

"No, thanks," I said. "I'm a Christian. I believe in Jesus Christ."

"Oh, *I* believe in Jesus, too! Jesus is a very great lord. If you believe in Jesus, you should believe in Lord Krishna, too!"

Similar encounters with the eastern mystical subculture have occurred hundreds of times. For it is one of the ironies of our day that all of the mystical cults have simultaneously claimed Jesus Christ as their personal prophet. To the TM people He is one of the original Transcendental Meditators.[6] Others, like the Eckankar cult, see Jesus as some kind of temporary ticket agent to outer space. When Jesus said, "Follow Me," they say, He was really talking about "astral travel" to the "worlds beyond."[7] And as far as Guru Maharaj Ji is concerned, Jesus was primarily involved in passing on Divine Light Mission techniques to His 12 disciples.

Which Jesus?

Probably most confusing for the Christian is the fact that virtually all of the new eastern sects honor Christ as being "divine" and a "Savior." In fact, they all "believe" in Jesus. But the question is, *which* Jesus do they believe *in*? To answer that, let's take a look at the profile of Jesus that emerges from the mystical subculture.

Many of the ideas about Christ that are prevalent in mystical circles come from a fabricated biography of His life called *The Aquarian Gospel of Jesus the Christ*. According to *The Aquarian Gospel*, much of the early influence in Jesus' life was from the mystic East.

The wise men, for instance, were really Persian astrologers who read the prophecy about Jesus' birth in the signs of the zodiac. Their warning sent Mary, Joseph and Jesus off to Egypt where Mary received three years instruction in occult teachings from an Egyptian priest. Supposedly, she later passed these teachings on to her son.

But the primary focus of *The Aquarian Gospel* is on the so-called "Silent Years" of Jesus' life between the ages of twelve and thirty. It was during this time, says "Levi," the *Gospel's* author, that Jesus visited ashrams, or spiritual communities, in India, Nepal, Tibet and Greece. There He is said to have been steeped in the teachings of the mystic orient, and He became adept in the occult sciences. Jesus then returned to Palestine a fully-developed yogi and spiritual master.

Re-interpreting Scripture

Why all this biographical speculation? The main advantage to the mystic is that it allows him to re-interpret all of Jesus' teachings with an eastern slant. For instance, the mystic would insist that when Jesus said, "the kingdom of God is within you," He was teaching the inner divinity of all men. (I'll be covering several of these mystical interpretations in the next chapter.)

Before continuing with the eastern mystic's view of Jesus, let's look for a minute at *The Aquarian Gospel* itself to determine its source and its accuracy.

Though presented as a "historical document," *The Gospel* reflects the classic mystical bias against written history. Actually, none of the information comes from written records of any kind. The author, whose full name was Levi Dowling, was a turn-of-the-century mystic who was given to trances and visions. Between the hours of two and six each morning,[9] Dowling would slip into a trance in which he would "come (into) rapport with the tones and rhythms of Jesus of Nazareth."[10] Dowling became a kind of "psychic transcriber" during these sessions and *The Aquarian Gospel* was born.

The Gospel also deeply reflects the mystic's lack of concern for historical *accuracy*. Eva Dowling writes in the Introduction, "Of course, all of (Levi's) transcriptions are true to the letter."[11] But in actuality, the book has a number of historical inaccuracies[12] that disqualify it from being taken for legitimate history. By way of comparison, no discovery of archeology or secular history has ever contradicted a single event recorded in the New Testament Gospels.[13] But then to the mystic, if a story "feels right," that's more important than whether the events really happened.

As we've seen, *The Aquarian Gospel* teaches that Jesus was a person heavily influenced by eastern and occult thought in His early years. This is the first view of Jesus prevalent in the eastern mystical subculture today. Second, the eastern sects would agree with Christians that Jesus' mission was to be a savior. But the mystical meaning attached to the term is completely different than the idea of "Savior" found in the Bible.

Avatar or Savior?

Actually, the Hindu concept of the *"avatar,"* or "divine Savior," developed fairly late in the history of eastern religion. Most scholars believe that Hinduism picked up the concept from Christianity after St. Thomas brought the gospel to India in 52 A.D. Before this time, the Hindu scriptures described only a vague, impersonal God. It would have been a contradiction to talk about the Impersonal Absolute assuming a personal form.

As a matter of fact, a number of fascinating stories were added to the Hindu scriptures in the first through third centuries, especially to the *Bhagavad-Gita* (Bah-gah-vahd Gheé-tah), the most popular of these scriptures. These stories describe a god who took on a human form and ministered personally on the earth.

Some of the stories about the god Krishna, for example, are exact parallels to the gospel accounts of Jesus. For instance, Krishna was supposedly born in a shepherd's hut while his parents were on their way to their home town to pay taxes. There was a massacre of innocent babies during that time that forced them to flee to a neighboring country; there was the anointing of Krishna's body with ointment provided by a maiden, as well as various miracle stories. Some even suggest the name Krishna itself is a derivative of Christ.[14]

At any rate, the biblical concept of the "Savior" definitely lost something in the Hindu translation.

The biblical concept of Jesus as *Savior* is different in at least three ways from the Hindu concept of the *avatar*:

(1) *Jesus is a permanent Savior.*

In the eastern view, a new *avatar* is needed in every age "whenever there is a decline of religion."[15] In the *Bhagavad-Gita*, Krishna says,

"In every age I come back
To deliver the holy,
To destroy the sins of the sinner,
To establish righteousness."[16]

By contrast, Hebrews 10:12 tells us that Christ "offered one sacrifice for sins *for all time.*" The result is that "we have been sanctified through the offering of the body of Jesus Christ *once for all*" (Hebrews 10:10).

(2) *Jesus is a uniquely qualified Savior.*

There are at least 22 different *avatars* mentioned in the *Bhagavad-Gita* alone, and every one of them is considered to be equally divine. As one Indian monk says, "It is one and the same Savior that, having plunged into the ocean of life, rises up in one place and is known as Krishna . . . and diving down again rises in another place and is known as Christ."[17] A common eastern belief is that there is one eternal "Christ spirit" that merely inhabits a new body in each age.

The Bible, however, describes Jesus as God's "*only* begotten Son" (John 3:16). And in answer to the question, "Can men be saved just as easily in the name of Krishna, Rama, or Buddha?" the New Testament says regarding Jesus: "And there is salvation in no one else, for there is *no other name* under heaven that has been given among men, by which we must be saved" (Acts 4:12). Jesus is not only unique in His divinity, but also in His sinlessness. As we've seen before, because He alone had no bad *karma* of His own to pay for, He was uniquely qualified to die in our place.

(3) *Jesus is an atoning Savior.*

In a little metaphysical word-play, the eastern cults refer to the *avatar's* purpose as being *not* to make "atonement" for man's sin, but to help man experience "at-one-ment" with God. Man's problem is not sin, they say, but ignorance of his own divinity. Therefore, the *avatar's* purpose is not to atone for sin, but to teach and guide spiritual seekers toward gradual enlightenment. One of the supposed sages in *The Aquarian Gospel* puts it this way: "There are no supernatural acts of God to lift a man from carnal life to spirit blessedness; he grows as grows the plant, and in due time is perfected."[18]

But Jesus was far more than some glorified guide. The Bible teaches that He was God's unique Son, sent as an atonement for our sins. Jesus said of His mission, "The Son of Man did not come to be served, but to serve, and to give His life as *a ransom for many*."[19] The writer to the Hebrews adds, "Without shedding of blood there is no forgiveness."[20]

The fact of the matter is, the Hindu *avatar* is not a "savior" at all, because he can't "save" anyone. He merely tries to point the way; the individual has to "save" himself!

Buddhism adopted the *avatar* idea from Hinduism and turned it into the concept of the "Bodhisattva" (Bo-dee-saht-vah). The *Bodhisattva* is one who has reached Enlightenment, but who sacrifices his right to enter Nirvana in order to point others to the way. But, just as He was not just another *avatar* in the Hindu tradition, Christ was *not* some sort of Jewish *Bodhisattva*. There's a vast difference between postponing Nirvana in order to point out the way to others and *becoming* "the Way" by dying in our place.

In past centuries, Satan's master plan in the Western World has focused on convincing men of the *falsehood* of Jesus' claims. Using scientific skepticism as a tool, scorn was heaped on His claims to be an incarnation of God, the Savior of mankind, "the Truth." The very existence of a person named Jesus was even called into question.

A Multitude of Messiahs

But in our generation, Satan has very cleverly reversed his entire strategy. His attacks are no longer focused on the *truthfulness* of Christ's claims, but on their *uniqueness*. Satan is using eastern mysticism today to exert a great leveling influence on Jesus' role and identity. The mystics are willing to honor Jesus as an incarnation of God, a Savior, the Truth, as long as He agrees to be but *one of many* incarnations, one of many saviors, and one of many truths. Christ is forced to yield His rightful position as King of kings and Lord of lords, and the crucifixion becomes just one more insignificant event in the life of a middle-eastern *avatar*.

Klaus Klostermaier analyzes the East's condescending acceptance of Jesus Christ this way:

"Men reject him because he unmasks their lies and hypocrisy, because he cannot be bribed. They would be willing to place him next to the gods, to offer him incense, even a little money, to cleanse themselves of sin. They would like to have him as a statue — but not as a man, not so immediate and provoking."[21]

I'm reminded of a Yoga Society ceremony I witnessed in San Francisco earlier this year. At the end of the ceremony a long list of deities and demi-gods were chanted in Sanskrit, the sacred Hindu language. One after another, I picked out the names of Krishna, Rama, Shiva, and others being hailed. And then at the very end, in the spirit of eastern tolerance, the priest threw in a final chant to "Jesu Christo and all the other prophets."

The issue of the "tolerance" of the eastern religions and the seeming "intolerance" of Christianity is central here. Os Guinness, exposes the fallacy of that comparison in this superb analysis:

> "If Christianity is true, Hinduism cannot be true in the sense it claims. *Even though on the surface it appears that Hinduism is more tolerant, both finally demand an ultimate choice.* Many Indians admit this. Some speak of the subtlety of Hindu toleration as 'the kiss of death.' Radakrishnan has described it as 'being strangled by the fraternal embrace'. . . . The best way for Hinduism to contain the rampant reform movement of Buddhism in India was to declare that the Buddha was only a further *avatar* of Krishna. Buddha's uniqueness was thus 'strangled by the fraternal embrace.' "[22]

Western mysticism is offering the same "fraternal embrace" to Christ today. But it is equally "strangling," for behind the offer is the monistic presupposition that "all truth is one; the sages merely call it by different names."

One of the popular stories told in mystic circles to illustrate this belief concerns four blind men who were sent out to feel an elephant and return with a description. In their blindness, they each feel a different part of the elephant and return with a different description: one feels the tail and declares the elephant is like a rope; one feels the elephant's trunk and says, "No, he is like a snake." The third feels a leg and says the elephant is like a great pillar, etc.

The moral that's usually drawn by the mystic is that *all* the men were right. They all had *part* of the truth, but in their blindness none of them could see the *whole* truth. In the same way, says the mystic, the various religions may have different conceptions of God, but each concept is just part of the whole — the total concept — they're really *all* true.

The Visible Expression . . .

The weakness of the analogy is that we are not blind. We can't use that excuse. God has openly visited this planet in the person of Jesus Christ, "the *visible* expression of the invisible God."[23] Referring to Jesus as "the light," John says, "And the light shines in the darkness; and the darkness did not comprehend it."[24] The problem is not lack of light today; the problem is lack of comprehension.

A more analogous story would involve four people with perfect vision. They're asked to go together into a room and return with a description of the person sitting there.

After they return, the first person says, "He's a white male, well-built, in his early twenties."

The second person says, "What do you mean? He's black, and he's eighty years old if he's a day!"

The third person says, "You're *both* wrong. It's not a 'he' at all; it's a 'she.' An oriental female. And she's really overweight."

The fourth person looks at the others strangely and says, "You're *all* crazy. There wasn't anyone in that room."

Now, there are just two possibilities here. The first is that only one of these people is telling the truth; the second is that none of them are. But, in any case, the theory that *all* of them are telling the truth is not an option.

Who Is Ultimate Reality?

The parallel is obvious. Is Ultimate Reality the god Krishna, who supposedly seduced thousands of women, turned others into cripples and claimed to be beyond normal standards of morality? Is it an impersonal force, completely without qualities or attributes as claimed by the Hindu monists? Is it the Buddhist "Void"? Or is Ultimate Reality Jesus Christ?

Either all of these views are false — or one *is* true and the rest are false. But they can't all be true. Jesus can't be both "*Avatar* Number Twenty-Three" and God's "*only* begotten Son." Nor can He be both a temporary *Bodhisattva* and "the one mediator between God and man."[25]

To say Jesus is several contradictory things at one time is like the Sufi story about Nasrudin. "Nasrudin is made a magistrate. During his first case the plaintiff argues so persuasively that he (Nasrudin) exclaims, 'I believe you are right.'

"The clerk of the court begs him to restrain himself, for the defendant had not yet been heard.

"Nasrudin is so carried away by the eloquence of the defendant that he cries out as soon as the man has finished his evidence, 'I believe you are right.'

"The clerk of the court cannot allow this. 'Your honor, they cannot both be right.'

" 'I believe you are right,' says Nasrudin."[26]

Are all possibilities right? Mystic monism would say "yes." Truth and falsehood, good and evil, are all ultimately the same. So it makes no difference which "savior" you choose, or how you view Jesus, as long as you honor Him in some way. Or is that true?

In Matthew 7, Jesus warns His disciples about false prophets:

"Not every one who says to Me, 'Lord, Lord,' will enter the kingdom of heaven; but he who does the will of My Father who is in heaven.

"Many will say to Me on that day, 'Lord, Lord, did we not prophesy in Your name, and in Your name cast out demons, and in Your name perform many miracles?'

"And then I will declare to them, 'I never knew you; depart from Me, you who practice lawlessness.' " [27]

We can't barter with Jesus. He has little patience with those who would offer Him a token title, but not the throne of their hearts. Those who fail to accept Him as Savior in the biblical sense now, will one day kneel before Him as Judge.

At that time every tongue *will* confess that "Jesus Christ is Lord." [28] But for many, that confession will merely be the bitter recognition of an opportunity lost. May we be living the lives and sharing the words that will draw thousands to Jesus as *Savior* — while there's still time.

For further reading on eastern mysticism's view of Christ please turn to page 234 *in the Supplementary Research Section.*

SOME PRACTICAL HELPS

I. Sharing the Uniqueness of Jesus' Claims

There's a tendency on the part of the mysticism movement to deny the exclusive nature of Jesus' claims about Himself. The mystic will even use certain Scriptures out of context to serve his own purposes in this regard.

Here's an example from Maharishi Mahesh Yogi:

"Christ said, 'Be still and know that I am God.' Be still and know that you are God and when you know that you are God you will begin to live Godhood, and living Godhood there is no reason to suffer, absolutely no reason to suffer."

(*Meditations of Maharishi*, p. 178)

First of all, Christ never said it. The quote is actually found in Psalms 46, and Jehovah God is the speaker. And the last thing God intended when He said it is that someone would use it to deify man!

A. *Jesus' claims.*

We need to be prepared to share those Scriptures that

clarify the uniquenesses of Jesus' claims. Here are a few of the most important:

1. Jesus is the only way to God.
   John 14:6: Jesus said, "I am the way, and the truth, and the life; no one comes to the Father, but through Me."

2. Salvation is found only in Jesus of Nazareth.
   Acts 4:10, 12: "Let it be known to all of you, and to all the people of Israel, that by *the name of Jesus Christ the Nazarene*, whom you crucified, whom God raised from the dead — by this name this man stands here before you in good health.... And there is salvation in no one else; for there is *no other name* under heaven that has been given among men, by which we must be saved."
   See also I John 2:23; 5:11, 12; John 8:24; II John 9.

3. Jesus will one day return as Judge of all men.
   John 5:22: "For not even the Father judges any one, but He has given all judgment to the Son."
   Matthew 25:31, 32, 34, 41: "But when the Son of Man comes in His glory, and all the angels with Him, then He will sit on His glorious throne .... And all the nations will be gathered before Him; and He will separate them from one another, as the shepherd separates the sheep from the goats .... Then the King will say to those on His right, 'Come, you who are blessed of My Father, inherit the kingdom prepared for you from the foundation of the world.'... Then He will also say to those on His left, 'Depart from me, accursed ones, into the eternal fire which has been prepared for the devil and his angels.'"

4. The prophecies about Jesus' return do not refer to other *avatars*.
   Acts 1:9-11: "And after He had said these things, He was lifted up while they were looking on, and a cloud received Him out of their sight. And as they were gazing intently into the sky while He was departing, behold, two men in white clothing stood beside them; and they also said, 'Men of Galilee, why do you stand looking into the sky? *This Jesus*, who has been taken up from you into heaven, will come in just the same way

as you have watched Him go into heaven.' "

B. *Countering the "all truth is one" attitude.*
   Often the mystic will respond to the gospel with, "Well, we're both really saying the same thing; we're just describing it in slightly different ways." At that point you need to be able to clarify that the eastern concept of God and of Jesus is *not* the same as the biblical view. Here are some suggestions based on the material in this chapter:

   1. Share the illustration about the four people going into the room and returning with four completely different descriptions of the person sitting there (p. 88). Point out that this story and its implications (the descriptions can't *all* be true) parallels the problem of the three eastern views of God versus the biblical view of God.

RELIGION	ULTIMATE REALITY
Krishna worshipers	Krishna (amoral lifestyle)
Monistic Hinduism	An Impersonal Force (without attributes)
Buddhism	A Void
Christianity	Jesus Christ (specific attributes, specific claims)

   2. Share the exclusive claims Christ made as listed in Section I above. Point out that if these claims are true, they exclude the validity of the Hindu and Buddhist views. A person has to make a choice.

   3. If necessary, point out the distinctions between Christ the *Savior* and the concept of *avatar* or *Bodhisattva*:
      a. Jesus is a *permanent* Savior.
         Hebrews 10:10, 12.
      b. Jesus is a *uniquely-qualified* Savior.
         (1) John 3:16.
         (2) Acts 4:12.
      c. Jesus is an *atoning* Savior.

    (1) Matthew 20:28.

    (2) Hebrews 9:22.

C. *A good "summary passage."*

If you forget the individual verses I've listed above, just remember to turn to Hebrews 9 and 10. That one passage contains several key clarifications for a mystic. You might want to mark these in your Bible for easy reference:

1. Hebrews 9:27 — "And inasmuch as it is appointed for men to die once, and after this comes judgment."

   - There is no reincarnation, or cycle of rebirths.

2. Hebrews 10:10, 12 — "By this will we have been sanctified through the offering of the body of Jesus Christ *once for all.*... But He, having offered one sacrifice for sins *for all time,* sat down at the right hand of God."

   - Jesus' sacrifice was effective for *all* time. We don't need "new *avatars*" to complete something impermanent.

II. Suggestion

Spiros Zodhiates, *Was Christ God?* (Erdmans, 1970).

Bibliography

1. Quoted by Faye Levine in *The Strange World of the Hare Krishnas* (Fawcett Publications, NY, 1974), p. 102.

2. Maharishi Mahesh Yogi, *Meditations of Maharishi* (Bantam Books, NY, 1973), pp. 123, 124.

3. Sun Myung Moon, *Divine Principle*, p. 212.

4. Ibid., p. 211.

5. *Divine Light* Magazine, January, 1972, quoted in *God and the Gurus* by R. D. Clements (Inter-Varsity Press, Downers

Grove, IL, 1976), p. 24.

6. Maharishi Mahesh Yogi, op. cit., pp. 122, 123.

7. Twitchell, Paul, Eckankar the Key to Secret Worlds (Illuminated Way Press, San Diego, 1969), p. 12.

8. Cameron, Charles, Who Is Guru Maharaj Ji? (Bantam Books, NY, 1973), p. 27.

9. Dowling, L. H., The Aquarian Gospel of Jesus the Christ (De Vorss and Co., Los Angeles, 1969), p. 7.

10. Ibid., p. 17.

11. Ibid., p. 17.

12. The very first verse, for instance, identifies Herod Antipas as "ruler in Jerusalem" when, in fact, he was ruler in Galilee, a completely different province.

13. Glueck, Nelson, Rivers in the Desert; History of Neteg (Jewish Publications Society of America, Philadelphia, 1969), p. 31. , ibid.

14. Walker, Benjamin, The Hindu World: An Encyclopedic Survey of Hinduism Vol. I (Frederick A. Praeger Inc., NY), p. 1.

15. Swami Abhedananda, The Sayings of Shri Rama Krishna (The Vendanta Society, NY, 1903), quoted in Huston Smith, The Religions of Man (Harper & Row, NY, 1958), p. 87.

16. The Song of God: Bhagavad-Gita, translated by Swami Prabhavananda and Christopher Isherwood (Mentor Books, NY, 1964), p. 50.

17. Smith, op. cit., p. 87.

18. Dowling, op. cit., p. 100.

19. Matthew 20:28.

20. Hebrews 9:22.

21. Klostermaier, Klaus, Hindu and Christian in Vrindaban (SCM Press, 1969), pp. 49ff.

22. Guinness, Os, The East, No Exit (Inter-Varsity Press, Downers Grove, IL, 1974), p. 50, italics mine.

23. Colossians 1:15.

24. John 1:5.

25. I Timothy 2:5.

26. Shah, Idries, The Pleasantries of the Incredible Mulla Nasrudin (E. P. Dutton & Co., NY, 1972), p. 67.

27. Matthew 7:21-23.
28. Philippians 2:11.

- Are the various eastern sects really compatible with the Christian faith as they claim?
- Is reincarnation taught in the Bible?
- Is the Bible an authoritative, reliable record?
- Isn't meditation condoned in the Bible?
- Didn't Jesus teach the inner divinity of all men when He proclaimed, "The Kingdom of God is within you . . ."?
- Can't yogis today perform the same miracles Jesus did — including resurrections?
- Are mind/body spinoffs like hatha yoga and the martial arts legitimate Christian activities?

Reincarnation and Other Questions

ARE THE VARIOUS EASTERN SECTS REALLY COMPATIBLE WITH THE CHRISTIAN FAITH AS THEY CLAIM?

"TM is not a religion; absolutely not."[1]

—Maharishi Mahesh Yogi, head of the Transcendental Meditation movement

"Christians as well as Buddhists can practice Zen just as big fish and small fish are both contentedly living in the same ocean. Zen is the ocean...."[2]

—Zen Master D.T. Suzuki

" 'Is Arica a new religion?' Oscar was asked. 'A new church?' 'Oh, no,' Oscar said. 'The disciplines are old: Buddhist, Tao, Islamic, Christian, but we don't ask for belief or faith; we just say, "Try these things and see what happens." ' "[3]

—Oscar Ichazo, founder of the Arica sect

> "There is a misconception that the Krishna
> consciousness movement represents the Hindu
> religion. In fact, Krishna consciousness is in no
> way a faith or religion. . . ."[4]

> —Swami Prabhupada,
> founder of the Hare Krish-
> na movement

In one of the boldest bits of semantic juggling to date, virtually all of the new eastern sects claim to be religiously neutral and thus compatible with the Christian faith. Even young Guru Maharaj Ji has decided to hang up his title as "Lord of the Universe" and begin cultivating a secular image. At any rate, this metaphysical double-talk has created confusion among many Christians regarding the appropriateness of their involvement in the eastern disciplines.

Though they claim to be non-religious, lurking somewhere beneath the carefully constructed public images of the mystical sects is a definite set of doctrinal beliefs. These beliefs are generally camouflaged by one of two non-religious labels.

Science or Religion?

The first of these is the "science" label. The Transcendental Meditation movement, for instance, seeks to promote a scientific image by focusing on its supposedly non-religious meditation technique and by pushing its doctrinal beliefs into the background. Numerous lab tests are produced to document the results of the practice, inferring that because TM can be tested scientifically, it should be classified as a science and not as a religion.

This is tantamount to saying that Christianity is in fact a science because one could produce tests indicating whether conversion to Christ brings inner peace, liberates drug addicts, etc.

The error of this kind of thinking, it would seem, lies in the fact that although science can sometimes measure the results of a religious practice, the religion itself is not explainable in terms of scientific data and thus cannot be considered a science.

The truth of the matter is that TM, like Christianity, holds a world view that is decidedly religious in nature. It sets out to define ultimate reality and claims to have a monopoly on the solution to the human dilemma.[5] These are religious issues.

The majority of the eastern sects take a more subtle tack than does the TM movement. They claim that their movements deal with something *more basic* than religion. The Hindu sects, for instance, would deny that they draw on "religious tradition" by basing their beliefs on the *Vedas* (Hindu scriptures). Instead, they would tell you that they are drawing on "the wisdom of the ages" or on "that Eternal Truth from which all religions spring," etc.

Ultimate Truth

Suzuki exhibits the mystical claim of going beyond religion to some higher truth when he says, "Zen is the ocean" in which all religions swim. By this statement, he is claiming that Zen focuses on truths that are deeper, more basic, and, ultimately more important than "religious truths."

Interestingly enough, however, when Suzuki goes on to list the key steps in the practice of Zen, he very clearly describes a religious view of ultimate truth:

> "Hush the dualism of subject and object, forget both, transcend the intellect, sever yourself from the understanding, and directly penetrate deep into the identity of the Buddha-mind; *outside of this there are no realities.*"[6]

A monistic view of the world if ever there was one.

So, in sum, most mystic sects, through a kind of metaphysical double-talk, skillfully say one thing while really meaning another. While claiming to be non-religious, they cling tenaciously to a religious (usually monistic) world view and to a definite set of doctrinal beliefs. They claim that their faith is not one "that seeks to defeat other faiths or religions,"[7] as Swami Prabhupada puts it, but then asserts out of the other side of his mouth that *his* faith is based on ultimate reality and all other faiths are mere subheadings under this reality. Krishna, speaking in the *Bhagavad-Gita*, says, "Abandon all varieties of religions and just surrender unto Me."[8]

Religion by any other name is still religion. And as we have seen in earlier chapters, the eastern brand is in direct conflict with biblical Christianity as regards man's identity, the human dilemma, the ultimate solution to that dilemma, the nature of God, the way to determine truth, and the identity of Jesus. Aside from these minor issues, the two systems are quite compatible!

SOME PRACTICAL HELPS

1. *The next time a mystic tells you that the teachings of his sect are compatible with your Christian faith, question him in depth about his sect's views of God's nature, man's identity, the identity of Jesus, etc. Then share with him the biblical view of each of these issues in turn.*

2. *Members of sects such as TM that promote a scientific image will say, "Our movement doesn't take a stand on any of those religious issues; we just offer a simple, scientific technique."*

   There are two key questions to ask here: 1) What, according to your movement, is man's basic problem? 2) What is the solution to the problem?

   The biblical answer to these questions is that man's problem is sin and self-will; the only solution is the cross and the reconciliation with God that is available there. Any other answer (such as the practice of a technique as the solution) is in direct conflict with the teachings of the Christian faith.

IS REINCARNATION TAUGHT IN THE BIBLE?

The dual concepts of *karma* and reincarnation lie at the heart of the eastern system of salvation. Along with many truths and many saviors, one is given many lives in which to work out his sin and achieve perfection. Such a view of the human situation is consistent with Satan's current strategy to divert man from his need to make a decision regarding eternity *now* — in *this* life.

The East claims to honor all religious scriptures, including the Bible; the great saints and prophets of the various faiths were supposedly all saying the same thing in the final analysis. Therefore, it is important that the eastern sects somehow reconcile their own concepts of *karma* and reincarnation with the biblical teaching. This is generally accomplished by citing isolated verses from Scripture without any regard to their true meaning.

It has been said that one can make the Bible say anything one wants it to say by simply taking verses out of their proper context and using them to support one's own views. Although Christians are by no means exempt from this practice, the eastern cults seem to have made it a specialty.

Karma

Let's look first at the concept of *karma*. This view is often substantiated biblically with the second half of Galatians 6:7: ". . . for whatever a man sows, this he will also reap." The cultists will tell you this means that the results of actions perpetrated in this life will be felt in the next and other lives.

In reality, the phrase is emphasizing man's accountability to a personal God who, according to the *first* half of the verse ". . . is not mocked. . . ." The next verse clarifies what it is that a man reaps. This turns out to be either "corruption" or "eternal life," not a higher or lower station in a subsequent reincarnation.

Jesus further refutes the idea of karma by explaining in John 9:1-3 that a certain individual who was born blind did not somehow bring the situation on himself by sins committed in a previous life.

The truth of the matter is that the concept of salvation as taught in the Bible and the mercilessness of *karmic* law are at serious odds. With Christ there is complete forgiveness and a fresh start in this life: "Therefore if any man is in Christ, he is a new creature; the old things passed away; behold new things have come" (II Corinthians 5:17).

Reincarnation

Let's move on now to the mystical concept of reincarnation. Jesus' references in Matthew 11:11-14 and Mark 9:11-13 regarding John the Baptist being Elijah are often cited by the eastern mystics as documentation of Jesus' belief in reincarnation. Luke 1:17, however, clarifies the issue by stating that John came "in the *spirit* and *power* of Elijah," that is to say, he had the same prophetic zeal as his Old Testament predecessor.

The Transfiguration account in Matthew 17 further refutes the idea that John the Baptist was the incarnate Elijah. This chapter describes the transfiguration of Jesus before His disciples Peter, James and John. Both Moses and Elijah, whose earthly lives had long since ended, appeared with Jesus at this time. Elijah had apparently retained his identity, for he was recognizable to the disciples as Elijah — he had *not* become John the Baptist. And, finally, to seal the issue, John the Baptist was directly·asked in John 1:21, "Are you Elijah?" His answer: "I am not."

As illustrated by this account, the Bible teaches *resurrection* after death rather than reincarnation. The Christian whose earthly life has ended is resurrected into eternity with a glorified body that still somehow retains its unique identity.[9]

A Reincarnated Jesus?

Another biblical passage used by the reincarnationists to substantiate their view is Jesus' statement in John 8:58: ". . . Before Abraham was born, I AM." The mystic points to this claim as proof positive that Jesus Himself existed on earth in previous reincarnations.

As usual, the context in which the phrase is written refutes this idea. Jesus, it turns out, is quoting here from Exodus 3:14. In that passage, Moses questions Jehovah as to what he should say when men begin to ask just who it is that sent him. God's reply: ". . . Say to the sons of Israel, 'I AM has sent me to you.' "[10] Now "I AM" is actually a derivative of the word "Jehovah,"[11] and is thus another way of referring to God. In his John 8 statement, Jesus is claiming to be God Himself, appearing in the flesh. The Jews certainly understood what He meant, for they immediately began to gather stones with intention of killing Him — a common reaction in those days to *blasphemy*.[12]

Perhaps the clearest biblical refutation of the concept of reincarnation is the succinct statement of Hebrews 9:27: ". . . It is appointed for men to die once, and after this comes judgment."

About a year ago, I spent some time counseling a new Christian on a campus in the southern United States. Until his conversion, he had been involved in the Eckankar cult, and though he was now committed to Jesus Christ, a few remnants of eastern doctrine — including the concept of reincarnation — had accompanied him into his new life.

In our conversations I tried to point him to the biblical perspective on the issue of reincarnation. After he had read Hebrews 9:27 for the first time, he raised his head and said, "I guess they can't *both* be true can they?"

As is the case for so many in the mystical subculture today, this student's belief in reincarnation was simply a matter of innocent ignorance regarding biblical truth.

For further information on this issue please turn to page 238 in the Supplementary Research Section.

SOME PRACTICAL HELPS
I. Summary of Key Points

1. *When discipling new Christians with a background in eastern mysticism,* make a mental note of the two key passages refuting *karma* and reincarnation: John 9:1-3 (*karma*); Hebrews 9:27 (reincarnation).

   Remember that the issue with Christians is *resurrection* versus reincarnation. The Bible teaches the resurrection of our bodies with our earthly identity intact. (See I Corinthians 15:35-54.)

2. *When dealing with non-Christians,* you may want to bear in mind this comment by Robert Brow:

   "Incidentally, you won't win a reincarnationist by attacking his views. He needs the system to hold on to till he knows he is loved and accepted as he is with his present body. Introduce him to Jesus, and if he goes along with Him, you will find that his reincarnation ideas have gone within a month."[13]

II. Suggestion for Further Reading

Phillip J. Swihart, *Reincarnation, Edgar Cayce, and the Bible* (Inter-Varsity Press, 1975).

IS THE BIBLE AN AUTHORITATIVE,
RELIABLE RECORD?

Before we begin to answer this question, let's consider the following conversation between a Hare Krishna devotee and a Christian:

Krishna
Devotee: "Chanting God's name is the only way to be purified spiritually. Even the Bible says so. Just look at this quote from the Krishna magazine *Back to Godhead*:

"God has an unlimited variety of names. Some of them — Jehovah, Adonai, Buddha and Allah — are familiar to us, while the names of Krishna and Rama may be less so. However, whatever name of God we may accept, all scriptures enjoin us to chant it for spiritual purification . . . *(for example)* Saint Paul said, 'Everyone who calls upon the name of the Lord shall be saved' (Romans 10:13)."[14]

Christian: "But you've taken Paul's statement out of context. What he means by 'calling on the Lord' here is 'believing on the Lord.' Also, Christ Himself said in Matthew 6:7: 'And when you are praying, *do not use meaningless repetition*, as the Gentiles do. . . .' "

Krishna
Devotee: "Well, I don't believe Jesus really said that. Jesus never wrote anything down Himself, you know. His words were all recorded long after His death. And the Bible's been translated so many times since then. . . ."

The mystics' denial of the Bible's authority is one of their most common responses to the gospel. As a matter of fact, this is exactly the response given by Maharishi Mahesh Yogi when confronted with the biblical emphasis on Christ's suffering and death. He simply refused to believe that Jesus said anything about it, or if He did, then He must have been talking about a "painless suffering."[15]

The point here is that the mystic feels free to use the Bible when it serves his own purposes or seemingly substantiates his own doctrine. But when it *refutes* his ideas, he is more than willing to flatly deny the Bible's ultimate authority.

In actuality, the mystic gives his ultimate allegiance to one of two completely different authorities:

Authority of Inner Intuition

Zen master Suzuki says, ". . . External authority is rejected by Zen. Absolute faith is placed in a man's own inner being. For whatever authority there is in Zen, all comes from within. . . . For this reason, all the scriptures are merely tentative and provisory; there is in them no finality."[16] In other words, if a scriptural teaching conflicts with a person's intuitional impulse, the impulse is to be the final authority rather than the scriptures.

Authority of a Living Spiritual Master

In contrast to the Zennist's rejection of external authority, members of certain of the "messiah cults" give their supreme allegiance to a specific individual. Typical of this perspective is the following comment by Guru Maharaj Ji: "Many people want to go and read scriptures. They think that they will get something out of them. I think, as a matter of fact, that *if you read scriptures you might end up getting more confused*. . . . That is why when a Perfect Master comes, whenever He comes in this earth, He does not need any scriptures. He does not come to write scriptures. He has come to reveal Knowledge. . . . It is only after a Perfect Master leaves that all these scriptures are made. And then *people get into the scriptures and never look for the living Perfect Master*."[17]

In the final analysis, the Zennist and the member of the "messiah cult" concur: Ultimate authority is not to be found in scripture, Christian or otherwise.

The Christian, of course, does believe in the ultimate authority of the Bible. And his belief is not a blind one; it is based on some very solid evidence.

Accuracy of the Copies

Although we do not have the original New Testament documents, scholars tell us that the copyists took such great care in transcribing the Scriptures that the New Testament today is "98.33% pure."[18] In other words, it is very accurate.

Numbers of Manuscripts

If only one ancient manuscript of the New Testament had survived, we would not have been able to compare it with others to determine whether any of the copyists had changed the text. Such is not the case, however; there are more than 13,000 ancient manuscripts or manuscript portions in existence today! By comparing all of these, scholars have been able to affirm that the text is highly accurate.[19]

Evidence from Archeology

No archeological discovery has ever contradicted a single biblical fact. Archeology has served rather to substantiate the amazingly accurate historicity of the document.[20]

Eyewitness Reports

All of the gospels were written by eyewitnesses or from first-hand information.[21] The popular conception that Jesus' words were written down hundreds of years after His death could not be further from the truth.

The concern over whether the Bible can indeed be trusted as an ultimate authority is well-founded.

If the Scriptures *can* be trusted, then one can know without a doubt that Christ did, in fact, say the things attributed to Him. And if one knows for sure that Christ said the things attributed to Him, then he can go on to ask, "Is there any objective evidence to help us determine the validity of these claims?" (Such evidence is discussed in Chapter II.)

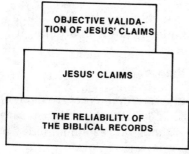

In the diagram, one proceeds from the bottom level to the top level. Only by establishing the reliability of the biblical records can one know that Jesus did, in fact, make certain claims. Once one knows what these claims are, he can go on to objectively determine their validity.

SOME PRACTICAL HELPS

I. *When a person refuses to believe that Jesus really made a claim attributed to Him in the Bible, you might try taking him through the following steps:*

A. Briefly share with him the evidence for the reliability of the biblical documents. The reliability of the Bible as an accurate historical record has not usually been investigated by the mystic. This is generally due to his overall bias in favor of the experiential as opposed to the historical. However, to the extent that he's willing to listen, do point the mystic to the overwhelming evidence for the Bible's veracity.

B. Ask him whether, in light of the seriousness of the issues, he's willing to study with you further on this matter.

C. If he responds positively, make an appointment and look together at the material in Josh McDowell's *Evidence That Demands a Verdict.* Concentrate on the New Testament since it contains Jesus' own words.

D. If he says he's not interested in further study, but has no good reason for rejecting the evidence you initially offered, gently ask him if he has other reasons for rejecting Christ's claims. The idea here is to help him realize that his rejection of Christ is not based on the insufficiency of the evidence, but on his own self-will.

II. *When dealing with Zennists and members of the "messiah cults," the issue becomes, "Where exactly is ultimate authority to be found?" The Zennists claim it is within the self while the "messiah cultists" claim that their spiritual leader is the only valid authority. You might try the following approach when dealing with these individuals:*

A. Ask them how they know their respective authorities are legitimate. Ask them on what basis they have made that decision.

B. Both will probably point to the mystical experience as a validation. Ask them how they can be certain that they're not being spiritually deceived. Show them the dangers of such an experiential approach as discussed in Chapter II.

III. Suggestions for Further Reading:

1. F. F. Bruce, *The New Testament Documents — Are They Reliable?*, Inter-Varsity Press.
2. Josh McDowell, *Evidence That Demands a Verdict, More Evidence That Demands a Verdict.* Campus Crusade for Christ, Inc.

ISN'T MEDITATION CONDONED IN THE BIBLE?

The meeting room was packed. Dozens of businessmen and their wives were gathered to hear a local priest speak on the subject: "TM — Conflict or Complement?" Since I knew the meeting was sponsored by the TM organization, I wasn't surprised when the speaker ultimately endorsed the practice. What did surprise me was his attempt to give it a biblical basis.

"As you know," the priest began, "the practice of meditation is encouraged throughout the Bible. Jesus Himself often drew apart for times of prayer and meditation. And as He looked within Himself during those times, and realized His own divinity, so we, too, can look within ourselves through Transcendental Meditation and realize that spark of divinity within us."

As I'll share in a later chapter, the evening proved to be an exciting one. For our purposes here, however, I would like to direct your attention exclusively to the priest's opening remarks, for they serve beautifully to illustrate the kind of statements being made today that foster confusion in Christian circles regarding the eastern and the biblical varieties of meditation.

Biblical Meditation

In actuality, the contrast between eastern meditation and its biblical counterpart could not be greater.

Biblical meditation always has as its object one of three things: *the works of God* ("I will meditate on all Thy work . . ." Psalms 77:12); *the Word of God* ("Thy word I have treasured in my heart . . ." Psalms 119:11); or *the person of God* ("I meditate on Thee in the night watches . . ." Psalms 63:6).

Conscious thought and the rational mind are both involved in the process. As Psalms 49:3 declares: "My mouth will speak wisdom; and the meditation of my heart will be *understanding*." [22]

The purpose of biblical meditation for the Christian is to replace old thought patterns with the thoughts of God, or, as Romans 12:2 puts it, to ". . . be transformed by the renewing of your mind. . . ."

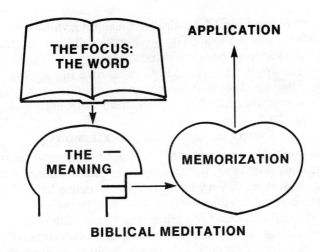

APPLICATION

THE FOCUS:
THE WORD

THE
MEANING

MEMORIZATION

BIBLICAL MEDITATION

Such transformation does not take place mystically or automatically, however. Rather, it involves, first of all, our meditation on the meaning of a specific biblical passage. We then "treasure it in our hearts" by committing it to memory, and God's Holy Spirit convicts us of the need to *apply* the truth contained in the passage to some area of our lives. As a result, we become more conformed to the image, or character of Jesus Christ.[23]

Psalms 119:9, 11 provides a clear summary of the process and purpose of biblical meditation: "How can a young man keep his way pure? By keeping it according to Thy word. . . . Thy *word* have I treasured in my heart, that I may not sin against Thee."

Eastern meditation is not even remotely similar to the biblical practice. The most basic difference between the two lies in the purpose for meditating. The purpose of eastern meditation is not to "renew the *mind*" but rather to "raise the *psychic* consciousness." In fact, the rational mind is shifted into neutral during meditation so that the psyche can take over. No conscious thoughts are involved, no scriptural input is considered, and, therefore, no opportunity exists for conviction of sin in the life.

Interestingly enough, however, eastern meditation claims that one of the results of meditating is that "very easily a sinner comes out of the field of sin and becomes a virtuous man,"[24] to quote Maharishi Mahesh Yogi. Whereas biblical meditation causes a person to grapple with God's perspective as seen in His Word and to apply this perspective to his own life in obedience to God, it is very clear that eastern meditation tries to promote perfection without repentance and without reference to any objective standard.

Danger of Pantheistic Programming

The fact that eastern meditation does not involve conscious thought does *not* mean that the mystical experience is without content, however. A very real message is communicated *subliminally* during the practice.

As the rational mind is hushed and the meditator ceases all conceptualizing, he eventually arrives at a state where he no longer makes distinctions between one thing and another. A feeling of "unity" or "oneness with all things" comes over the meditator, a sensation that can easily be mistaken for an experience with the One, the impersonal Absolute of pantheistic thought. The result is usually a subtle form of pantheistic programming.

The result of a Christian's involvement with mystical experience is demonstrated by Meister Eckhart, one of the so-called "Christian mystics" who have appeared from time to time through the ages. Eckhart was a 13th century Dominican monk who began to indulge in the eastern variety of meditation. As with our clergy friend at the TM meeting, Eckhart's theology was ultimately affected. "My eye and God's eye are one and the same," he said. "God and I, we are one."[25]

To summarize, eastern meditation involves merging with the "One"; biblical meditation centers on appreciating and worshipping the Lord. The same word may be used to identify both practices, but their respective meanings are as far apart as the East from the West.

For further information on this issue please turn to page 240 in the Supplementary Research Section.

SOME PRACTICAL HELPS

I. Summary

A. *Biblical meditation.*

    1. Focus is *outward* on Lord: His Word, His works, His person.

2. Involves conscious thoughts.
3. Purpose: to "renew the mind," become more like Christ.

B. *Eastern meditation.*
    1. Focus is *inward,* on "inner divine self."
    2. Purpose: self-perfection through "raising the psychic consciousness."

II. The Best Defense

The best defense against the false promises of eastern meditation is a strong personal walk with the Lord. If you haven't begun the personal discipline of memorizing and meditating on God's Word, why not begin today? Then, the next time someone tells you about eastern meditation, you can share from personal experience what God is doing in your life through biblical meditation.

DIDN'T JESUS TEACH THE INNER DIVINITY OF ALL MEN WHEN HE PROCLAIMED, "THE KINGDOM OF GOD IS WITHIN YOU"?

The verse quoted most often from Scripture by the mystical subculture is undoubtedly Luke 17:21. The biblical passage in which it's found reads as follows in the King James version:

> "And when he (Jesus) was demanded of the Pharisees when the kingdom of God should come, he answered them and said, 'The kingdom of God cometh not with observation: neither shall they say, Lo here! or, lo there! for, behold, *the kingdom of God is within you*'" (Luke 17:20-21).

Members of virtually every one of the eastern cults use Christ's statement regarding the kingdom of God to support the view that man is essentially divine. Maharishi Mahesh Yogi cites the verse no fewer than 10 times in his *Meditations of Maharishi!* The following comment typifies his thinking: "It should be possible for the followers of Christ to first seek the kingdom of God, and the kingdom of God is within you.

. . . Everybody has the capacity, everybody has it, has his own God within himself."

But, indeed, was Christ *really* pushing pantheism on the Pharisees? An examination of the original Greek in which Luke's gospel was written provides the answer.

The King James version of the Bible erroneously translates the Greek adverb "entos" as "within," giving rise to the idea that Jesus was telling the Pharisees that God was actually *within* them. If Christ had meant to say that the kingdom of God was *inside* each Pharisee, He would have used the Greek word "eso," meaning, literally, "inside."

The mistranslation of the King James has been corrected in the most respected of subsequent translations. The New American Standard reads: "The kingdom of God is *in your midst*." And both the New Scofield and the Revised Standard versions read: "The kingdom of God is *in the midst of you*."

Since the Pharisees were self-righteous individuals who had rejected Christ, His description of the kingdom of God as being *in their midst* (which is precisely where Jesus and His believing disciples were) as opposed to being within them was an accurate statement of fact.

SOME PRACTICAL HELPS

A good passage to help explain the meaning of the kingdom of God is John 3:1-8. The crux of the matter is actually found in verse 3: "Truly, truly I say to you, unless one is *born again*, he cannot see the *kingdom of God*." Explain to the mystic that if he really wants to be part of the kingdom of God, that entrance to the kingdom is contingent on a spiritual birth through Christ.

CAN'T YOGIS TODAY PERFORM THE SAME MIRACLES JESUS DID, INCLUDING RESURRECTIONS?

There are two ways to diminish the impact of the resurrection as a proof of Jesus' unique deity: 1) Deny that it happened, or 2) grant that it happened, but add, "Resurrections aren't such an unusual phenomenon. Anyone who has developed his psychic abilities to their fullest can resurrect from the dead."

The second position is the one taken by most of the eastern subculture today. Subscribing as he does to a world view replete with magic, supernatural beings and paranormal powers, another resurrection more or less makes little difference to the modern mystic.

In fact, the same indifference accorded the resurrection is extended to every other miracle recorded in the Bible. For,you see, the mystic does not view the supranormal happenings in Scripture as "miracles," that is to say, he doesn't see them as evidences of a transcendent God intervening in human affairs and overruling the natural laws of the universe. He views these happenings more in *magical* terms, seeing them rather as examples of the superhuman powers within all men.

A Psychic Moses?

Biblical healings and resurrections are thought to be demonstrations of mind over matter; visions and angelic appearances become the result of normal mystical experience. As one eastern spokesman put it: "In the mystical sense of the term, intuition . . . can also operate during altered states of consciousness, such as the burning-bush experience of Moses and the descent-of-dove experience of Jesus."[26] As far as this commentator is concerned, Moses didn't actually see a bush burning in time and space, but was involved at the time in an inner *psychic* experience.

This way of interpreting the supranormal happenings in the Bible reflects the mystic belief in subjective experience as the only basis for religious faith. Charles Tart expresses the mystic stance this way:

> "Faith in religious teaching brought about by witnessing miracles, for example, can be seen as a rather inferior form of faith because it still uses physical reality as its ultimate testing point, *while the faith that has an experiential basis in spiritual realities alone can be a very important tool in spiritual growth.*"[27]

Another expression of the eastern mindset on this matter came about following a campus lecture I gave in which I had presented the resurrection as a piece of objective evidence for the deity of Christ. As soon as I had finished speaking, a student came up to me in the hopes of "setting me straight" and said, "Christ believed that men shouldn't follow His miracles to God, but should follow God to the miracles." What he meant here was that a person begins his spiritual growth by having an experience with God, an experience that reveals to the individual his own divine potential. He is then ready to fully develop his own latent powers. In this case, and indeed throughout eastern mysticism, self, and not God, was the ultimate focus.

With this bit of background behind us, let us now look directly at the question, "Can yogis today perform the same miracles Jesus did, including resurrections?"

Masters of Metabolism?

There are really two answers here. Yogis and others have on occasion demonstrated an amazing mastery of their physical bodies, managing to lower their metabolic rates, slow their heart beats, reduce their oxygen consumption, etc. Many of these cases of "mind over matter" have been scientifically validated.[28] Resurrection from the dead, however, is a horse of a different color, and claims to this effect require the most careful scrutiny.

In his *Autobiography of a Yogi*, the former head of the Self-Realization Fellowship, Paramahansa Yogananda, writes of several alleged resurrections effected by such yogis as his own guru, Sri Yukteswar. For those in the mystical subculture, with their magic-filled world view, no further validation is necessary; just to state that such resurrections occurred is sufficient.

But how should a Christian evaluate these claims? In fact, God has given us two resources in this regard: our common sense and the Word of God.

Let us look first to our common sense and compare the objective evidence for the resurrection of, say, Sri Yukteswar, with the evidence for Jesus' resurrection.

(1) The witnesses.

Yukteswar allegedly appeared after his death to only two people: one elderly lady and Yogananda himself. Each was alone at the time of the experience. Jesus, by comparison, spent 40 days after His death talking to His disciples in groups of two, three, a dozen and even up to five hundred at one time! Multiple witnesses greatly reduce the possibility of hallucination, whether mystically-oriented or grief-induced.

(2) Public nature of the resurrection.

Jesus prophesied that He would die and then be raised again on the third day following His death. This prophecy was public knowledge. In fact, the Jewish authorities mounted guard over the tomb to prevent such an occurrence from happening. As a result, Jesus' resurrection took place in the midst of public scrutiny. In contrast, Yukteswar died quietly and was buried privately by his own disciples. His alleged resurrection was "public" only to Yogananda and the one elderly woman.

(3) The grave.

The ultimate test to determine whether or not a resurrection has occurred is to look to the grave and see if the body is still there. Yogananda makes no mention whatsoever of there being any change in the grave of his guru. Christ's grave on the other hand has been empty since the third day following His death.

Let's turn now to the Word of God which will give us further insight as to the veracity of Yogananda's claim regarding his guru. Checking such claims against God's Word in addition to using our common sense is crucial, for miraculous events can occur by means of *Satan's* power as well as by God's. Satan has always been able to counterfeit the miraculous.

The apostle John gives us a very significant biblical test for determining the validity of a claim; it applies perfectly in this case:

> "Beloved, do not believe every spirit, but *test the spirits* to see whether they are from God; because many false prophets have gone out into the world.
>
> "*By this you know the Spirit of God: every spirit that confesses that Jesus Christ has come in the flesh is from God;*
>
> "And every spirit that does not confess Jesus is not from God; and this is the spirit of the antichrist ..."
> (I John 4:1-3).

In a "post-resurrection" conversation, Yogananda tells his guru how grieved he was upon first hearing of his death. Chiding Yogananda for such an attitude, the guru explained, "You were only dreaming on earth; on that earth you saw my dream body. Later you buried that dream image. . . . All dream bubbles must eventually burst. . . ."[29]

As he relates this account, Yogananda explains to the reader that in Vedantic thought the physical universe does not really exist, but is only the "dream of God." "All creation or separate existence is *maya* or illusion."[30]

These comments give us two significant insights. First of all, if physical existence is mere illusion, and we possess only "dream bodies," then Yogananda could *not* really believe that Jesus came in the flesh. Thus, according to John's test, Yogananda and his claim qualify for the designation of "antichrist."

Furthermore, Yogananda, in keeping with eastern thought in general, considers the whole concept of resurrection from the dead as being virtually meaningless. For if everything in this life is a mere dream and is not real, then nothing that occurs here can have any ultimate significance. Knowing that Yogananda possesses such a view, the Christian can safely discount the resurrection of Sri Yukteswar as being an event that actually happened.

As for Christ's resurrection, it was of a different order altogether, for Jesus Christ was God in the flesh. He bled *real* blood, he felt *real* pain and He *really* died. And His resurrection, far from being a mere exchange of one "dream body" for another, was a victory over a *real* enemy: death and all the forces of hell. And, ultimately, Christ's resurrection has very real eternal consequences for all who follow Him and who will one day, like Him, be "raised in the newness of life."

MIND/BODY SPINOFFS

In the wake of the eastern cultic invasion, a whole spate of eastern spinoffs have caught the fancy of the western mind. From vegetarianism and Zen macrobiotics to yoga exercises and the martial arts, all share a common focus: the development of the powers of the body. Some of the practices are relatively innocent; others have definite cultic overtones. How, then, can a Christian judge what his own involvement should be, if any?

To answer this question, let's look at two of the most popular eastern imports in the body conditioning field: *hatha* yoga and the martial arts.

Yoga has been practiced in India for thousands of years as a way of attaining oneness with Brahman, the impersonal Absolute. In fact, the word "yoga" literally means "union," referring to the mystical state that results from the practice.

According to Indian metaphysics, there are at least six different forms of yoga, and thus at least six different ways of attaining the desired "union":

The yoga of bodily control (*hatha*)
The yoga of mind control (*raja*)
The yoga of action (*karma*)
The yoga of love (*bhakti*)
The yoga of knowledge (*jnana*)
The yoga of life-energy (*kundalini*)

Exercise Eastern-style

The "union with God" idea is greatly de-emphasized, however, in the mass marketing of *hatha* yoga in the West. In much the same way that the so-called "neutral" meditation techniques are marketed, *hatha* yoga is presented to a gullible western public as being mere "exercise eastern-style."

But *hatha* yoga, as much as any of the other "paths to God" from India, has an inherent religious purpose. Journalist Arthur Koestler, following extensive research, observes that the impression given in the West is "that Hatha yoga is merely a superior system of gymnastic exercises, designed to relax the body and mind by adopting a suitable posture, a natural way of breathing, and thus to facilitate a meditative attitude. At the same time, it is usually denied that there is anything 'mysterious' or 'occult' about its doctrines.

"In fact, every Indian-born practitioner of Hatha yoga, from the Himalayan hermit to the Bombay insurance clerk who spends an hour a day at a yoga institute, knows that Hatha yoga does promise the attainment of supernatural powers; and he also knows that every posture and exercise has both a symbolic meaning and a physiological purpose related to the tenets of ayurvedic medicine, and is not considered a fit subject for discussion with foreigners."[31]

Biological Enlightenment

Unknown to most westerners, *hatha* yoga is actually based on the eastern assumption that enlightenment can be *physically* induced. Let us examine this assumption.

Hatha yoga literally means "forced union." It's believed that spiritual oneness with the impersonal Brahman can be achieved through perfecting the body. Gopi Krishna, a respected Indian yogi, says,"Enlightenment, therefore, is a natural process *ruled by biological laws . . . .*"[32]

There is not the division in Hindu thought that there is in that of the Christian between the physical and the spiritual. All is ultimately one. Therefore, to perfect the physical is also to perfect the spiritual, or "to bring the soul to a clear realization of its own divine nature,"[33] to again quote Gopi Krishna.

We have to remember that while we westerners may be concerned with the simple conditioning of our physical bodies,

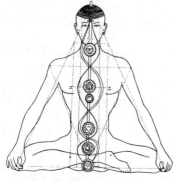

Kundalini Yoga's view of
THE PSYCHIC CENTERS OF THE BODY

the eastern concern is with the "psychic self" or "subtle body." *Hatha* yoga is not primarily focused on muscle tone, as is commonly thought in the West, but aims at raising the psychic consciousness of the individual to the level of oneness with the Absolute. Thus, the physical discipline of *hatha* yoga is considered to be an essential step down the evolutionary path to full divinity.

Two Dangers

There are two primary dangers for the Christian practicing *hatha* yoga. As with eastern meditation, there is the danger of pantheistic programming. The breathing exercises, the physical postures — all combine to create an artificial experience of the "oneness of all things."

But there is a further danger. Within the eastern system,

hatha is universally viewed as the *experiential* preparation for the more philosophical approaches to enlightenment, such as *raja* yoga. French scholar Alain Danielou states that "the sole purpose of the physical practice of Hatha yoga is to suppress the physical obstacles on the spiritual or Royal path of Raja yoga; and Hatha yoga is therefore called 'the ladder to Raja yoga.'"[34]

For the Christian, there are better ways to condition the body than through yoga, *hatha* or otherwise. Consciousness-alteration should have no place within the "temple of the Holy Spirit."

The Martial Arts

The second major mind/body spinoff from eastern religion comes to us primarily from the lands of Buddhism: China, Japan and Korea. These Buddhist offshoots, the martial arts, have caught the western imagination as have few other diversions in recent years. Martial arts studios have proliferated in all the major cities of the West, and Kung Fu movies and TV programs continue to command large audiences. Interest is especially high in the new influx of "soft" martial arts, such as aikido and Kung Fu, as opposed to the more traditional "hard" varieties, such as judo and karate.

What about the Christian's participation in the martial arts?

We'll focus, in this discussion, on the new "soft" forms of the martial arts. For, in contrast to the more traditional forms, these new disciplines have arrived on the western scene loaded with Buddhist and Taoist philosophy which bears close examination.

According to Taoism, one of the dominant religions in China, there is a great energy flowing through the universe and our bodies. This energy consists of two forces, Yin (female) and Yang (male), which constantly complement and harmonize with each other. When one is in harmony with this energy, then his life and body are also in harmony.

**The Taoist
"Yin-Yang" Symbol**

Monism in Motion

The "soft" martial arts of Kung Fu and aikido are physical ways of expressing these monistic beliefs. All attacks, for example, must be met in accordance with the Yin-Yang concept. This is accomplished by "harmonizing" or "flowing" with the attacker and leading him harmlessly in a circle. As aikido expert George Leonard says, "There is a flow in the universe. Our task is to join it . . . . I am part of the universe. The (attacker) is part of the universe . . . . In these delightful moments, the thrower is not separate from the thrown. We blend in a single motion, a small ripple in the endless sea of existence."[35]

Not only is the philosophy behind Kung Fu and aikido pure eastern monism, but, as with eastern meditation and with yoga, the actual performance of the techniques is viewed as a way of directly experiencing ultimate reality. There is often an emphasis on emptying the mind of conscious thought and becoming one with the universe. George Leonard comments that through the practice of aikido, an individual "will certainly know the Divine Ground, the repository of all truth, by a direct intuition superior to discursive reasoning."[36]

In sum, eastern meditation, yoga and the *philosophical* varieties of the martial arts all share the same pitfalls for the Christian: an experience that tends to condition his view of reality, and the possible impartation of an underlying monistic philosophy that directly conflicts with the Bible.

SOME PRACTICAL HELPS

I. Summary

A. *Hatha yoga.*
   1. Origin: India.
   2. Underlying philosophy: Hindu.
   3. Promoted as "exercise eastern-style."
   4. Actually considered a physical means to enlightenment.
   5. Dangers:
      a. Pantheistic programming.
      b. Prepares one for philosophical yoga.
B. *"Soft" martial arts (Kung Fu, aikido).*

1. Origin: China, Japan, Korea.
2. Underlying philosophy: Buddhist and Taoist.
3. Promoted as purely self-defense.
4. Actually considered means of becoming "one" with universe.
5. Dangers:
   a. Conditions view of reality.
   b. Imparts monistic philosophy.

II. Judge for Yourself

Virtually all of the eastern mind/body spinoffs down-play their religious overtones and promote themselves as being "natural techniques." Following are some questions to help you evaluate for yourself the advisability of involvement in these disciplines.

A. *What is the philosophy behind the technique? What is the underlying view of ultimate reality?*

B. *How does that philosophy compare with the biblical view of life?*

C. *Is the philosophy communicated directly or indirectly? How?*

D. *How would you describe the feeling you derive from the experience? Are you left with a sense of the "oneness" or "unity" of all things?*

E. *What fruits has the practice produced in your Christian life? Do you have a greater desire to study God's Word or a lesser one? Has your zeal for sharing Christ with others increased or decreased?*

III. Suggestion for Further Reading

Arthur Koestler, *The Lotus and the Robot* (Harper & Row, 1960).

Bibliography

1. Quoted in *Religion Maharishi Style: The Camouflage Technique* by John E. Patton, 1976, p. 41.
2. Suzuki, D. T., *An Introduction to Zen Buddhism* (Grove Press, NY, 1964), p. 45.

3. Smith, Adam, *Powers of Mind* (Random House, NY, 1975), p. 262.

4. A.C. Bhaktivedanta Swami Prabhupada, "Divine Culture," *Back to Godhead* Magazine, No. 68, 1974, p. 3.

5. For a fuller treatment of the religious nature of TM, see chapter VI. See also *What Everyone Should Know About Transcendental Meditation* by Gordon R. Lewis, (Regal Press, Glendale, CA, 1975).

6. Zen master Yengo, quoted in Suzuki, op. cit., p. 46.

7. Prabhupada, Swami, op. cit., p. 3.

8. *The Bhagavad-Gita As It Is*, Chapter 18, Text 66, p. 835.

9. I Corinthians 15:35-54; John 20:14-28.

10. Exodus 3:14.

11. " 'I AM' is related to the name of God. *YHWH* (Jehovah) is derived from the verb *HAYAH*, to be." Marginal note, Exodus 3:14, NAS.

12. Compare the Jews' reaction in John 10:30-33.

13. Brow, Robert, "Reincarnation," *His* Magazine, March 1975, p. 18.

14. *Back to Godhead* Magazine, Vol. 11, No. 7, p. 1.

15. Maharishi Mahesh Yogi, *Meditations of Maharishi* (Bantam Books, NY, 1973), pp. 123, 124.

16. Suzuki, D. T. op. cit., p. 44.

17. "Editorial" by Guru Maharaj Ji, *And It Is Divine*, June, 1974, p. 6.

18. Geisler, Norman L. and William E. Nix, *A General Introduction to the Bible* (Moody Press, Chicago, 1968), p. 365, quoted in *Evidence That Demands a Verdict* by Josh McDowell (Campus Crusade for Christ, 1972), p. 45.

19. Robertson, A. T., *Introduction to the Textual Criticism of the New Testament* (Broadman Press, Nashville, 1925), p. 29, quoted in McDowell, ibid., p. 46.

20. Glueck, Nelson, *Rivers in the Desert; History of Neteg* (Jewish Publications Society of America, Philadelphia, 1969), p. 31, quoted in McDowell, ibid., p. 68.

21. See McDowell, pp. 64, 65.

22. I am indebted to David Haddon for these insights on biblical meditation.

23. Romans 8:29.

24. Maharishi Mahesh Yogi, op. cit., p. 119.

25. Quoted in Walter T. Stace, *The Teachings of the Mystics*. (New American Library, NY, 1960), p. 127.

26. Maharishi Mahesh Yogi, op. cit., pp. 65, 77, 88, 89, 100, 113, 118, 124, 151, 155.

27. Tart, Charles, *Transpersonal Psychologies* (Harper & Row, NY), 1975, p. 94.

28. Chaudhuri, Haridas, "Yoga Psychology," in *Transpersonal Psychologies*, ed. by Charles T. Tart (Harper & Row, NY, 1975), pp. 234-280.

29. Yogananda, Paramahansa, *Autobiography of A Yogi* (Self-Realization Fellowship, Los Angeles, 1946), p. 494.

30. Ibid., p. 494.

31. Koestler, Arthur, *The Lotus and The Robot* (Harper & Row, NY, 1960), pp. 85, 86.

32. Quoted in John White, *Everything You Want To Know About TM — Including How To Do It*, (Pocket Books, NY, 1976), p. 103.

33. Ibid., p. 103.

34. Danielou, Alain, *Yoga: The Method of Re-Integration* (University Books, NY, 1955), p. 17, quoted in "Yoga" by David Fetcho, Spiritual Counterfeits Project Newsletter, April/May, 1976.

35. Leonard, George, *The Ultimate Athlete*, (Viking Press, NY, 1975), pp. 52, 53.

36. Leonard, George, Ibid., p. 50.

PART TWO

THE CULTS: PSYCHIC SLAVERY IN THE WEST

So far, our analysis of the new western mysticism has focused on the growth of a pervasive eastern mindset throughout the West. Now it's time to take a look inside four of the most influential of the new eastern sects themselves: Transcendental Meditation (TM), the Hare Krishna movement, the Buddhist sect known as Nichiren Shoshu (NSA), and Sun Moon's Unification Church.

What attracts millions of westerners from every walk of life to these groups?

For most, the initial contact with an eastern cult is relatively low-key. You might be invited to share a vegetarian meal at a Hare Krishna temple or attend a weekend "rap session" sponsored by the Unification Church. Someone might ask you to come with them to a group chanting session sponsored by the NSA group. Or you might be encouraged to initiate into TM "purely for the physical benefits."

This initial contact is generally followed by a period of programming of one kind or another. The Unification Church relies heavily on non-stop lectures and around-the-clock chaperonage to wear down a newcomer's defenses and begin to win his allegiance. On the other hand, the pantheistic programming of TM is much subtler. The conditioning process of the meditation experience is generally combined with advanced lectures on quasi-scientific topics, all designed to condition the meditator's world view, and to deepen his commitment to the movement. Eventually in each of these cults, individuals are encouraged to step over the line into the "inner circle." For the Krishna movement, that usually means moving into the Krishna temple, and adopting the dress and discipline of a full devotee. In the TM organization, that final step involves becoming a TM teacher and accepting TM head Maharishi Mahesh Yogi as one's spiritual master.

It is at this point that the relationship between guru and disciple, master and devotee, intensifies. For many hard-core cult members it eventually leads to a kind of psychic slavery. Rational thought and analysis is discouraged, and the guru appears to develop an actual supranormal influence over his disciples.

One of the followers of the American guru called Bubba Free John describes the guru-disciple relationship this way: ". . . The Guru *literally* enters and transforms. It is a kind of possession. It is God-possession. Bubba animates this body. I feel Him all the time, not as an experience, but *as Him*."[1]

In a similar vein, the Swiss coordinator of the Transcendental Meditation movement once confided to me that "you can sit outside Maharishi's room and get all your questions answered." Other advanced meditators have shared similar stories of Maharishi's psychic influence over them.

However it may be manifested from cult to cult, the power of the cult leader over his "inner core" is great. The result is that thousands today are being blinded by the Enemy "with all power and signs and false wonders, and with the deception of wickedness . . ." (II Thessalonians 2:9, 10).

Step with me now into the strange world of the eastern cults — and bring a heart of compassion with you as you come.

---

[1]Bubba Free John, *Garbage and the Goddess* (The Dawn Horse Press, Lower Lake, CA, 1974), p. 151, quoted in Spiritual Counterfeits Newsletter, August, 1976.

"*I don't see any conflict between TM and my Christian faith. I do it every day during my quiet time.*"

—a young California Christian

Transcendental Meditation "*is the only way to salvation and success in life; there is no other way.*"

—Maharishi Mahesh Yogi

Transcendental Meditation: Hinduism in a Scientist's Smock

Increased energy, heightened creativity, reduced stress, lowered blood pressure — the graphs and slogans on Transcendental Meditation (TM) posters across the nation boldly proclaim Nirvana on earth. Television talk shows, the news media, state legislatures — all are paying homage to the little guru from the Himalayas and the mushrooming movement he heads. Some 17 years after he brought Transcendental Meditation to the West, Maharishi Mahesh Yogi today finds himself atop a following of more than a million meditators in the U.S., with 30,000 new initiates joining each month.

Though originally just a fad for the jet set and the counter-culture, then a phenomenon found basically among collegiates, the TM ranks today have been swelled by educators, politicians, sociologists, businessmen and military personnel — all looking for the ultimate elixir for a profusion of societal problems, from drug abuse to employee inefficiency.

Nevertheless, the practice of TM continues to increase on college campuses throughout the U.S. Students' International Meditation Society chapters meet on 95% of all public universities, and more than 100 campuses and adult education programs offer the Maharishi's academically oriented Science of Creative Intelligence course for credit.

Why would so many college students — in fact, westerners of every race, creed, color and profession — be attracted to something as occult-sounding as Transcendental Meditation?

Probably because TM claims to offer a low-commitment, non-religious way to experience inner peace. And, TM appears to deliver on at least part of its promises; many Americans will attest to being more relaxed after beginning meditation.

But is TM merely a "scientific technique for relaxation," as the organization claims? Or is it, as Colin Campbell put it in *Psychology Today*, "clearly a revival of ancient Indian Brahmanism and Hinduism"?[1] I believe the facts clearly show the religious mold from which TM is cast.

The Mantra

The secret Sanskrit word used by a person in his meditation is called a *mantra*. For 20 minutes in the morning and again in the evening, the meditator is to sit quietly and silently repeat his *mantra* over and over. According to TM instruction, the silent repetition of the word produces psychic vibrations that positively affect mental and physiological functions. The *mantra*, then, becomes the key to the TM experience.

New initiates are never told the deeper, religious purpose of the *mantra*, however. Maharishi explains it:

> "We do something here according to Vedic rites, particularly, specific chanting to produce an effect in some other world, draw the attention of those higher beings or gods living there. The entire knowledge of the *mantras* or hymns of the Vedas (Hindu scriptures) is devoted to man's connection, to man's communication with the higher beings in different strata of creation."[2]

Recent research has revealed, in fact, that, far from being "meaningless sounds," the TM *mantras* are actually inseparably related to the names of Hindu deities![3]

Maharishi's Own Writings

Introductory TM lectures and literature are filled with vigorous disclaimers of TM's religious character. But the published writings of Maharishi clearly contradict the organization's carefully constructed public image. Consider these statements:

"Transcendental Meditation is a path to God."[4]

"A very good form of prayer is this meditation which leads us to the field of the creator, to the source of creation, to the field of God."[5]

"(TM) is the only way to salvation and success in life; there is no other way."[6]

Maharishi's motivation in promoting a non-religious facade is clearly that of shrewd opportunism, as seen in his book, *The Science of Being and Art of Living*:

"Whenever and wherever religion dominates the mass consciousness, transcendental deep meditation should be taught in terms of religion. . . .Today when politics is guiding the destiny of man, the teaching should be primarily based on the field of politics and secondarily on the plane of economics. . . .It seems, for the present, that this transcendental deep meditation should be made available to the peoples through the agencies of government."[7]

So hoping to avoid the constitutional issue of separation of church and state, Maharishi falsely claims that TM is purely secular.

The Initiation Ceremony

Perhaps the clearest outcropping of underlying Hinduism shows up in the initiation ceremony in which all potential meditators are required to participate.

Former TM teacher Vail Hamilton gives us these insights into the ceremony she led many initiates through:

"At the beginning of the ceremony the candidate is asked to bring an offering of six flowers, three pieces of fresh fruit, and a white handkerchief, which are placed on an altar before a picture of Guru Dev (which means 'Divine Leader'), who is the Maharishi's departed Master. The small room is candlelit and filled with incense. The candidate is asked to stand before this altar while the teacher sings a hymn of thanksgiving and praise to the entire line of departed Hindu masters who have passed down the knowledge of the *mantras*. At the end of the song, the teacher indicates to the person that he is to kneel for a few moments of silence, and then, both still kneeling, the teacher repeats the *mantra* selected for the person and has him repeat it until he has correctly pronounced it, and then they are seated for further instruction.

"Many candidates I encountered while teaching TM objected to this religious aspect, but went along with it in order to learn the technique. Once they experienced the pleasant sensation of meditating, they quickly forgot their immediate objection to the religious nature of the ceremony and rapidly embraced all that TM had to offer them."[8]

TM teachers generally respond that the ceremony is just a ritual of thanksgiving to the line of departed TM teachers through the centuries. However, a recently obtained English translation of the hymn, or *puja*, chanted in Sanskrit by the initiator clearly shows the hymn to be a form of Hindu worship. The invocation reads, in part:

"To Lord Narayana, to lotus-born Brahma, the Creator . . . to Shankaracharya the redeemer, hailed as Krishna . . . I bow down. To the glory of the Lord I bow down again and again, at whose door the whole galaxy of gods pray for perfection day and night. Adorned with immeasurable glory, preceptor of the whole world, having bowed down to him, we gain fulfillment."[9]

Of course, because this is chanted in Sanskrit, the TM initiate never knows the nature of the ceremony in which he is taking part.

The TM public relations pattern is consistent. The *mantra*, they insist, is a "meaningless syllable," part of a scientific technique. Maharishi's own words, however, show it to be a spiritual tool to be used to call on spiritual beings "on other levels of creation."

So what if Transcendental Meditation is religious in nature? Are there any inherent dangers involved in the practice of TM? Yes, there are several very real dangers, both on the physical and the spiritual levels.

"Unstressing" Can Cause Severe Physical Reactions

TM's alleged purpose is to relieve the meditator of built-up stress, both from this life, and from "previous lives" (reincarnation is a central TM/SCI doctrine). This process is known as "normalization of the nervous system," or simply, "unstressing." Introductory TM lectures are filled with glowing descriptions of the supposed positive benefits of the technique, but potential meditators are never warned of the violent reactions experienced by many advanced initiates.

Greg Randolph, another former TM teacher who has become a Christian, has observed this reaction often: "When you're unstressing for a long time, large amounts of this (stress) can come out and actually condition angry moods and cause heart attacks and all kinds of different experiences."[10]

But what about all the "scientific tests" supposedly documenting the positive benefits of TM? Dr. Peter Fenwick, consultant neurophysiologist at St. Thomas Hospital in England, has this to say about the TM tests:

> "All of these studies need to be looked upon with reservations. Few include adequate control groups, and none that I am aware of have yet used a blind control procedure, where neither the subject nor the observer is aware of the treatment given or the aims of the experiment. Until this sort of study is carried out in meditating groups, it is almost impossible to draw any conclusions."[11]

Transcending Thought Causes Spiritual Dullness

Recent studies reported in Psychology Today have indicated that TM "may have the side effect of decreasing our ability to think creatively."[12] This side effect is common to most forms of eastern meditation because they supposedly "transcend" conscious thought. The goal is to put your mind in neutral and to "get beyond" intellectual analysis and rational thought processes. TM initiates experience this twice a day at first, but eventually you're encouraged to keep your mantra on "the back burner," and to slip into a passive meditative state throughout the day.

This de-emphasis on the mind carries with it at least one inherent danger, namely, the dulling of the mind's ability to make judgments, to discern, and to evaluate. Of course, much of eastern philosophy says this is a good thing. As we've seen, they say the mind is not really to be trusted; instead, their emphasis is on raw experience.

TM/SCI also says transcending thought not only relieves stress, but "automatically" and "spontaneously" produces moral character. No mental concentration or self-evaluation is necessary. The mind is set aside as an active participant in this supposed transformation.

Dr. Jacob Needleman, chairman of the philosophy department at San Francisco State University, asks this about TM: ". . . To what in a man does the idea of easy spiritual progress appeal? What sort of pleasure or 'happiness' does it bring to accept the thought that no struggle or sacrifice of any sort is needed for the radical transformation of the inner life?"[13]

The biblical perspective, on the other hand, is that God has given us a mind to help us evaluate the truth and error in the things we become involved in, as well as to help us evaluate the right and wrong within ourselves. The Bible gives us an objective standard for us to measure ourselves by, thus avoiding the trap of a totally subjective, experiential orientation.

TM Can Become a Substitute
for a True Experience with God

The most serious danger involved in the practice of TM, then, is not physical or mental, but spiritual. What starts for many meditators as merely a search for an effective relaxation technique ends with embracing TM's pantheistic philosophy in hopes of reaching "the field of God."

All meditators are encouraged to go on to the advanced Science of Creative Intelligence course. There, meditators learn of the ultimate spiritual goals of the movement in terms of the "seven states of consciousness" through which an individual is to evolve. These states include the three that everyone experiences: (1) waking, (2) dreaming and (3) deep sleep, plus four additional levels, attained only through the practice of TM: (4) bliss consciousness, (5) cosmic consciousness, (6) god consciousness and (7) unity consciousness.[14]

The sixth state, god consciousness, specifically refers to a pantheistic self-deification. As Maharishi explains, "He who practices Transcendental Meditation becomes acquainted with the inner divine consciousness. [15]

"Although we are all 100% Divine," the Maharishi elaborates, "consciously we do not know that we are Divine, so

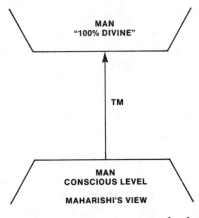

MAN
"100% DIVINE"

TM

MAN
CONSCIOUS LEVEL

MAHARISHI'S VIEW

there is no connection, there is no bridge and we suffer on the conscious level."[16] The practice of TM, then, is supposed to help the meditator realize his true divine essence, and bridge the gap between the "conscious level" and the "transcendental level." Through TM, the Maharishi concludes, "a sinner very easily comes out of the field of sin and becomes a virtuous man."[17]

This promise is typical of the low-commitment nature of TM: presumably, little or no change in lifestyle is required to become "morally excellent or good." This assumes, of course, that there is nothing in man's basic nature that needs changing, and that a radical spiritual transformation can take place virtually effortlessly.

Oddly enough, ex-TM teacher Vail Hamilton experienced just the opposite in her search for "inner divinity." "As I began meditating more and more," she recalls, "I noticed a growing pride and insensitivity to others in myself — even though I felt more calm and confident than ever before. I realized I was becoming, in fact, my own god."

How could a meditator be feeling more calm and confident, and simultaneously sense a growing ego problem? The answer is simple.

TM attempts only to suppress the *symptoms* that self-centeredness and sin produce, symptoms like guilt and lack of peace. The *root problem* of self-centeredness is never dealt with. This approach is appealing for a couple of reasons:

(1) No humbling is necessary. There's no need to admit to anybody, God included, that you've been wrong.

(2) The TM experience reinforces an individual's autonomy and independence and ultimately points him toward a belief in his own divinity.

God's words through the prophet Ezekiel reveal the foolishness of man's attempts at self-deification: "Thus says the Lord God, '. . . You have said, "I am a god, I sit in the seat of gods, in the heart of the seas"; Yet you are a man and not God, although you make your heart like the heart of God.' "[18] This attitude of self-will and independence is at the heart of what sin is all about. And it's been man's primary obstacle in establishing a close relationship with God ever since Lucifer decided second-best wasn't good enough in the heavenly hierarchy.

Still, God has always desired to have a relationship with men and women. So He Himself bridged the gap between His 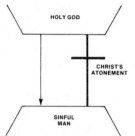 perfection and our sinfulness. At a point in history, God reached down to man through Jesus Christ, and through His sacrificial death on the cross for our sins, made it possible for us to experience His cleansing and forgiveness and inner peace.

TM Can Open a Person to Demonic Activity

One of the most serious dangers for advanced meditators is the possibility of involvement in demonic activity.

The danger here comes from combining the mental passivity of the meditation state with the active repetition of the mantra, the purpose of which is "to produce an effect in some other world, draw the attention of those higher beings or gods living there,"[19] to again use Maharishi's words.

Vail first began experiencing activities of this kind during her TM teacher training course in Italy in 1972. She relates: "One night I awoke with a sense of fear because a spirit was putting pressure all over my body and head in an attempt to enter my body. I commanded it to leave and resisted it until it left. Other supernatural experiences also began to occur — ESP and clairvoyance, telepathy and the beginnings of astral travel."

The dangers involved in the practice of TM are clear — and needless. To the Christian, Jesus promised, "Peace I leave with you; My peace I give to you; not as the world gives, do I give to you. . . [19] All of the resources of Jesus Christ are available to us if we are willing to yield the various areas of our lives to His gracious control.

Why turn to a dangerous spiritual counterfeit when the time-tested promise of Scripture is to "let your requests be made known to God. And the peace of God, which surpasses all comprehension, shall guard your hearts and your minds in Christ Jesus"?[20]

For further reading on the subject of Transcendental Meditation, please turn to page 240 in the Supplementary Research Section.

SOME PRACTICAL HELPS
I. Summary of Key Points

A. *TM: Science or Religion?*
   1. The *mantra* — designed to call on Hindu deities.
   2. Maharishi's own writings — reveal TM to be "a path to God."
   3. The initiation ceremony is religious.
      a. The offerings to "Guru Dev."
      b. The kneeling.
      c. The *puja* (worship ceremony) praising Hindu deities.

B. *Dangers of TM.*
   1. "Unstressing" can cause severe physical reactions.
   2. Transcending thought causes spiritual dullness.
   3. TM can become a substitute for a true experience with God.
   4. TM can open a person to demonic activity.

II. Some Practical Suggestions

A. *Distinguish between new initiates and TM teachers.*
   1. The vast majority of new TM initiates are involved in TM purely for the physiological benefits. They generally have no knowledge of the religious aspects of the practice. In fact, they generally have heard the organization deny being a religion so many times, that they find it hard to believe even when confronted with the facts.
   2. In summary, you may or may not be talking to someone with an "eastern mindset" when you talk to a new TM initiate. *Use the same approach you would for anyone else: share a straight-forward presentation of the gospel.*

3. Although it may be helpful to point out some of the dangers of involvement in TM, don't make TM's religious nature the main emphasis of your interaction. Focus instead on their personal need to accept Christ as Savior and Lord.

4. For your Christian friends involved in TM obtain copies of the article "Transcendental Meditation: Relaxation or Religion?" from the Publications Department, Campus Crusade for Christ, San Bernardino, CA 92414, or let them read the information on TM in this book. Share with them the biblical principles for inner peace found in the presentation "Have You Made the Wonderful Discovery of the Spirit-filled Life?" which is found in the Supplementary Research Section, pp. 269 .

5. For almost all TM teachers and many advanced meditators who have gone on to take the Science of Creative Intelligence course or other advanced seminars, TM has become their religion, and Maharishi is their spiritual master. I've had several TM teachers admit this to me. In their advanced training they are exposed to the doctrines of reincarnation, *karma* and spiritual evolution through the practice of meditation. *TM teachers are also trained to answer questions deceptively about TM's religious nature.*

6. For teachers, as well as new initiates, it's best not to become involved in a long discussion about TM being a disguised form of Hinduism. Instead, focus on their personal need for Christ. Because they claim TM is not a substitute for any religious belief, they will generally be open to discussing it. You might introduce the gospel by asking, "Could I share what I believe as a Christian? Then you can tell me if it does conflict with anything in TM." Stress Christ's death on the cross and the need to ask forgiveness in order to know God and to experience peace. (TM says peace and a sense of "cleansing" come only by "clearing your mind" of all guilty thoughts through meditation.)

B. *An encouraging encounter.*

    1. In a previous chapter I mentioned a TM meeting where a priest spoke on "TM: Conflict or Complement?" The evening was an exciting one that I think could be duplicated elsewhere.

    In the question and answer time, I asked the priest if he was aware of the meaning of the *puja* or hymn that's chanted during the TM initiation.

    "No," he said. "It's all in Sanskrit. He could have been chanting through the telephone directory for all I knew."

    "Would you mind if I read a couple lines from the English translation?" I asked. "I'd like to ask you a question about it."

    "No. Go right ahead."

    I read the section that appears in this chapter on page 136 and then asked, "In view of the Hindu deities that are praised here, could you, being a priest of the Christian religion, now that you know the meaning of the *puja*, ever initiate someone into TM yourself?"

    There was a long pause. "I don't know," he said. "I'd have to think about that."

    At that point, several people who were meditators began asking questions. One couple in particular wanted to know why they hadn't been told the significance of the initiation ceremony before. "It seems like you're trying to keep something from us," they said.

    When the meeting finally broke up we were surrounded by people wanting to know more about the hidden religious aspects of TM and how they could get copies of the material we had. We were able to share the gospel with several individuals and made appointments with several others to talk later.

    2. Be prepared.

    In public situations like this keep in mind two principles: be prepared with fully documented facts, not just opinions, and be very courteous. *Do not* dominate the question and answer time if there are others who have questions.

Be prepared also for little tricks from the TM teacher designed to undercut the impact of your questions. Often, if a teacher senses that the questions are reflecting negatively on TM, he'll say, "We need to get off this topic. If there are some who are interested in these religious questions, you can stay after the meeting and we'll discuss them."

If this happens, try to talk to several people as soon as the meeting ends and make appointments to talk further. But, interestingly enough, a large number usually stay behind for the second meeting anyway.

C. Don't argue. Reflect love.

III. Suggestions for Further Reading

1. Gordon Lewis, *What Everyone Should Know About Transcendental Meditation* (Regal Press).
2. David Haddon, *TM: A Christian Analysis* (Inter-Varsity Press).
3. John White, *Everything You Want to Know About TM — Including How to Do It* (Pocket Books, Simon Schuster).

Bibliography

1. Campbell, Colin, "The Facts on Transcendental Meditation: Part I," *Psychology Today*, April, 1974, p. 38.
2. Maharishi Mahesh Yogi, *Meditations of Maharishi Mahesh Yogi*, (Bantam Books, NY, 1973), pp. 17, 18 (Italics are mine).
3. See Supplementary Research Section on "The Meaning of the Mantras," p. 247.
4. Maharishi Mahesh Yogi, op. cit., p. 59.
5. Ibid., p. 95.
6. Maharishi, *On the Bhagavad-Gita: A New Translation and Commentary* (Penguin Books, Baltimore, 1967) p. 228.
7. Maharishi, *Science of Being and Art of Living* (New American Library, Bergenfield, NJ, 1963) pp. 299, 300.

8. Haddon, David, "Transcendental Meditation Wants You," *Eternity*, November, 1974, p. 22.

9. "The Translated Puja" from *The Holy Tradition*, uncopyrighted TM teacher's manual, quoted in *Right On*, November, 1975, p. 10.

10. Alexander, Brooks and Fetcho, David, "TM Behind Closed Doors," *Right On*, November, 1975, p. 10.

11. *London Times*, May 17, 1975; quoted in *Right On*, November, 1975, p. 8.

12. Martindale, Dr. Colin, "What Makes Creative People Different?", *Psychology Today*, July, 1975, p. 3.

13. Needleman, Jacob, *The New Religions* (Doubleday, 1970), pp. 134-135.

14. Campbell, Anthony, *Seven States of Consciousness: A Vision of Possibilities Suggested by the Teaching of Maharishi Yogi* (Harper & Row, NY, 1974).

15. Maharishi, *On the Bhagavad-Gita: A New Translation and Commentary*, p. 14.

16. Maharishi, *Meditations of Maharishi*, pp. 177, 178.

17. Ibid., p. 119.

18. Ezekiel 28:2.

19. Maharishi, *Meditations of Maharisha*, pp. 17, 18.

20. John 14:27.

21. Philippians 4:6, 7.

7

Hare Krishna: A God in Saffron?

In a Krishna Consciousness temple on Detroit's east side, the great-grandson of wealthy auto maker Henry Ford and the daughter of union leader Walter Reuther wear loose-fitting robes and chant prayers to a blue-skinned deity named Krishna. Alfred Ford and Elizabeth Reuther are just two of more than 10,000 young people in the U.S. alone who have turned their backs on material comforts and joined the Hare Krishna movement.

It all started in the mid-sixties in New York. There a 70-year-old newly-arrived immigrant from India began quietly gathering disciples among Greenwich Village's counter-culture. His message was simple: drop out of material life and give yourself in devotion to the Hindu god Krishna.

Today, this same man, now referred to as "His Divine Grace," A. C. Bhaktivedanta Swami Prabhupada, heads a movement known as the International Society for Krishna Consciousness (ISKCON). ISKCON boasts some 68 centers worldwide where the ascetic life of Krishna Consciousness is diligently practiced.

The Pharmaceutical Philosopher

Who *is* this man and exactly what *is* his movement? Prabhupada, né Abhay Charan De, entered this world in Calcutta, India, in 1896. He eventually studied philosophy, English ~~ '

147

economics at the University of Calcutta, though he did not graduate from that institution. In subsequent years, he earned a living as a pharmaceutical manager until 1959 when he left his wife and five children to devote himself to full-time study under Siddhartha Goswami.

For his part, Goswami had also abandoned a career, surrendering a professorship in mathematics and astronomy in 1908 in order to spend his days spreading the teachings of the 16th century Indian sage, Chaitanya. Among other things, Chaitanya had declared Krishna supreme amidst the galaxy of Hindu gods.

At any rate, Goswami eventually commissioned student Prabhupada to carry the message of devotion to Krishna to the Western World, a mission which Prabhupada was more than willing to carry out in devotion to his respected master. In 1965, he hopped a slow freighter to America where he found fertile ground for his philosophy among the New York "hippies."

The swami was indeed welcomed with open arms. Former "beats," such as poet Allen Ginsberg, took to eulogizing Krishna Consciousness in iambic pentameter, and Beatle George Harrison declared its virtues in song. A "hip" publication, "The Village Voice," began to publicize the movement, and an assorted congregation, comprised mainly of young people within the drug culture, soon flocked to the grandfather figure in the saffron robes. Prabhupada's mission was well on its way to full fruition.

Self-denial Krishna Style

The Krishna Consciousness movement is, in a word, "ascetic." While TM and others of the watered-down imports from the East would stress that no change in lifestyle is necessary in order to attain "god-consciousness," ISKCON makes a strenuous attempt to regulate every aspect of a devotee's life. The men shave their heads, believing that the sole purpose for hair is sexual attraction. (A shiny scalp is also a symbol of submission to Krishna.) Only a pigtail is left sprouting from the back of the head; devotees believe Krishna will use this one day to "pull them into heaven."

Male devotees wear a "kirtan" (shirt) and a "dhoti" (loose trousers). Female devotees wear a sari, a single wide piece of thin cloth that is wound around the body. The garb for both male and female is strategically designed to de-emphasize the body, one of the evil aspects of the physical world, believe Krishna followers.

Each devotee carries with him at all times a string of 108 beads, similar to Catholic rosary beads. The beads represent the 108 cowherdess lovers of Krishna, and each must be chanted upon with the 16-word "mahamantra" or "great mantra" which proceeds as follows:

HARE KRISHNA, HARE KRISHNA,
KRISHNA, KRISHNA, HARE, HARE
HARE RAMA, HARE RAMA,
RAMA, RAMA, HARE, HARE.

In addition to the attire and the beads, both designed to help devotees forget the physical realm so that they can dwell upon Krishna, asceticism is carried over into every other phase of life.

Blessings by the Mouthful

The Krishna follower's diet is vegetarian, consisting primarily of a white substance called "prasadam" which is made with milk, yogurt and diced fruit. This concoction, supposedly blessed by Krishna himself, provides a subtle way of "blessing" nonbelievers. Food is offered to the public in the belief that Krishna's energy floods the body of the unsuspecting diner when the food is digested.

Even the smell that emanates from the devotee is regulated as it, too, must be a reminder of his god. ISKCON owns a lucrative incense business called "Spiritual Sky" that manufactures a vast assortment of heavenly aromas. Devotees actually believe Krishna is physically present in the aromatic fragrance!

Musical instruments such as bells, drums and finger symbols provide "transcendental sound vibrations," and temple idols of Krishna and his lover offer visual reminders of the god they worship.

As if such regulations were not enough, Krishna followers are faced daily with a regimen that begins at 3 a.m. and doesn't end until 10 at night. In between, the devotee is called on for a variety of chores including temple cleaning, working in the incense factory, or street chanting and begging. In addition, he is also responsible for keeping up with the required number of *mahamantra* chants and must participate in the group dancing that westerners are accustomed to seeing on the streets of most major cities.

The Devotee and the Counter-culture

Strict adherence to the so-called "Four Rules" is also required. These involve a personal restraint from gambling, intoxicating drinks, illicit sex and the eating of meat. Further elaboration is given in each of these categories. All sexual contact between husband and wife, for example, except for the sole purpose of procreation, is considered illicit. And according to the law of *karma*, meat eaters will be born in a future life either as animals or as humans doomed to violent death in war.

What kind of individual would be motivated to adopt such a lifestyle? A personal profile of the typical Hare Krishna devotee is revealing. In his book *Hare Krishna and the Counter Culture*, J. Stillson Judah writes:

"Most of the converts to Hare Krishna come from the counter culture. They have rejected the goal of material success through competitive labor, education that promotes that end, sense gratification, parental or civil authority that favors the status quo, war and hypocrisy, especially in matters of racial discrimination."[1]

Statistics reveal that more than 30% of all practicing devotees have spent at least one year in college, over 91% smoked marijuana before joining, and 75% had unfavorable attitudes toward authority. Former church-goers include 70% of all devotees.[2]

Krishna followers claim they were drawn to the movement through "the sound of the *mantra*, the friendliness of the devotees, the philosophy of the movement, the food served and the power of the spiritual master, Prabhupada." In addition, the communal living offers to those who would seek it an alternative to a more traditional lifestyle.[3]

The doctrine underlying ISKCON is clearly Hindu in the Vaishnavistic (as opposed to the Vedantic) tradition. The major difference between the Vaishnavistic and the Vedantic traditions is the way in which each views ultimate reality.

The Vedantic movement emphasizes the *impersonal* nature of God — called Brahman. Brahman is the Absolute, Ultimate Reality, the Force that lies behind the universe. When oneness with Brahman is attained through enlightenment, individual personality disappears.

In the second century B.C., the Vedantist position was challenged by Vaishnavism which claims that ultimate reality is to be found in the *personal* god Vishnu, or Krishna. Thus, thanks to the Vaishnavistic movement, a personal god finally broke through the impersonal world of Hindu pantheism to vie for man's devotion.

Salvation Through Devotion

A subsequent development which added greatly to the popularity of the Vaishnavistic movement was *bhakti* yoga. This form of yoga taught devotion as the way of release from the endless round of rebirths known as the *wheel of samsara*. Previous forms of yoga had taught good works as the way of release (*karma* yoga), or had stressed knowledge as the key (*jnana* yoga). But *bhakti* yoga taught devotion to a personal deity, and this concept clearly paved the way for the future acceptance of Krishna Consciousness.

The basic tenets of ISKCON's doctrine today include the following:[4]

(1) Krishna is the highest of all deities.

(2) The body is illusory; the soul is individual and at the same time part of the divine soul.

(3) By chanting the divine name, one is delivered from suffering and experiences ecstasy — transcendental love without sexual contact.

(4) Devotees should surrender completely to their gurus.

Now when the Krishna follower speaks of the "oneness of souls" as in (2) above, he does not mean this in the pantheistic sense. ISKCON doctrine states that individuals maintain a distinct identity in relation to Krishna. So when he speaks of oneness, the Krishna devotee is referring to the "fact" that Krishna's "super soul" or energy pervades the universe and all living things.

Pantheism with a Personal Touch

ISKCON's belief in Krishna's partial representation in every living thing is really a compromise between the *bhakti* yoga tradition of devotion to a personal god and the pantheism that has held sway in eastern thought for centuries. In fact, there are many such compromises within ISKCON. For example, the gods of the Hindu trinity are explained by Krishna apologists as "forms or expansions" of Krishna, as are the myriad of lesser gods of Hinduism.

ISKCON does lean toward more traditional eastern thought in its belief that the physical world is simply *maya* or illusion, a mere figment of man's depraved perception. Now an important moral point emerges here. If everything in this world is mere illusion, then the concepts of good and evil must inevitably fall within that category also. (Krishna is considered to be above good and evil.) Hence, suffering of all kinds, war and injustice are blinked off as passing unreality by Krishna devotees.

At any rate, if the physical world is only *maya* or illusion, why does man view it otherwise? How did his perception become depraved in the first place? These are difficult questions to answer, but at least the ISKCON cosmologists make the attempt.

An Over-inflated God

Aeons ago, they allow, Krishna grew and grew until he became the over-inflated deity "Maha-Vishnu" or "Great Vishnu." A result of Krishna's strange and irresponsible expansion was the creation of the material universe and of all living creatures. Since such expansion was not in keeping with the normal behavior of the Hindu gods, the resultant material universe was not a *real* one but was merely illusory.

The people who inhabited the material universe did not surrender in love to Krishna as they should rightfully have done, so, consequentially, their perception of the world became depraved. They began to frolic in the material universe, turning to sense gratification and filling their days with the allurements of illusion while an unrequited Krishna wept in the skies.

Earth, Hell or the Spirit Planets

Among the many illusory diversions that sidetrack mankind, three stand out prominently in ISKCON thought: goodness, passion and ignorance. It is the way in which a man responds to these three illusions while on earth that determines where he will spend his next life. If he is governed by ignorance, then his next destination will be hell; if passion rules him in this world, then he will experience future rebirths on earth. But a life based on goodness (total repudiation of the material world and total devotion to Krishna) will reap for the fortunate devotee a future life on other planets in the higher spirit realms.

In view of this somewhat ponderous cosmology, what would the Krishna devotee state as man's basic problem? It would certainly not be "sin" in the Christian sense of the term. The answer would rather be that man has forgotten Krishna. As a result he has become preoccupied with all things temporal. The Krishna follower will tell you that man is possessed with the desire to harness the physical realm for his own benefit.

What man *should* concentrate on is the fact that he is really a spirit-soul. "I am not this body," devotees will tell you. Man should wage a continual war with his libido, they say, which pulls him toward a preoccupation with his own body and the physical realm and away from the spiritual.

A God Without Grace

It is interesting to note here that Krishna offers no assistance to his followers in their 24-hour-a-day struggle for total purity. Krishna is not a god of grace. It is up to each devotee to keep his own mind and body pure through various works and by chanting the *mahamantra*.

Since Krishna is so far removed from his followers, a "spiritual master" is called for to help usher devotees along the path to Krishna Consciousness. To be considered genuine, a spiritual master must come from within the line of "disciplic succession." In other words, it is only those masters who can trace their ancestry back to such spiritual stalwarts as Chaitanya who are considered the legitimate middle-men between Krishna and his followers. Prabhupada claims such an ancestry and is himself worshipped as a manifestation of God.

Let's look now at a biblical assessment of some of the key points of ISKCON doctrine.

Works Orientation

The Krishna follower pursues a myriad of different *works* — chanting, keeping the Four Rules, etc. — in the hopes of compensating for his sin of failure to love Krishna.

The Bible teaches that only one work was necessary to obliterate forever the repercussions of sin. It occurred on Calvary. When Jesus Christ suffered death on the cross as a payment for the sins of mankind, He freed men forever from both the penalty and the power of sin. Our part is merely to understand what Jesus did for us (and this is clearly delineated in the Bible) and to *believe* that He did it. That is why Paul says in Romans 3:28, ". . . A man is justified by *faith apart from works* of the law," and in Ephesians 2;8, 9, "For by grace you have been saved *through faith* . . . not as a result of works . . . ."

World of Illusion

The Krishna follower believes that the human body and the physical world are not real commodities but simply *maya* or illusion. This "fact" results from the capriciousness of his god whose irresponsible "expansion" created an unreal universe.

The Bible teaches that the true God is anything but a capricious deity who delights in playing cosmic pranks. He is a real God, and His creation is equally real, for it is the result of His responsible and determinate will. This is evidenced in the first chapter of Genesis.

If all of God's creation is real, then man's body is no exception. And this, by the way, includes the body of Jesus Christ who was God incarnate.

In addition, the Bible teaches us something further about the human body and the physical universe. In Genesis 1:31, after creating everything that exists in heaven and on earth, ". . . God saw all that He had made, and behold, it was very *good*."

Divine Indifference

The Krishna follower believes that the object of his devotion, "The Supreme Personality of Godhead," resides beyond our universe on a "heavenly planet" and is thus relatively inaccessible and remote. Although he imitates many of man's actions, Krishna cannot really understand man, because he is, and always has been, 100% divine. The *Bhagavad-Gita* teaches that "the Lord Krishna neither hates nor likes anyone though he appears to."[5]

The Bible teaches that God *identifies* with man, for He became a man in the person of Jesus Christ. According to Hebrews 2:17, 18, ". . . He had to be made *like His brethren in all things*, that He might become a merciful and faithful high priest in things pertaining to God, to make propitiation for the sins of the people. For since He Himself was tempted in that which He has suffered, He is able to come to the aid of those who are tempted."

The Bible further teaches that God *loves* man: "For God so loved the world that He gave His only begotten Son, that whoever believes in Him should not perish, but have eternal life" (John 3:16).

While the Krishna devotee feels that he must try to compensate for his sin through devotion to a capricious deity, the Christian knows that he need only respond to the love that has been abundantly bestowed on him through the person of Jesus Christ.

God's Moral Character

The deity of the Krishna follower has a character that is marked by such traits as thievery and lust. Before he obtained his 16,000 wives, Krishna had relations with numerous country girls called "gopis" (cowgirls). In one account, he manages to lure them with his flute into the forest where he hides their clothes as they bathe in a river. He returns the stolen clothes only after forcing the girls to come before him and beg for them.

Ultimately, this god who considers himself beyond good and evil openly claims for himself the title of "Master of demons."[6]

The Bible teaches that the true God, as revealed to us through the person of Jesus Christ, is impeccable in character. Hebrews 4:15 tells us that "we do not have a high priest who cannot sympathize with our weaknesses, but one who was tempted in all things as we are, *yet without sin*." Christ's entire life was a picture of moral perfection.

The Law of *Karma*

The Krishna follower believes that if he fails to compensate for his sin in this life, he will have another chance in the next, and the next.

This second-chance doctrine has no basis in Scripture, for as Hebrews 9:27 relates, ". . . It is appointed for men to die once, and after this comes judgment . . . ." Those who believe they are living under *karmic* law figure they are under no moral accountability. The Bible refutes this theory with the notion that we must all appear before the judgment seat of Christ.

For further reading on the subject of Hare Krishna please turn to page 254 in the Supplementary Research Section.

SOME PRACTICAL HELPS

I. Sharing Christ with a Krishna Devotee

The following is an excerpt from an actual testimony of a young man who was saved out of the Krishna Consciousness movement. This is presented as an example of how God can use you to reach out in love to Krishna devotees:

". . . So I went out and collected two bowlfuls of money for the temple and I got so involved in collecting that I wandered away from my 'god-brothers.' We were always supposed to stay with our brothers so that if they saw a brother falling into *maya* — the illusions of worldly life — they could bring him back.

"But I wandered away from them and then I ran into Dale. He started talking to me about Jesus. Actually, we weren't supposed to talk about philosophy on the streets for more than a minute but I was interested so I talked to Dale. We went into the park and sat on the grass and he read to me out of the Bible.

"First, he asked me if we accepted the Bible as bonafide scripture. At that time the temple did accept the Bible. Since then they have changed their opinion of the Bible and they now say it has 'the ring of truth,' but isn't true scripture. But I said I accepted the Bible so he read me some passages. First he read the part when Christ said, 'I am the way, the truth, and the life; no man comes to the Father except through Me.' But that didn't work, because I told him there was another interpretation to that. The Krishna temple says that to have Christ is to have His *teaching*, His Word, and to come to the Father through Him is to follow His teaching — to praise the Father, Krishna.

"So then he gave me the words of Jesus when He said, 'When

you pray, use not vain repetitions, as the heathen do.' This struck me, because Christ prayed to His Father just like He was talking to another person instead of chanting.

"So we decided to pray that God, whoever He was, would show me the truth. When we finished praying, I felt that Krishna was far away, or that I was far away from him. So then we talked some more and then I told him I wanted to receive Jesus, which blew his mind. But I had just felt something building up in me since I started talking to him, and finally realized what it was, that I wanted to receive Jesus."

(For a full transcription of this testimony, and for other helpful material on the eastern cults, write Spiritual Counterfeits Project, Box 4308, Berkeley, CA, 94704).

II. Summary

God may lead your conversation in a different direction, but note the key points in this exchange:
- Dale asked him if he believed the Bible.
- He then shared with him John 14:6.
- Then he shared Matthew 6:7.
- Finally, he asked him to pray that God would show him the truth.

Above all, remember this is a sovereign work of God's Spirit. Ask Him to be opening the hearts of devotees that you have a chance to share with.

III. Suggestions for Further Reading

1. William Petersen, *Those Curious New Cults* (Keats Publishing, 1973).
2. J. Stillson Judah, *Hare Krishna and the Counter Culture* (John Wiley and Sons, 1974).
3. Faye Levine, *The Strange World of the Hare Krishnas* (Fawcett Publications, 1974).
4. Ted Patrick, *Let Our Children Go!* (E.P. Dutton and Co., 1976).

Bibliography

1. Judah, J. Stillson, *Hare Krishna and the Counter Culture* (John Wiley and Sons, NY, 1974), pp. 112-127.

2. Judah, Ibid., pp. 112-151.

3. Judah, Ibid., p. 153.

4. Sorma, D.S., *Hinduism Through the Ages* (Bharatiza Vidya Bhavan, Bombay, 1967), p. 284.

5. Prabhupada, A.C. Bhaktivedanta, *Bhagavad-Gita As It Is* (Bhaktivedanta Booktrust, Los Angeles), Chapter V, Text 15, p. 289.

6. *Bhagavad-Gita*, Chapter X, Text 37. See Prabhupada's note in *Bhagavad-Gita As It Is*, p. 533.

The Buddhist Paradox: Mystical Atheism

by Bryan Pollock

Whereas in previous chapters we have focused on two of the most popular versions of westernized *Hinduism* — Hare Krishna and Transcendental Meditation — let us now turn our attention to another eastern import which is claiming thousands of converts throughout America and the West.

Buddhism is sold to the Western World in many different packages, and there are buyers for all of them. More than a quarter million Americans, for example, are involved in Nichiren Shoshu/ Sōka Gakkai, a sect that advocates "chanting for happiness." Others are seeking enlightenment through Zen Buddhism or have chosen est (Erhard Seminars Training) as a means of fulfillment. A minority has espoused the more esoteric offshoots of the religion, such as Tantric and Tibetan Buddhism, which condone meditation, magic and soul travel among other pursuits.

Before examining the various Buddhist cults themselves, let us first take a look at the origins of the religion that has spawned them.

The Birth of a Brahmin

Gautama Buddha, né Siddhartha Gautama, entered this world around 560 B.C. in northern India. His father was a brahmin, that is to say, he was a member of the highest ranking caste in the Hindu world, and he held a position similar to that of a feudal lord. With such a background, it appeared that little Siddhartha was headed for a life of leisure — whether he liked it or not.

To ensure that this *was* the case, Gautama's father carefully supervised his young son's upbringing, ordering that he remain within the confines of the palace compound where he was to be exposed only to the pleasant side of life. As Gautama grew older, however, he longed to see the world beyond.

During his forbidden travels, the young brahmin saw four sights which touched him deeply: an old man, a sick man, a corpse and a Hindu holy man. The sight of human suffering and death haunted Gautama upon his return to the palace and greatly tainted the pleasures of his brahmin existence. Inspired by the sight of the holy man, Gautama eventually left his mother and father, and his wife and child, and set off on a journey to seek the cause of man's suffering.

Gautama began his famous search by visiting the various gurus of the day, but these failed to give him any satisfying answers. Next, he joined a group of ascetics and turned his back on all convention, including the brahminical teachings of his youth. In Hermann Hesse's novel, *Siddhartha*, the hero plainly states his case: ". . . I have become distrustful of teachings and learning, and . . . I have little faith in words that come to us from teachers."[1]

Even his diet during this period was unconventional. In an attempt to tame his body, Gautama existed on oddities such as seeds and herbs and, for a time, even on dung.[2]

When after almost six years he saw the futility of such efforts, Gautama abandoned the ascetic life and took up residence in a nearby village. He was now 35 years old, and the meaning of life still eluded him. Determined to persevere, however, Gautama retired to the shade of a fig tree to meditate on his dilemma. Seven short weeks later, Siddhartha Gautama arose from his cross-legged "lotus posture" an enlightened man. He was now the "Buddha" or "enlightened one." He had discovered the root cause of all suffering, and he had a solution.

Before revealing Buddha's two-fold discovery, let us first look at his concept of human existence in general.

In Buddha's way of thinking, the universe is comprised of eternal energy, boundless and uncreated. Human existence, equally eternal and uncreated, is nothing more than a by-product of this universal energy. "According to the Buddhist," states former Buddhist Gene Aven, "man is not a being, he is nothing but a bundle of sensations, thoughts, feelings and energy, and he is constantly in a state of flux. He believes that there is no individual self, but *everything in the universe is one essence.*"[3]

Spinning Wheels

Buddha taught that the human personality, or "soul" in western terminology, is a mere mental compilation of five transient conditions: the physical body, one's feelings, ideas or understanding, will and pure consciousness. This personality is locked into a process that Buddha called the "existence wheel." Governed by the *karmic* law of cause and effect, the existence wheel spins a man's ever-changing personality around an endless cycle of births and rebirths. And because in each successive life a man must pay for the improprieties of former lives, each new reincarnation only brings him added suffering and death. Man's goal, then, is to free himself from the "infernal" existence wheel.

Now this brings us to Buddha's fig tree revelations. While meditating under the leaves, Buddha discovered what it is that keeps a man chained to the existence wheel: It is his own selfish craving or *desire*. Desire is thus man's root problem for it causes him to commit actions that must be paid for in future lives. If desire can be overcome, then a man will be able to live a life that will ultimately lead to enlightenment, and he will be freed forever from his fleshly existence(s). When enlightenment has been attained, a man is said to be in Nirvana, a blissful state of mind where all desire and illusion of self have been extinguished.

So Buddha's first discovery was that desire is man's root problem. As a solution to the problem he proposed the "Eightfold Path," or eight basic steps designed to stifle desire and thus pave the way to enlightenment. These include: 1) right viewpoint, 2) right aspiration, 3) right speech, 4) right behavior, 5) right occupation, 6) right effort, 7) right mindfulness and 8) right meditation. So, in sum, a man is to effect his own salvation by doing everything "right"!

After he discovered these "truths," Buddha returned to civilization where he became involved in a most active ministry. His first converts included the five ascetics with whom he had lived for nearly six years. To them and to the thousands of monks who subsequently joined him, Buddha preached the message of salvation through self-effort. This was the theme of his entire 45-year ministry and was even the subject of his death-bed utterance: "Subject to decay are all component things. Strive earnestly to work out your own salvation."[4]

Seek for Your Self

In *The Religions of Man*, author Huston Smith observes: "In a time when the multitudes were passively relying on the brahmins to tell them what to do, *Buddha challenged each individual to do his own religious seeking*."[5] "Do not accept what you hear by report," admonished Buddha. "Do not accept tradition, do not accept a statement because it is found in our books, nor because it is in accord with your belief, nor because it is the saying of your teacher."[6] Each man is to effect his own salvation through right living, and he alone must determine what that is.

As for his concept of God, Buddha maintained an icy silence whenever a monk would question him about the Deity. Buddha reasoned that since all we know about ourselves is what we and others perceive with the finite senses, we shouldn't speak at all about a "god" which, if He exists, is beyond our knowing.

Buddha's life purpose was not to direct a man to God but rather to delineate his problem (suffering caused by desire) and to postulate a cure (the Eightfold Path). "One thing I teach," pronounced Buddha, "suffering and the end of suffering. . . . It is just Ill and the ceasing of Ill that I proclaim."[7] "If indifference to a personal creator is atheism," writes Smith, "Buddha was indeed an atheist."[8]

While Buddha spoke of man's ills, he never once mentioned sin as a source of his dilemma. "It is ignorance, not sin, that struck Buddha as the offender,"[9] to quote again from Smith. Sin, in the biblical sense, is simply not an issue to the Buddhist.

As for heaven and hell, these are considered conditions of the here and now rather than the loci of an afterlife. As one Buddhist priest in California put it: "Sometimes we feel the state of hell through hunger, animality (sensual desire) or anger.

Other times we experience heaven through noble thoughts and actions. But both of these states exist within man, not without."

Enlightenment on Parade

With a cursory examination of the basics of Buddhism behind us, let us now look to its various forms as they appear in the West. There is such a diversity of these that one can choose from literally dozens of ways to effect his salvation or "attain enlightenment."

Buddhism began to gain a foothold on western soil in the fifties when Alan Watts wrote his books on Zen Buddhism. The "beat" generation, ever-ready to embrace an alternative to the conventional lifestyle of the day, accepted Watts' writings with enthusiasm. With his Buddhist-oriented poetry, Allen Ginsberg further nurtured the budding Zen movement which began to bloom almost overnight.

In the sixties, Buddhist influence in America temporarily waned as a hoard of Hindu offshoots, including Transcendental Meditation, began to muscle in on Buddhist territory. Today, however, Buddhism has begun to regain the ascendency through such phenomena as the militant proselytizing of Nichiren Shoshu practitioners and the popular appeal of est and other Zen offshoots.

Chanting for Change

NSA (Nichiren Shoshu Academy) was at first an inconspicuous invader, landing quietly on western soil with the Japanese war brides who espoused it. Today, through its "shakabuku"(literally "break and subdue") or proselytizing techniques, the movement is quickly gaining ground.

NSA devotees believe that the way to enlightenment is through chanting, which proceeds in a very specific manner, which I'll describe later in this chapter. Chanting is thought to lead to a merging of one's Buddha nature with that of the universe. Practitioners are fond of using the phrase "getting in rhythm with life" when speaking of this process.

Less aggressive but equally serious are those who seek "satori"or enlightenment through the silence of Zen. At some 10 or 12 Zen centers in the United States, practitioners can be found meditating on such famous riddles as "What is the sound of one hand clapping?" or "What was the appearance of your face before your ancestors were born?" These riddles or "koans"are designed to neutralize the mind, preparing it for the sudden onslaught of *satori*, which is described in Zen as "the mystic state in which you appreciate your own original inseparability with the universe."[10]

Forgetting You Remember

A westernized offshoot of Zen, est (Erhard Seminars Training) offers the would-be practitioner 60 hours of intensive training in a philosophy that manages to combine Zen, Vendanta Hinduism, Scientology and the power of positive thinking. More than 100,000 Americans have paid $250 each to sit through the est sessions, which amount to a one man *tour de force* in which Erhard explains his "experiential philosophy." The idea is to discard the memory of everything experienced thus far in life and to begin to experience the ever-present "now." This process is referred to as "getting it."

In addition to the more traditional Zen and its offshoots, there are several extremely esoteric forms of Buddhism which are now beginning to advance toward the western front.

Tantric Buddhism, for example, deriving its name from the ancient Hindu texts or *Tantras*, involves such practices as ritual nudity and the worship of sexual union. (There are also Tantric sects within Hinduism, it might be mentioned.) This cult has a number of followers in the United States.

Originating from deep within the Himalayas of Tibet where it was originally practiced by the ancient lamas, Tibetan Buddhism is also becoming a part of the American scene.

Tibetan Buddhism, among other things, has a perverse fascination with death. One of its chief writings, *The Tibetan Book of the Dead*, or *Bardo Thodol*, has become an occult classic, and is one of the most popular books on the college campus today.

First translated in 1927, *The Tibetan Book of the Dead* purports to unlock the secrets of the *Bardo*, or the three mystic states of existence. It also serves as a guide for the dead during the *Bardo* existence, or period of 49 days falling between the moment of death and the moment of rebirth.

Because of their belief in the *Bardo* existence, lamas spend years studying the intricacies of the *Bardo* and developing the spiritual powers necessary to guide their dying clients into "the clear light of the void," an eternal state of consciousness free from all limitations.

Ceremony, too, plays an important part in Tibetan Buddhism. Western lamas meditate on *mantras* (sacred words or syllables) or *mandalas* (sacred symbols) in an attempt to gain mastery of their bodies so that they can perform such ceremonial feats as walking over hot coals, showering in ice water, etc.

As our brief survey of Buddhist infiltration in the West comes to a close, we are perhaps most struck by the diversity of thought and technique that exists within this particular spiritual counterfeit. Though the goal is always the attainment of some form of enlightenment, the pathways to this mystical state are as diverse as the cults that have devised them. In sum, there is something for everybody within the Buddhist world today.

To gain further insight into the Buddhist phenomenon, let us now take a closer look at one of its largest movements, the militant Nichiren Shoshu sect.

Bibliography

1. Hesse, Hermann, *Siddhartha* (New Directions, NY, 1951), p. 18.

2. Walker, Benjamin, *The Hindu World*, Volume I (Frederick A. Praeger, NY, 1968), p. 178.

3. Aven, Gene, "My Search" (Life Messengers, Seattle, WA, 1974), p. 21.

4. Quoted in Walker, op. cit., p. 182.

5. Smith, Huston, *The Religions of Man* (Harper & Row, NY, 1958), p. 93.

6. Burtt, E.A., *The Teachings of the Compassionate Buddha* (Mentor Books, NY, 1955), pp. 49, 50, quoted in Smith, ibid., p. 93.

7. Woodward, F.L., *Some Sayings of the Buddha* (Oxford Press, London, 1939), p. 294, quoted in Smith, ibid., p. 97.

8. Smith, ibid., p. 112.

9. Smith, ibid., p. 108.

10. Petersen, William, *Those Curious New Cults* (Keats Publishing, New Canaan, CT, 1975), p. 177.

NICHIREN SHOSHU/SŌKA GAKKAI

On a college campus in Portland, Oregon, a handful of students were seen handing out small cards bearing the cryptic phrase *"Nam Myoho Renge Kyo."* With smiling faces, they encouraged passers-by to pronounce the foreign words and to expect positive results from doing so. A few curious souls ventured an attempt at mouthing the words, but their efforts met with little success.

To the majority of students on the Portland campus such audacious tactics to gain recognition were nothing new. One more group had merely surfaced to make its presence known, joining the already prodigious pantheon of campus cults. Nichiren Shoshu/Sōka Gakkai, however, is one of the most zealous in terms of outreach, and is thus one of the fastest-growing of the new oriental religions.

From a mere foothold of 300 members in 1960, most of them Japanese war brides, the movement has scored impressive gains. Today, estimates of the number of practitioners range up to 250,000.

This stunning growth has been accompanied by a sharp drop in the number of oriental members. In 1960, 96% of the Nichiren Shoshu membership was oriental. By 1965 it had dropped to 77%, and in 1970, only one in three practitioners could claim oriental descent.[1]

Active Nichiren Shoshu chapters can also be found today in many Latin American countries including Colombia, Venezuela and Peru. In Europe, the movement boasts active outreaches in England, France and Germany, and further plans call for expansion throughout Western Europe.

Missionary Buddhism

Such aggressive outreach stems from a burning missionary zeal to spread "True Buddhism" on a worldwide basis, thereby achieving "kosen rufu" or "world peace through individual happiness." The means for achieving such a goal involves nothing less than "human revolution."

Richard Okamoto, former LOOK magazine correspondent in Japan, penned the following assessment of Nichiren Shoshu in that country:

> "Sōka Gakkai regards itself as not only the one true Buddhist religion, but the one true religion on earth. Its principal aims are the propagation of its gospel throughout the world, by forced conversion if necessary, and the denunciation and destruction of all other faiths as 'false' religions. . . . Sōka Gakkai is unmistakably a church militant in Japan geared for a determined march abroad. Its significance to America and all nations cannot be ignored. Its target is world domination."[2]

To determine just what insight occasioned such a warning, we will be taking a closer look at this sect, known commonly in the West as Nichiren Shoshu Academy (NSA). But first, perhaps a bit of history is in order.

In the 13th century, a Japanese monk named Nichiren Daishonen pledged himself to the study of the teachings of Gautama Buddha (also known as Sakyamuni Buddha). Unlike his devoted colleagues, Nichiren found few answers in the teachings of Sakyamuni. As he studied, one question in particular continued to plague him: "Why had so many different religious traditions emerged from the teachings of one man?"

In his efforts to find the answer, Nichiren turned to a Buddhist teaching known as the *Lotus Sutra*. (Although NSA attributes this teaching to Sakyamuni, it was actually written much later, according to eastern scholar Kenneth Latourette.)[3]

As he poured over the text, one sentence stopped Nichiren dead in his tracks: "Honestly discard the *provisional* teachings." To Nichiren this seemed like the answer he had been looking for: simplify the Buddhist teachings by cutting out such ponderous doctrine as had accrued through the years. Retaining only the *Lotus Sutra*, Nichiren did just that, and "True Buddhism" was born, with Nichiren Daishonen as its "True Buddha."

Short-cut to Enlightenment

The only prerequisite to enlightenment in Nichiren's new cult was devotion to the *Lotus Sutra* which bears the appropriate title "Nam Myoho Renge Kyo" (devotion to the mystic law of cause and effect through sound). Being freed as it was from the burden of doctrine, Nichiren envisioned the lightning-like spread of "True Buddhism" throughout the world.

Some 700 years later, Nichiren's burning dream was unfulfilled, but its embers were still alive in the heart of a certain Japanese school teacher named Makiguchi. Spurred on by a fervent zeal, Makiguchi founded the Sōka Gakkai (Value Creation Society) and endeavored to show all Japan that Nichiren Shoshu is the only true religion. For all of his efforts, the unfortunate Makiguchi merely landed in jail where he died in 1941. One of his disciples, however, Josei Toda, took over where Makiguchi left off, and Nichiren Shoshu began to come alive.

Conversion by Force

Under Toda's direction, the number of believers increased dramatically, often through ruthless proselytizing techniques or *shakabuku* meaning, literally, "break and subdue." Members would break into new converts' homes and destroy family Shinto altars, or would chant round the clock at the homes of prospective members until they broke down and joined. Such tactics were finally abandoned in the sixties due to public opposition.

In 1960, a practitioner by the name of Masayasu Sadanaga became the head of Nichiren Shoshu of America, a position he still holds today. In keeping with the movement's westward push, Sadanaga obligingly changed his name to George Williams. Such a name change reflects the amazing adaptability that has made the sect such a potent force throughout America and the Western World. Nowhere is this blend of East and West more

curiously felt, however, than at the weekly NSA chapter meetings held on Wednesday and Friday evenings around the
country.

The Chanting Meeting

On one particular Friday evening in April, I attended one of
these meetings in San Bernardino, California. As I approached
the innocent-looking, one-story stucco house, my first impression was that I had the wrong address. But when I opened the
door, the sight of 30 pairs of shoes on the entry-way floor, the
smell of incense and the deep-toned chanting confirmed the
proper destination.

I discarded my shoes and entered the living room where
nearly 30 people were deeply involved in "daimoku," which is to
say they were chanting the words in the Lotus Sutra title, "Nam
Myoho Renge Kyo." The chanters faced a large black box, the
"butsodon" which houses the "gohonzon," a scroll containing
the names of the Buddhas in the Lotus Sutra. Many were fingering
a string of 108 beads that resembled a Catholic rosary. Some of the
people smiled as I weaved my way through them, headed for
less conspicuous territory in the back of the room.

No sooner had I sat down than one young man in his mid-
twenties came over and introduced himself. He held out a
gongyo or small booklet containing the words of the Lotus Sutra,
and encouraged me to follow along. I declined the offer,
explaining that I was quite content just to listen.

The eerie and sonorous rhythm of the chanting continued for
a few minutes until it was terminated by the sound of a bell. A
brief pause, then the beginning of a rapid-fire rendition of the
Lotus Sutra. Twenty minutes later the bell rang again, this time
to retransition the practitioners back into their chanting, which
finally ended the ceremonial part of the meeting.

Chanting to Cheerleading

What followed seemed like a page out of my high school
yearbook. Riotous cheers and applause broke from the tiny
crowd, and three young girls jumped up to lead songs in a cheer-
leader fashion. Hits of the evening included "I've Been Doin'
Shakabuku" sung to the tune of "I've Been Workin' on the
Railroad" and "Have a Gohonzon" belted out in the refrains of

"Havah Nagila." The singing was followed by one final chant, this time rendered in pep-rally English. "Let's go NSA, NSA all the way!" they screamed, slowly at first, but faster and faster with each succeeding round until the room erupted in sound.

Following the frivolity, the atmosphere resumed a more serious tone. Guests were introduced, and an explanation of NSA offered for their benefit. "Nichiren Shoshu is 'True Buddhism,'" explained Ray. "We believe that by chanting we can find individual happiness in life and eventually obtain world peace. We believe that chanting can overcome any obstacles to this goal and that it can give us the benefits we seek in life." Another girl added that you didn't have to believe in chanting for it to "work." She challenged the visitors to "try it and see for yourselves."

I might mention here that, following the meeting, I talked with several members in hopes of obtaining an expansion of this token explanation. Instead I was met with a contradictory barrage of opinion that only served to convince me that NSA is many things to many people. One person referred to it as "true humanism," and another said I could call it anything I wanted to. "Only the practical benefits from the philosophy are what count," he explained. Perhaps the most accurate assessment came from a man who observed, "It's very difficult to explain what NSA is; it's better if you see what NSA does."

At any rate, the speaker's original explanation of Nichiren Shoshu was followed by testimonials from various practitioners. A middle-aged lady literally jumped to her feet to relay how chanting to the gohonzon had rid her of two bothersome sons. Both, it seemed, had enrolled in colleges outside of California. Another lady told of entering a shopping center and encountering a friend with whom she had been wanting to talk. Others spoke of chanting for such diverse items as driver's licenses and new homes.

Mystical Materialism

Everything under the sun, it seems, has been longingly chanted for at one time or another by some NSA member. And herein lies the subtle aspect of NSA doctrine that has done more than anything else to propel it to such overwhelming success in the West. Nichiren Shoshu is a religion based on *materialism*.

In NSA's unorthodox philosophy, man's material desires

become his life's goal. Materialism is thus given a sanctity that enables members to selfishly serve Mammon under the auspices of religion. This whole concept is a drastic departure from the original teachings of Sakyamuni, though members claim he authored the doctrine. In reality, if Sakyamuni were alive today, he would throw the NSA "money changers" out of Buddhism altogether.

What these views are really based on is an incredible doctrine, "bon' no soku bodai," meaning, literally, "worldly desires equal enlightenment." This doctrine teaches that if one continually pursues his desires through chanting, he will eventually acquire riches and wisdom, which will in turn lead to his enlightenment. His bondage to the *karma* law of cause and effect will be broken as he escapes from the endless round of births and rebirths (*wheel of samsara*) into Nirvana.

Physical Equals Spiritual

A corollary to the doctrine of *bon' no soku bodai* is that of "shikishin funi" which states that the spiritual and physical are not separate entities but are one and the same. Therefore, what makes the body happy must do the same for the spirit since there is absolutely no distinction between the two.

One result of these two doctrines is that a man's material or physical acquisitions are given a higher footing than his moral character. If a person chants for, say, a house, and gets it, the acquisition serves to bring him nearer enlightenment. The concept of greed disappears altogether.

A logical extension to the *shikishin funi* doctrine is the concept that all physical suffering is an outward sign of an inward spiritual malady. Consequentially, not even poverty is to be tolerated by NSA members. One NSA official was once quoted as saying that "the poor will go to hell."[4]

Buddhist Monism

Another NSA doctrine, "esho funi," translates as "subject and object, not two." According to *esho funi*, when a person chants before the *gohonzon*, his life essence is brought in tune with the life essence of the universe. The things that he concentrates on are drawn to him as all subject-object distinction disappears.

Marc   Gould, a former NSA Buddhist, sheds more light on this shadowy doctrine. "By looking constantly at the *gohonzon*," he explains, "you begin to take on the qualities you are chanting for. They believe the more you look at the gohonzon while chanting, the more you become like it. There's also a visual effect imparted by the gohonzon because it is written in Sanskrit," a language that possesses both audible and (non-linguistic) visual effects.

As for the problem of sin, NSA doctrine regards it as irrelevant. Sin is real and is thought to stem from man's basic bad character, but it requires no forgiveness. For, as the NSA "mystic principal of the true cause" states: ". . . Anyone who practices this life-philosophy is making a fresh start with each new day, regardless of his past."[5]

Nirvana, Not Heaven

The concept of heaven and hell is also dispensed with. At NSA meetings, questions regarding an afterlife often receive the common answer, "Heaven and hell are right here on earth. It's what you make of the present that counts." NSA members further believe that when one breaks his bad karma through chanting, he escapes into Nirvana, leaving the earthly heaven and hell behind him.

It should be mentioned, however, that attaining Nirvana is not really so easy as it might appear. In addition to their endless chanting, NSA members are encouraged to maintain a frenetic pace, participating in a number of outreaches including the NSA drum and bugle corps, parades and professional musicals which feature a sort of "down home, apple pie and America" theme. (Patriotism and appreciation for one's historical heritage are highly encouraged by NSA.) National conventions, drawing members from across the country, provide yet another activity. As if all of this were not enough to keep them busy, George Williams recently challenged members to chant two million daimoku before an upcoming convention in San Francisco.

The Biblical Perspective

At this point, let's look to the Bible for a Christian assessment of some of the doctrine within NSA.

The concept of shikishin funi asserts that the spiritual and physical are really one and the same. In Matthew 4:4, however, Jesus clearly reveals that man is both body and spirit, requiring both physical and spiritual nourishment. God the Father is revealed in the Bible as being pure spirit, distinct from all matter; thus, according to John 4:24, it is appropriate for man to worship God in his spirit. In Matthew 6:24, Christ sheds more light on the matter by asserting that a man "... cannot serve God *and* Mammon (money or material goods)," the two being separate and distinct from each other.

The NSA idea that man's suffering is the outward manifestation of a spiritual disorder is also discounted in the Bible. While they are, in fact, consequences of man's fall, poverty and suffering are by no means the barometers of a man's spiritual status.

When the disciples questioned Christ about the martyred Galileans, He replied, "Do you suppose that these Galileans were greater sinners than all other Galileans, because they suffered this fate? I tell you, no ..." (Luke 13:2, 3). In the Old Testament, we learn that Job's suffering was not a result of a faulty spiritual condition, but was rather brought on by an adversary, Satan. As for poverty, specifically, the moral character of the poor is generally exalted above and beyond that of the rich throughout Scripture.

The NSA view that a man can break his own bad *karma* is predicated on the notion that man is basically good. Ignorance has simply clouded man's basic goodness.

The psalmist, however, says otherwise:

> "The fool has said in his heart, 'There is no God.'
> They are corrupt, they have committed abominable deeds;
> There is no one who does good.
> The Lord has looked down from heaven on the sons of men,
> To see if there are any who understand,
> Who seek after God.
> They have all turned aside; together they have become corrupt;
> *There is no one who does good, not even one.*"

Psalms 14:1-3

Confirming the prognosis, the apostle Paul writes in Romans 3:23: "For all have sinned and fall short of the glory of God." The basic depravity of man is amply supported in the secular chronicles of history as well. *The Guinness Book of World*

Records calculates, for example, that in the 3,467 years since 1496 B.C., there have been only 230 years of recorded peace throughout the *civilized* world![6]

Man is clearly in need of assistance, but who has the cure? The NSA answer calls for chanting to achieve individual happiness, but happiness founded on hopelessness won't work. The answer clearly lies beyond the panaceas of NSA, in the person of Jesus Christ.

SOME PRACTICAL HELPS

I. Sharing Christ with the NSA Member

Although the NSA's official quarterly publication lists the birth of Jesus Christ on a timeline of noteworthy historical events, NSA president Daisaku Ikeda has stated that "Christianity and the Bible" have been "researched and evaluated" and found to be "false, unbelievable" and "full of myths."[7]

One NSA priest gave the following response when specifically asked about Christ: "This is a very knotty problem." (Pause.) "I don't think Jesus was ever a person of history — I think He was a myth."

When confronted with such an attitude, it's best to avoid a defensive stance and just seek an opportunity to share the simple gospel. Following is a suggested approach:

A. *Ask the NSA member what he does believe.* Listen politely and ask questions that will clarify, not challenge. Remember, you are "winning the right to be heard" here, as well as gaining a clearer understanding of NSA beliefs.

B. *Ask him, "May I share with you what I believe? It's summarized in this little booklet. I'd like to go through it with you and have you tell me how it compares with what you believe."*

(I'd strongly recommend that as you share the gospel you use a tool such as the Four Spiritual Laws booklet. This will help keep you on track when talking with any cultist.)

C. *Be prepared to clarify several misunderstandings that NSA members have of Christianity:*

1. *The Bible is full of myths.*
   a. Point out proofs of historical reliability of Scripture.
      (1) Accuracy of copies transcribed from original documents.
      (2) Number of ancient manuscripts.
      (3) Evidence from archeology.
      (4) Eyewitness reports.
   b. See Chapter V, "Is the Bible an Authoritative, Reliable Record?," p. 106 for a discussion of the above proofs.
2. *Jesus was just a man.*
   a. Point to the two main evidences of Jesus' deity: His miraculous works and His consistent fulfillment of prophecy. See Chapter II, p. 47 for a discussion of these evidences.
   b. You may want to use the trilemma argument (Jesus was either a liar, a lunatic or the Son of God) to lead the member to a fair consideration of Christ's deity.
3. *The Christian Church has had a very insubstantial impact on society.* (Remember, the NSA goal is to "promote world peace through individual happiness.")
   a. Point out some of the social achievements of the church in history.
      (1) Arthur Koestler stated, "Welfare work in the slums and care of the poor in general was, and still is, a monopoly of the Christian missions in Asia." (See Chapter III, p. 65 for full quote.)
      (2) Benjamin Walker in *The Hindu World* writes, "Every significant movement for social reform in Hinduism in recent times has received an impetus in some measure from the Christian religion." (For full quote, see Supplementary Research Section p. 233 .)
      (3) Kenneth Latourette, in his *History of the Expansion of Christianity*, stated that "the initiative and the early leadership in the creation of the system of free public schools supported by the state" came almost entirely from persons who had been inspired by Christianity.

(4) Out of the first 119 colleges and universities in the United States, 104 — including Harvard, Princeton, Dartmouth and Yale — were established by Christians for the express purpose of perpetuating the Christian faith.

(5) "I learned to know a whole host of institutions that minister to the bodies and souls of men. I inspected their schools and prisons. I observed their homes for the poor and the sick and the orphaned. I studied ... their societies for the improvement of prisons, and so forth. I particularly noted that practically all of these institutions and organizations were called into being by a living faith in Jesus Christ and that nothing but this vital faith sustains them," stated Theodore Fliedner upon returning from a trip to England in the 19th century. Quoted from *Fliedner the Faithful* by A.D. Wentz, p. 29.

D. *Be prepared to deal with the NSA member's misunderstanding of God.*

Because of his basic atheistic mindset, the NSA member does not believe in the one Jehovah God, but in several "gods." Even these are not considered personal beings, but are rather thought of as the various protective functions of life such as certain of man's human characteristics and certain material things like the sun, the moon, etc. Actually, any person or thing can be a god according to this belief. You will want to share with the NSA member your view of the true Jehovah God.

1. Point out that the best picture we have of what God is like is in the person of His Son Jesus Christ. Share such verses as Colossians 1:15 — "And He (Jesus) is the image of the invisible God ..."; and John 1:18 — "No man has seen God at any time, the only begotten God (Jesus) ... He has explained Him."

2. Point out some of the attributes of God as described in verses from the Four Spiritual Laws.

   a. He is perfect love — Romans 5:8.

   b. He is perfect truth — John 14:6.

   c. He is perfect holiness — Romans 3:23.

    d. He is the source of real life — John 10:10.

E. *Point out to the NSA member the insecurity of depending on transient material goods for happiness.* Stress the security you've found in knowing God loves you, in knowing that if you died tonight, you'd go directly to be with the Lord.

Bibliography

1. Ellwood, Robert, *The Eagle and the Rising Sun* (Westminster Press, Philadelphia, PA, 1974), p. 101.
2. Okamoto, Richard, "Japan," *LOOK*, September 10, 1963, p. 16.
3. Latourette, Kenneth, *Introduction to Buddhism* (Friendship Press, New York, NY, 1956), p. 38.
4. Flagler, J.M., "A Chanting In Japan," *New Yorker*, November 26, 1966, p. 152.
5. NSA Quarterly, Summer 1976, p. 143.
6. McWhirter, Norris and Ross, *Guinness Book of World Records* (Sterling Publishing, NY, 1974 edition), p. 378.
7. Okamoto, Richard, "Japan," *LOOK*, September 10, 1963, p. 10, 1963, p. 23.

Sun Moon:
The Militant Messiah

One can see them on practically any given day in any given city throughout the Western World. On downtown street corners, at international airports and in shopping centers they can be spotted soliciting buyers for an odd assortment of wares including ginseng tea, candy, flowers and candles. But before you mistake these people for ordinary street peddlers, consider the following: their humble inventory nets at least $15 million annually, financing one of the most controversial cults in the West — the Holy Spirit Association for the Unification of World Christianity, Inc., or, as it is more simply known, the Unification Church.

While many have had some sort of contact with the fresh-faced members of this cult, there's another side to the Unification Church that few have glimpsed. Once a week members rise in the early morning hours, not to sell their wares, but to kneel before a picture of their "leader" and to pledge their allegiance to him and to the Unification Church he founded. A portion of that pledge proceeds as follows:

"As the center of the cosmos, I will fulfill our Father's Will (purpose of creation), and the responsibility given me for (self perfection). I will become a dutiful son (or daughter) and a child of goodness to attend our Father forever in the ideal world of creation (by) returning joy and glory to Him. This I pledge."

The object of all this adoration is a full-faced, 56-year-old former Presbyterian from Korea named Sun Myung Moon. To his followers, he's known as "Father" or "Messiah," which reflects the very reason for the existence of his cult: Mr. Moon thinks he's God's only valid representative on earth today, and nearly two million people worldwide agree.[1]

Communing with Jesus?

The Unification Church stems directly from a vision that Moon supposedly had while "deep in prayer on a Korean mountaintop in 1936."[2] The 16-year-old youth claimed he saw Jesus Christ, who informed him that his (Moon's) services were needed for the fulfillment of "God's providence." Later, he allegedly communed with Jesus, Moses and Buddha as well. These events supposedly launched the young Moon into a search for the spiritual and the physical meaning of the universe.[3]

As regards Mr. Moon's history during the forties, the accounts diverge curiously. Unification Church apologists give glowing reports of struggles against communist aggression and resulting imprisonment during this period. Other sources cite numerous imprisonments for less noble reasons including "irresponsible sexuality."[4] Marital failure is also recorded.

Moon, however, has remained undaunted by this somewhat shadowy history. Encouraged by successes in Korea, he headed West in 1972. In the United States, he watched his movement mushroom into a major cult, eclipsing even some of those which had been long established in this country.

Young people (18- to 25-year-olds mainly) flocked to the new group. Followers generally came from backgrounds characterized by a lack of love and family security and had been repelled at some point by the hypocrisy of their parent's churches. Today, however, with opposition mounting against it at every turn, the Church may have reaped more than it bargained for.

Recent articles tell of "brain washing" techniques employed by the cult to assure the continued devotion of its followers. Ted "Black Lightning" Patrick has gained publicity (along with a jail sentence) for his de-programming of cult members whom he's actually "kidnapped" from the Moonies, or Moonites, as they are colloquially called.

Innocent Victims

Rabbi Maurice Davis summed up the prevailing sentiment toward the cult in the following statement:

> "I hold this movement to be evil and dangerous. I hold Reverend Sun Myung Moon to be a charlatan and a manipulator of people. I hold his inner henchmen to be devious, unscrupulous and false. And I hold the kids that are caught up in this to be the innocent victims of their own dreams, the innocent victims of their own needs. But most of all the innocent victims of Reverend Moon."[5]

Despite any hard times it may be having, the Unification Church needn't worry about money. Moon himself is worth $15 million in industrial holdings in South Korea, and the Church can list a number of impressive assets and holdings of its own. It has even shown a reported interest in purchasing the Empire State Building![6]

So far, the most impressive of the Church's holdings, at least to Moonites, is the $8 million, Barrytown, New York, estate which houses the movement's official seminary. It is here that the cult's doctrine is explored, studied, memorized and, most of all, admired.

What type of doctrine does such a controversial figure as Sun Myung Moon espouse? The following doctrinal statement filed with the Korean government by the Church helps to answer that question:

(1) The one Creator is the only God and Father.

(2) The only Son, Jesus, is mankind's Savior.

(3) The second advent of Jesus is in Korea.

(4) Mankind shall become one united family centered around the event of the second advent.

(5) Ultimate salvation rests upon the elimination of hell and evil, while establishing good and the kingdom of heaven.

In addition to its *official* doctrine, the group believes the following *secret* doctrines:

(1) Founder Moon is the "Lord of the Second Advent," i.e., he fulfills the prophecies regarding the second coming of Jesus Christ.[7]

(2) Founder Moon is sinless.[8]

(3) Moon's "shed blood" (drawn during his supposed "persecution") provides for the forgiveness of man's sins. Indeed, without Moon, there is no forgiveness of sin.[9]

(4) In order for man to be saved, a change in "blood lineage" from Satan's blood to God's must be effected through a ceremony known as "Blood Cleansing," or simply, "the blessing," carried out by Moon. *Time* magazine reports that the "Blood Cleansing" ceremony regularly involved ritual sex in the early days of the movement.* Today, "the blessing" of sinlessness is conferred by Moon in a comparatively innocuous ceremony directly preceding the marriage rites of qualified Unification Church members.

(5) Members who have experienced Moon's "blessing" can produce a sinless generation.[10]

Before elaborating on the above doctrines, let's first examine some of the other basic beliefs within the Moon philosophy.

Divine Men

The Unification Church teaches a concept called "dual characteristic" which holds that the relationship between God and perfected man is like the relationship between a man's mind and his body. Any *external* appearance of the body (a frown, a smile, etc.) reflects the state of the *internal mind* (anger, happiness, etc.). In the same sort of relationship, God is reflected outwardly in the perfected individual.

The deity who is thus reflected in perfected man possesses a whole set of dual characteristics like "positivity" and

*"In those days, say early members of the sect, ritual sex characterized the Moon communes. Since Moon was a pure man, sex with him ("Blood Cleansing") was supposed to purify both body and soul, and marriages of other cultists were in fact invalid until the wives slept with Moon. As the cult became bigger, the blood-cleansing rites were abandoned, but today Moon arranges his disciples' marriages . . ." (*Time*, June 14, 1976, p. 50).

"negativity," masculinity and femininity, etc. This concept of God is very similar to the Taoist view of ultimate reality, as represented by the male/female forces of Yin and Yang.

One result of God's duality is that it permits Him to have a "give and take" relationship, first of all with Himself, then with His creation. In fact, perfected man enjoys a 100% give and take communion with God and is actually "one" with God. Fallen man, on the other hand, is cut off from God and his give and take relationship occurs with Satan with whom he is "one."

Two Falls

How did fallen man come into such a state? Moon teaches that two separate "falls" occured in Eden, a physical fall and a spiritual fall. Originally, it seems, God placed both Adam and Eve in the Garden where they began to pursue a course of "formation," "growth" and "perfection." (God hadn't created them perfect for, as the doctrine of give and take declares: "For the realization of God's ideal, both God and man must work together.")[11]

At any rate, while pursuing her course of perfection, Eve visited the tree of the knowledge of good and evil where she fell into "sin" by having sexual intercourse with the Serpent. The consequences of this act were dire, not only for Eve, whose chances for perfection were obliterated, but for all mankind, because his spiritual fall was thus instituted.

Subsequent to this event, Adam's premature sexual relations with his wife instituted man's physical fall. Moon teaches that "by responding to the temptation of Eve, Adam left his position as God's son and united with Eve prematurely, before he had reached individual perfection."[12]

Serpent Blood

Because of Eve's relations with Satan, and Adam's subsequent relations with Eve before his perfection, Moonites believe that "serpent blood" courses through human veins today![13]

Since the alienation from God is two-fold, the Unification Church teaches a two-fold or dual redemption; both a physical and a spiritual salvation are necessary.

Jesus Christ, in His earthly mission, made an attempt to

redeem mankind both physically and spiritually. But since Christ was not God *Himself* (though He *had* attained divinity as Moon has), His earthly task was too much for Him and He failed, at least in part. According to the Divine Principle (the Unification Church's "Bible" or statement of doctrine): "Jesus failed in his christly mission. His death on the cross was not an essential part of God's plan for redeeming sinful man."[14]

Christ's failure was not total, however, because He *was* able to achieve *spiritual* salvation at Calvary, thereby resolving half of man's dilemma. A person *can* be spiritually redeemed through belief in the resurrected Jesus and through union with Him. But, the Moonites believe, "the Messiah did not finish *physical* salvation."[15]

Presumably, had Christ lived long enough, He would have accomplished physical salvation through marriage to some equally perfect woman. The offspring from this union would have populated God's kingdom with perfect men. But Jesus' "untimely" death at Calvary cut this plan short, necessitating a second advent.

The 'Third Adam'

To the rescue at this point comes none other than Sun Moon. In a television documentary a few years ago, Reverend Moon informed the world that he had inherited Christ's unfinished mission to restore mankind *physically*. Since the original Adam and the Second Adam (Christ) both failed to father the perfect race, the task had apparently fallen to Mr. Moon who claimed to be the "Third Adam" or "Second Advent Christ."

When Moon married his second wife (fourth in some annals) in 1960, the marriage feast of the Lamb as recorded in Revelation 19 supposedly took place. Moon and his bride, Hak Ja Han, became the progenitors of God's kingdom of perfect individuals and thus the "True Parents" of mankind.

Such claims are rather remarkable even for cultic doctrine, but they don't end here. Moon describes the "Lord of the Second Advent" this way: "The Messiah is he who has subjugated Satan absolutely and has provided the pattern by which each person can subjugate Satan completely."[16] The Divine Principle goes on to claim:

"He (Moon) singly challenged Satan in cosmic battle for

over twenty years . . . . He discovered that God would restore man with the same Principle by which God created him. He pioneered the path to perfection — the cosmic restoration — of which no one had even dreamed."[17]

Instead of making extensive personal comment on the Moon doctrine, I would like to point the reader to a scriptual assessment of his various claims.

The Deity of Jesus

"Jesus was not the unique, only begotten Son of God who was pre-existent with the Father before all created things," states the Divine Principle. "Jesus attained deity, as a man who fulfilled the purpose of creation, but can by no means be considered God Himself."[18]

The Bible leaves no doubt as to the veracity of this doctrine: "For in Him," states Colossians 2:9, "*all the fulness of the Deity dwells in bodily form . . . .*" In Hebrews 1:8, God the Father says to His Son, Jesus: "Thy throne, *O God*, is forever and ever . . . ." In verse 6, when the Father commands all the angels in heaven to worship Him, Christ's unique deity is also clearly affirmed. Other verses relating to Christ's deity include John 8:58; 10:30 and 14:9.

The Mission of Jesus

The Divine Principle claims that Jesus failed in His "christly" mission.[14] The Bible, however, affirms that Jesus was ". . . delivered up according to the predetermined plan and foreknowledge of God . . ." (Acts 2:23). Moonites will say that Christ's fervent prayers in the Garden of Gethsemane regarding His impending crucifixion indicate that such a death was not God's will. What they do not take into account is the wording of Christ's prayer: ". . . Father, if thou art willing, remove this cup from Me; *yet not My will, but Thine be done*" (Luke 22:42).

As for fully completing His earthly mission, a fact which the Unification Church denies, Jesus states: "I glorified Thee on earth, *having accomplished the work which Thou gavest Me to do;* and now, Father, glorify Thou Me in Thy own presence with the glory which I had with Thee before the world was made"

190

(John 17:5).

Jesus' Miraculous Birth

Unification Church doctrine denies the miraculous birth of our Lord, believing instead that Jesus was the result of an illicit affair between Mary and Zacharias or some other man.[19] The Bible clearly proclaims that Mary was a virgin. (See Matthew 1:20-23.) For this reason, until an angel explained the situation to him in a dream, an embarrassed Joseph considered divorcing his wife, thinking her to be unfaithful.

A Female Holy Spirit

In keeping with their belief in the dual gender of God, Moonites assert that the Holy Spirit is female and was given to Jesus as a "spirit bride" in the "spirit world." In John 14:26, however, the Spirit is clearly referred to as "He." In Acts 5:3, 4, the Holy Spirit is considered to be God Himself not simply one aspect of God.

With the Unification Church, the central issue is Jesus. The Bible declares He was and is the *only* divine Son of God — not just one of many "gods." Far from failing 2,000 years ago, Jesus fully completed His mission, including His crucifixion and resurrection, according to a plan laid down "before the foundations of the world."

" 'I will conquer and subjugate the world,' says Sun Myung Moon. 'I am your brain.' "[20] Moon's goal is clear-cut: the fashioning of a militant messiah cult that will eventually extend his influence around the globe. But at the same time, God is preparing hundreds within his ranks to come to know the only true Messiah, Jesus Christ.

(For further reading on the subject of Reverend Sun Myung Moon and the Unification Church please turn to page 260 of the Supplementary Research Section.)
(For further reading on the subject of Reverend Sun Myung Moon and the Unification Church please turn to page 260 of the Supplementary Research Section.)

SOME PRACTICAL HELPS

I. General Sharing with the Moonite

If you encounter a Moonite, don't expect that you can persuade him to leave the cult right away. He is emotionally hooked. However, in love, through the power of God's Word, you can plant seeds which the Holy Spirit can use to open his mind to the truth. Following are suggestions from a number of individuals experienced in dealing with members of the Unification Church.

A. *Be sure that you know what the Bible says about Jesus and His total sufficiency in salvation.*

B. *Share your testimony with them.* Remember, many Moonites are ex-church goers and have joined Moon to escape hypocrisy they have seen within the church. Your personal testimony can do much to cut through this veil and demonstrate the genuineness of a personal relationship with Christ.

C. *Members of the Unification Church often fool Christians by using terms like, "I was born again."* Don't be taken in by this phrase. It simply means that the Moonite is learning doctrine about God and Jesus.

D. *Encourage them to read the Bible and make a comparison of what Moon says and what Jesus said.*

E. *Learn what the Bible says about:*
    1. Lying.
        Moonites are trained to call it "Heavenly Deception," especially when practiced during fund-raising. Moon has even attempted to give a far-fetched spiritual justification to the practice: "If you tell a lie to make a person better," Moon says, "then that is not a sin. . . . Even God tells lies very often."[21]

        When encountering this practice, share with them some of the following verses, trusting the Holy Spirit to convict their consciences:
        a. John 8:44 — Satan is father of all lies.
        b. Psalms 119:163 — God is hater of falsehood.
        c. I John 2:21 — No lie is of the truth.

d. Proverbs 21:6 — Treasures by lying only bring death.
2. False teachers.
    The Lord Jesus warned us, "See to it that no one misleads you. For many will come in My name saying, 'I am the Christ (Messiah),' and will mislead many" (Matthew 24:4, 5). "Then if anyone says to you, 'Behold, here is the Christ,' or 'There He is,' do not believe him. For false Christs and false prophets will arise . . ." (Matthew 24:23, 24).
    We can blanketly reject all mere verbal claims that Christ has come again, for the Second Coming is to be a highly visible event: "For just as the lightning comes from the east, and flashes even to the west, so shall the coming of the Son of Man be" (Matthew 24:27).
    Some verses to share include:
    a. Galatians 1:8 — contrary gospel.
    b. Romans 16:17 — contrary teachings.
    c. I Corinthians 3:11 — foundation in Christ.
3. Blood of Jesus.
    Verses to share include:
    a. Romans 5:8, 9 — justified by His blood.
    b. Romans 5:17 — free gift.
    c. Hebrews 9:22 — no forgiveness without shed blood.
    d. Hebrews 10:19 — holy place entered by His blood.
    e. Colossians 1:20 — peace through His blood.
    f. Ephesians 2:13 — brought near by blood of Christ.
    g. I Peter 1:18-20 — bought by blood of Christ.

II. Sharing the Four Spiritual Laws

When specifically sharing the Four Spiritual Laws with a Moonite, expect him to agree at least on the first two laws. After that he will begin to question you. If he feigns disinterest, don't be dismayed, be loving. Following is a sample of the kind of opposition you may encounter through the last two laws.

| Christian: | "Jesus Christ is God's only provision for man's sin." |
| Moonite: | "Jesus was a perfect man but as such He is not the only provision for man's sin." |

This reply refers to Moon's intercessory work in "completing" Jesus' unfinished task by providing physical salvation through Blood Cleansing or "the blessing." Show the Moonite that the Bible points to only one mediator between God and man, Jesus Christ. (See I Timothy 2:5.) He must also be made aware of the totality of Christ's atonement and of its finality. (See Hebrews 10:12-14.)

| Moonite: | "Jesus failed in His mission; that's why a third Adam is needed." |

This doctrine of the Adams means that Adam, Christ and Sun Moon are all would-be effectors of man's physical salvation; all are the hopeful progenitors of God's kingdom of perfect men. Sun Moon is considered the greatest of the three since he has come to fill in where the other two Adams failed. This concept is surprisingly similar to Hinduism's belief in recurring *avatars.*

The response shows an inaccurate view of Jesus. Point out Scripture that shows His unique deity. The Moonites will have trouble with the fact that Christ was a man, yet God Himself. (They believe He was only divine in the sense that all men potentially are.) Take them through such verses as Isaiah 9:6 where the Son is called the "Mighty God" and "Eternal Father." Share with them Paul's statement that "God was manifest in the flesh" (I Timothy 3:16). See also John 1:18.

Explain that Christ experienced such human phenomena as sorrow (Matthew 26:37), hunger (Luke 4:2) and weariness (John 4:6). Yet He continually charged His disciples to believe in His deity by the works which He did. (See Matthew 8:27; John 3:35.)

Point the Moonite directly to Jesus' empty tomb and explain that the resurrection, the greatest miracle that Christ performed, is also the greatest proof of His deity. In Romans 1:4, Paul speaks of God's Son, ". . . who was declared with power to be the Son of God by the resurrection from the dead, according to the Spirit of holiness, Jesus Christ our Lord."

The Moonite may balk at this and restate Moon's part in

salvation. If this is the case, then you might want to reiterate the verses concerning Christ's deity. Reason that if Christ is God, then His sacrifice is certainly sufficient atonement for man's sin. Once Christ's unique deity is established in the Moonite's mind, then you can show him that no task is too great for Him, not even the salvation of mankind. Also, if Christ is God then He is greater than anything or any one on earth, including Moon himself.

> Moonite: "Christ failed in His earthly mission by dying prematurely and not marrying the Bride mentioned in Scripture."

This response is based on a scriptural misinterpretation. Christ's Bride is the Church, not a perfect wife. Share with him such verses as II Corinthians 11:2 and Revelation 21:2 to set him straight on this issue.

> Moonite: "How do you know what the Bible really says? Only the *Divine Principle* can show us its real meaning."

If you encounter this objection, share with the Moonite that nowhere in the Bible is the usage of anything other than Scripture condoned. (See II Timothy 3:16.) Inform the Moonite that ". . . no prophecy of Scripture is a matter of one's own interpretation" (II Peter 1:20). This being the case, the truths of Scripture are not reserved only for those fortunate enough to have a *Divine Principle*, but are readily taught by the Holy Spirit to all who believe in Christ. (See John 14:26.)

III. Suggestions for Further Reading

1. William Petersen, *Those Curious New Cults* (Keats Publishing, 1975).
2. Ted Patrick, *Let Our Children Go!* (E.P. Dutton & Co., 1976).
3. J. Isamu Yamamoto, *The Moon Doctrine* (Inter-Varsity Press, 1976).

Bibliography

1. While it is difficult to pinpoint exact numbers involved in the Unification Church, this figure was verified by George Slaughter, member of the anti-Moon group, Committee Engaged in Freeing Minds.

2. "The Way of the World," Holy Spirit Association for the Unification of World Christianity, Inc., (Vol. VIII, #4, April 1976), p. 37.

3. "The Way of the World," ibid., p. 37.

4. Shin, Sa Hun, "The Criticism and Truth of the Unification Church," (Seoul University, Seoul, Korea), p. 3.

5. Patrick, Ted, Let Our Children Go! (E.P. Dutton & Co., Inc., NY, 1976), p. 259.

6. "The Register," May 30, 1976, p. 7.

7. Sudo, Ken, Unification Church 120 Day Training Manual, p. 40.

8. Sudo, Ken, ibid., pp. 40-42.

9. Sudo, Ken, ibid., pp. 40-42.

10. Sudo, Ken, ibid., p. 42.

11. Whi Kim, Young, "Divine Principle Lecture Outline and Study Guide," (Holy Spirit Association for the Unification of World Christianity, Belvedere Tarrytown, NY, May 1, 1973), pp. 7, 9.

12. Whi Kim, Young, ibid., pp. 73, 75, 76.

13. Sudo, Ken, op. cit., pp. 41, 42.

14. Oon Kim, Young, Divine Principle and Its Application (Holy Spirit Association for the Unification of World Christianity, Belvedere Tarrytown, NY, 1968), pp. 142, 143.

15. Whi Kim, Young, op. cit., p. 138.

16. Oon Kim, Young, op. cit., p. 196.

17. Oon Kim, Young, ibid., p. ix.

18. Oon Kim, Young, ibid., pp. 209, 210.

19. Oon Kim, Young, Unification Theology and Christian Thought (Golden Gate Publishing Co., NY, 1975), p. 116. See also interview of U.C. President Salonen in Albuquerque Tribune, Mar. 28, 1974, p. 6.

20. "Mad About Moon," Time, November 10, 1975, p. 44.

21. Master Speaks, March 16, 1972, p. 11.

THE
REFERENCE
SECTION

Glossary of Eastern Mystical Terms

Anatman — In Buddhism, the belief that the human being is not composed of soul or spirit, but of a changing variety of sensory impressions, thoughts, feelings and energy.

Asceticism — The view that the physical body is evil and detrimental to a holy life and that only through renunciation of the world can one reach a higher spiritual state.

Ashram — The Hindu name for a settlement of disciples living with or around a guru.

Atman — In Hinduism, the real spiritual self as distinguished from the empirical self or "false ego." According to Hare Krishna, it is that part of an individual which continues in various material forms through reincarnation until the self receives liberation. Also, spirit or world soul.

Avatar — In Hindu usage, any incarnation of the god Vishnu. General usage can refer to the descent of any god into the world in human form, usually to help mankind in a time of crisis.

Bhagavad-Gita — Sanskrit term for "Song of the Divine One." The so-called gospel of the Hindu scriptures containing dialogue between the warrior Arjuna and the god Krishna.

Bhakti or bhakti-yoga — The supposed way to salvation by loving devotion to a personal deity. Is actually a form of works salvation, in that the devotee's devotion *earns* the deity's favor.

Bodhisattva — In Buddhist terminology, one who is qualified to enter Nirvana and become a Buddha, but who prefers to remain a Buddha-to-be in order to work for the salvation and deification of beings on earth.

Bon' no soku bodai — Nichiren Shoshu concept where worldly desires equal enlightenment.

Brahma — The creator-god in Hindu thought. A member of the triad of Hindu gods along with Shiva and Vishnu.

Brahman — The Absolute; impersonal essence of the universe in Vedanta Hinduism.

Brahmin — Any member of the priestly caste of the Hindu world.

Buddha — An "Awakened One." Refers usually to Siddhartha Gautama, the Indian prince who became an enlightened man and the historic founder of Buddhism.

Butsodon — The black, box-like altar containing the *gohonzon* that Nichiren Shoshu members face when chanting.

Chaitanya — A 15th century Hindu who began the worship of Krishna as the Supreme Being. Later he was recognized as an incarnation of Krishna.

Chakra — In yoga, one of the so-called "psychic centers" of the human body.

Daimoku — In Nichiren Shoshu, the act of chanting *"Nam Myoho Renge Kyo.."*

Dharma — In Hinduism and Buddhism, the path toward enlightenment or "way of righteousness" which a man must follow. Similar to the concept of "good works."

Eightfold Path — Gautama Buddha's formulation of the eight steps which lead to enlightenment. These are: 1. right viewpoint, 2. right aspiration, 3. right speech, 4. right behavior, 5. right occupation, 6. right effort, 7. right mindfulness and, 8. right meditation.

Enlightenment — In Hindu usage, personal realization of that inward soul called *atman* which is a portion of the universal essence or Brahman. Hence a realization of man's oneness with the universe and a realization of his deity. In Buddhism, a merging of the personal Buddha nature with the universal Buddha nature or universal energy.

Esho funi — In Nichiren Shoshu, the oneness of man and his environment.

Esoteric — Hidden, secret, not accessible to the uninitiated.

Gautama — Family name of the historic Buddha; also spelled Gotama.

Gohonzon — In Nichiren Shoshu, a small scroll-like paper containing a list of names of the Buddhas and *Bodhisattvas* found in a teaching called the *Lotus Sutra*.

Gongyo — In Nichiren Shoshu, selections from two chapters of the *Lotus Sutra*. Practitioners chant the *gongyo* each morning and evening while facing the *gohonzon* or altar.

Guru — A spiritual guide, one who oversees others in religious instruction. Means literally "to lead from darkness to light."

Hatha yoga — The form of yoga stressing physical conditioning. It is based on purely Hindu philosophy and is designed to lead the practitioner to an eventual practice of the philosophical and religious aspects of yoga.

Intuition — The non-rational, feeling-oriented capacity of the human mind emphasized as the key to ultimate reality in mysticism.

ISKCON — Acronym for International Society for Krishna Consciousness, the official name of the Hare Krishna movement.

Jnana yoga — The school of yoga stressing the path of knowledge to spiritual enlightenment.

Karma — Literally, one's deeds; the effects of one's deeds, good or bad, which determine the place and condition in which one is reborn, and one's rewards or punishments after death. The so-called universal law of cause and effect.

Karma yoga — The yoga path that supposedly leads to release through selfless activity or good works.

Koan — In Zen Buddhism, a term or riddle which cannot be solved by the intellect alone.

Kosen Rufu — In Nichiren Shoshu, the attainment of world peace through the spread of the movement's beliefs.

Krishna — The Supreme Being of the Hare Krishna movement. A personal deity said by ISKCON to be an even higher manifestation of god than the impersonal Brahman. Other branches of Hinduism view Krishna as just one of many gods of similar rank.

Kundalini — A form of yoga in which "serpent power," or occult powers residing at the base of the spine, are summoned to the brain through certain yoga techniques. This endows the practitioner with superhuman psychic and spiritual powers which lead to *samadhi* or enlightenment.

Lama — A Tibetan Buddhist monk or spiritual leader.

Lotus Sutra — A teaching ascribed to Sakyamuni Buddha, though actually written much later than his time. It includes the *gongyo*, book of chants and prayers, in Nichiren Shoshu liturgy.

Mahabarata — The ancient epic poem of India, including the *Bhagavad-Gita*.

Mandala — A mystical diagram used as an aid in meditation.

Mantra — A sacred word, verse or syllable which embodies in sound some specific deity or supernatural power. An aid in meditation.

Maya — "Illusion" in Hinduism, the cosmic force which produces the phenomena of material existence. All that is finite and subject to decay, all that is not eternal and unchangeable is considered maya.

Metaphysics — The study of the nature of ultimate reality.

Moksha — The Hindu term for liberation from the bondage of finite existence. The identification of oneself with the ultimate reality — eternal, changeless, blissful — or in a state of complete indifference, either with or without loss of consciousness. A state supposedly beyond good and evil, pleasure and pain.

Monism — The philosophical doctrine that there is only one ultimate reality in existence, and that all things are parts of or composed of this reality.

Mudra — The "mystic seal" of oriental occultism; a series of occult signs made with the fingers, and considered to have magical effects.

Mysticism — Any philosophy or doctrine centered more on the worlds of the spirit than the material universe and aimed at the spiritual union or mental oneness with the universal spirit through an intuitive grasp of reality.

Nam Myoho Renge Kyo — The phrase Nichiren Shoshu practitioners chant to the gohonzon. One meaning ascribed to the phrase is, "Devotion to the mystic law of cause and effect through sound."

Nichiren Daishonen — A 13th century Japanese monk, and the historic founder of Nichiren Shoshu.

Nirvana — In Buddhism, the attainment of final enlightenment and freedom from rebirth. In the oriental philosophical doctrines, the absolute and final extinction of individuality, without loss of consciousness.

Om, also spelled Aum — The most revered mantra contained within the Vedas, ancient Hindu scriptures.

Pantheism — The doctrine that reality involves a single being of which all things are modes, moments, members, appearances or projections. Pantheism teaches the essential imminence of God in all creatures and things. It identifies God with nature and nature with God, teaching that the forces and laws manifest in the universe, the entire Cosmos, the whole of reality itself, are God.

Puja — In Hinduism, the term for worship; religious service. In Transcendental Meditation, a written portion of the controversial initiation ceremony that is read in Sanskrit by the TM instructor. The writing contains a listing of the principal deities of classical Hinduism and brings worship to the Maharishi's spiritual master, Guru Dev.

Puranas — Ancient Hindu texts telling stories of gods, goddesses and mythological events; part of the folklore of Hinduism embodying also social and religious instruction.

Raja yoga — The Hindu path to God involving psychological experimentation; usually involves practicing certain mental exercises and observing the effects of these on one's spiritual condition.

Rationalism — A system or doctrine which makes reason the sole guide in the interpretation of reality.

Reincarnation — Belief in many rebirths for each soul or spirit.

Rig Veda — One of the ancient authoritative scriptures of Hinduism.

Rishi — Sanskrit word meaning "seer" or "sage."

Sakyamuni, also spelled Shakyamuni — Sanskrit for "Great Sage." A name of Gautama Buddha, founder of Buddhism.

Samadhi — Sanskrit word for "putting together." Profound meditation, absorption in the spirit. The final stage in the practice of yoga, in which the individual becomes one with the object of meditation, thus attaining a condition of superconsciousness and blissfulness, which is called moksha.

Sanskrit — The ancient unwritten language of Hinduism. Believed to have magical effects when spoken or even thought.

Satori — The Japanese Zen Buddhist term for enlightenment.

Shakubuku — In Nichiren Shoshu, the act of telling nonbelievers about the practice of "True Buddhism" as embodied in NSA. The term literally means "break and subdue," and in Japan has come to be known as forced conversions.

Shikishin funi — Nichiren Shoshu belief asserting the oneness of the physical and the spiritual. From this doctrine springs a flat denial of the existence of a Supreme Being or a spirit world.

Shiva — One of the three gods of Hinduism, commonly termed the Destroyer.

Siddha — In Hindu mystic and occultic terminology, a man who possesses supernatural powers.

Sōka Gakkai — The lay movement within Nichiren Shoshu begun by a Japanese school teacher named Makiguchi in the 1930's. Nichiren Shoshu's aggressive proselytizing techniques can be attributed to Makiguchi's zealously intolerant attitude toward other religions. Sōka Gakkai means "Value Creation Society."

Sutra — The Sanskrit word for Buddhist scriptures, meaning a discourse by the Buddha, or a disciple, accepted as authoritative teaching.

Swami — A Sanskrit word meaning spiritual teacher or learned, holy man.

Tantra — A body of esoteric Hindu religious literature said to have been revealed by the god Shiva for man's guidance. These scriptures place emphasis on the worship of the female essence of the universe. From this foundation, an erotic religion known as Tantrism has formed, featuring worship of sexual union among other practices.

Taoism — Chinese religion based on the *Tao*, an ancient writing attributed to Lao-Tse. Foremost among Taoist concepts is the yin and yang, symbolizing the convergent and divergent aspects of the universe; good and evil, male and female, etc.

Theosophy — In general, a philosophical system claiming to hold divine wisdom and the true knowledge of the existence and nature of the deity. Specifically, a society founded in 1875 by Madame Helena Blavatsky in New York City for the study of occult and esoteric religions worldwide.

Unconscious mind — A compartment of the mind which lies outside the consciousness.

Upanishad — Sanskrit for secret teaching or esoteric doctrine. The *Upanishads* form the third of the Vedas, recording the speculations of Hindu sages on such topics as the nature of ultimate reality and the way to spiritual union with the Absolute.

Vedanta — The best known and most popular formulation of Hindu mystic philosophy. The Vedanta school teaches that the phenomenal world is mere illusion and has only seeming reality, as have also the apparent individual selves of the world. Vedantists say there is but one true self, *Brahman-Atman*.

Vishnu — One of the three gods of Hinduism (Brahma, the Creator; Vishnu, the Preserver; and Shiva, the Destroyer).

Wheel of Samsara — In Hinduism and occult terminology, the wheel of suffering in life, the chain of births and rebirths.

Yin and Yang — In Chinese thought, the two primary forces of the universe. The yin symbolizes the female, passive force and the yang, the male, active essence.

Yoga — Literally, "union." The Hindu path to God, taking various forms within the eastern sects.

Yogi — Literally, one who practices yoga.

A Who's Who of Gurus and Other Mystics

Carlos Castaneda — Mexican mystic who apprenticed himself to a Yaqui Indian sorcerer named Don Juan. His books, *The Teachings of Don Juan* (1968), *A Separate Reality* (1971), *Journey to Ixtlan* (1972) and *Tales of Power* (1974), contain accounts of the occult and the demonic and have all been best sellers on university campuses throughout the West.

Sri Chinmoy — Founder of the Lighthouse Mission. Sri Chinmoy is believed to have reached the highest state of *samadhi*, enlightenment, while still only a child of 13. At the age of 32, Chinmoy left his native Bengal and came to America. His movement, centered around an almost god-like worship of himself, has grown to where it includes a few hundred American participants. In keeping with their devotion to Chinmoy, followers maintain their own family altars where they meditate before a photograph of their spiritual leader every day. Chinmoy's followers believe that by totally surrendering their minds to him, they will experience enlightenment.

Baba Ram Dass — The former Richard Alpert and Harvard University instructor. In the aftermath of his LSD experimentation and subsequent dismissal from Harvard, Alpert headed east in search of more permanent "highs." In Nepal he met a young American who had spent five years studying with a guru in that area. The American escorted Alpert to an *ashram* near the Himalayas where he met Maharaj Nimcorola. Alpert studied under Nimcorola for six months, eventually returning to the States to share his insights. His book, *Be Here Now*, purports to offer spiritual advice for modern seekers. His teachings under the acquired name, Baba Ram Dass, underscore the eastern belief in total commitment to the guru to achieve enlightenment.

Werner Erhard — Founder of est (Erhard Seminars Training). Born John Paul Rosenberg, he changed his name in 1960 after deserting his wife and four children. He joined many cult groups including Scientology and Zen, the latter's philosophy providing much of the basis for est. The cult was formed in 1971.

Bubba Free John — Formerly Franklin Jones, Bubba Free John is considered by knowledgeable students of the East to be the first American-born *siddha*, one who possesses spiritual powers. He studied under *kundalini* practitioner, Swami Muktananda, among many others, and eventually regained the "enlightenment" he claims to have lost in his youth. Free John founded the Dawn Horse Communion near San Francisco where he presides as guru over a small colony of devotees. There Free John guides them through the techniques of *kundalini* yoga and displays, at times, extreme psychic and spiritual influence over his followers. Free John openly claims to be Brahman, the impersonal absolute of Vedantist Hindu doctrine.

Guru Maharaj Ji — Born Prem Pal Singh Rawat in Hardwar, India, Maharaj Ji became the leader of his father's disciples in 1966. Four years later he dropped out of the ninth grade to spread the message of the Divine Light Mission to the world. His movement reached a peak with Millenium '73, held in the Astrodome in Houston. Despite the fanfare, fewer than 20,000 of the expected 80,000 devotees attended. Today, Maharaj Ji is no longer considered the perfect spiritual master, in keeping with the movement's new Madison Avenue approach. His new position as mere corporate executive for Divine Light grew partially out of a 1974 schism which saw his mother, Mata Ji, harshly criticize him for alleged ungodly behavior. Before her statement, Maharaj Ji was considered by devotees to be God incarnate. The guru is now trying to put together the same "secular" image that the TM organization has found so useful.

Maharishi Mahesh Yogi — Founder of Transcendental Meditation (TM). His name, Maharishi, means "great sage." Born in north central India in 1911, Mahesh studied physics at Allahabad University and graduated at the age of 31. He studied under a Hindu swami named Guru Dev in the Himalayas for 11 years, emerging in 1959 to spread his teaching to the world. His movement blossomed briefly in 1968 when such notables as the Beatles and Mia Farrow joined up. Their devotion, however, proved temporary and the Maharishi's movement died out almost overnight. Today, a revitalized version of TM enjoys phenomenal success in the West, despite impending legal action aimed at proving TM to be religious in nature. The movement has deceptively claimed to be a science. Maharishi is considered to be a fully-realized form of divinity by his inner core of disciples.

Sun Myung Moon — Founder of the Unification Church. Reverend Moon was born in Korea in January, 1920. In 1936, young Moon had a vision in which Jesus Christ supposedly appeared to him, christening him for a mission to save mankind. Nine years later he began preaching, and in 1954, Moon founded the Holy Spirit Association for the Unification of World Christianity. He came to America in 1972, establishing his new headquarters in Tarrytown, New York. He is viewed by followers as the "Second Advent Jesus," mankind's co-redeemer along with Jesus Christ.

A. C. Bhaktivedanta Prabhupada — Founder and spiritual head of the International Society for Krishna Consciousness (ISKCON), commonly known as the Hare Krishna movement. Prabhupada was born Abhay Charan De on September 1, 1896, in Calcutta, India. He studied English, philosophy and economics at the University of Calcutta but failed to graduate. He left his wife and family in 1959 to study under a guru named Goswami. In 1965, Goswami sent him westward to bring the message of Krishna to the United States. Devotees look upon Prabhupada as an incarnation of their god, Krishna.

Chogyam Trungpa — Popular exponent of Tibetan Buddhist philosophy in the West. Trungpa, like many Tibetan monks (lamas), fled to the West in the late 1950's when the Red Chinese attacked Tibet. Trungpa founded the Naropa Institute in Boulder, Colorado.

A Compendium of Eastern Cults

Ananda Marga — Founded in India by Shri Anandamurti, this group features a mixture of *kundalini* yoga and good works. Western disciples involve themselves in humanitarian services such as disaster relief and visiting the old and the sick. There are 3,000 followers of Ananda Marga in the United States. The name *Ananda Marga* means "Joy" or "Bliss Path."

Arica — A cosmic consciousness movement founded by Oscar Ichazo. The movement features instruction designed to supposedly awaken the conscious mind and believes that it alone has been entrusted with the teachings that will "save the world." The movement's philosophy draws heavily from such eastern groups as Tibetan Buddhism, yoga and Zen. The group is named after the Chilean hometown of founder Ichazo.

Association for Research and Enlightenment — Famed psychic Edgar Cayce founded this group in Virginia Beach, Virginia, in 1931. Cayce, known as the "sleeping prophet," gained fame through self-induced trances in which he would predict future events and diagnose diseases, all with a seemingly high degree of accuracy. Cayce's popular "life readings," in which he would claim to describe a person's previous lives, fueled interest in reincarnation. Cayce's trance information was consistently in conflict with Jesus' own teachings on such subjects as life after death, however. Cayce died in 1945. His son, Hugh, now presides over the movement and its 13,000 U.S. followers.

Bahai — A religion based on Islam, Bahai stresses world peace through devotion to Bahá'u'lláh, a 19th century prophet who claimed he was the Messiah. Today this religion has nearly 100,000 followers in America. Its headquarters is in Wilmette, Illinois.

Divine Light Mission — A Hindu movement, the Divine Light Mission was founded in the U.S. by the then 13-year-old Guru Maharaj Ji in 1971. Known to his disciples as "Perfect Spiritual Master," Maharaj Ji gathered a large following throughout the world, at one time numbered at well over two million. *Premies* (disciples) learn how to "receive knowledge" from the guru in an effort to discover the "divine self" within. This discovery, they believe, leads to enlightenment. Today the Divine Light Mission appears to be remodeling its movement after the highly successful Transcendental Meditation organization.

Eckankar — Based on Tibetan Buddhist philosophy, Eckankar was founded by an American named Paul Twitchell. This cult, defined as the ancient science of soul travel, teaches the monist viewpoint that the world is one essence, composed of spirit. The physical world is considered to be unreal. The way to escape the illusory physical realm is through soul travel, a technique taught only by certified Eck masters. This cult has many of the earmarks of the first-century heresy called Gnosticism, a religion that denied the existence of the physical realm. Followers of Eckankar believe that Jesus is simply an advanced Eck master.

Erhard Seminars Training (est) — Werner Erhard, formerly John Paul Rosenberg, founded est in 1971. This movement is subtly based on Zen Buddhism and features an anti-authoritarian mindset. Instructees receive teaching designed to stop the rational mind and open them to experiencing the so-called "ever present now."

Healthy, Happy, Holy Organization (3HO) — A *kundalini* yoga sect founded by yogi Bhajan. This sect is based on *sikhism*, a mixture of Hinduism and Islam, and teaches both monotheism and reincarnation. Enlightenment is achieved within this cult through the awakening of the *kundalini* or "serpent power" located at the base of the spine. Through various yoga techniques this mystic power coils its way up the spine eventually uniting with the mind to produce a state of altered consciousness or enlightenment.

International Society for Krishna Consciousness (ISKCON) — Known popularly as Hare Krishna, ISKCON is a *bhakti* yoga sect of Hinduism stressing devotion to the god Krishna. Founded in the U.S. in 1965 by Indian swami A. C. Bhaktivedanta Prabhupada, the Hare Krishna movement features an ascetic lifestyle. Devotees must chant the name of Krishna daily in attempts to defeat worldly desire and train all thought totally on Krishna. When this is achieved, the devotee is said to be enlightened. Devotees recognize Prabhupada as an incarnation of Krishna.

Meher Baba — A small eastern cult founded on devotion to a deceased Indian, Merwan Sheriar Irani, who was better known as Meher Baba, "Compassionate Father." Irani thought himself to be a divine *avatar* or savior, and he claimed to be the last and greatest of the divine incarnations. A peculiar characteristic of Meher Baba was his self-imposed silence lasting from about 1926 until his death in 1969. During this time he communicated by means of hand signals and an alphabet board.

Nichiren Shoshu — A Buddhist sect also known as Nichiren Shoshu/Sōka Gakkai, NSA devotion is directed around the *butsodon*, an altar-like box containing a small scroll called the *gohonzon*. Members chant portions of a teaching called the *Lotus Sutra* while facing the *gohonzon*. They believe such devotion will enable them to attain their personal desires and also bring them enlightenment.

Ouspensky-Gurdjieff — The product of two Russian intellectuals, P. D. Ouspensky and George Gurdjieff, this movement stresses extreme self-awareness. At local meetings practitioners indulge in discussion and Sufi-style dancing designed to awaken the disciple to true awareness. This cult has fewer than 5,000 followers in the United States.

Scientology — A western religion founded by former science fiction writer L. Ron Hubbard. Scientology blends psychotherapy, science fiction and eastern religious philosophies in a teaching which stresses that each human being is a fallen god, or *Thetan*. Through scientology's training, the neophyte works his way out of a state of forgetfulness and back to a realization of his original deity.

Self-Realization Fellowship — A Hindu group founded in 1920 by Paramahansa Yogananda, the Self-Realization Fellowship is one of the primary popularizers of Vedanta philosophy in the West. As is the case with many cult groups, its headquarters is in Los Angeles, California.

Sufism — A system of Mohammedan mysticism and Hinduism stressing bodily movement as a means toward union with God. At Sufi gatherings, devotees dance in circular motion, leading to the description "whirling dervishes" in the Middle East. This is followed by an encounter session where devotees openly interact with one another, showing no inhibitions in expressing their aroused affections for one another. The leader of the Sufis is Idries Shah, who lives in England.

Transcendental Meditation (TM) — Founded by Maharishi Mahesh Yogi, Transcendental Meditation stresses a mind-clearing philosophy based on Hinduism. Meditators concentrate on a *mantra*, which is a Sanskrit word, usually associated with a Hindu god. The *mantra* induces the practitioner into a state of relaxation. The goal of TM is for the meditator to experience "bliss consciousness," a state where normal waking consciousness is transcended and a mystical union with other mental and spiritual realms is achieved.

Unification Church — Founded in the United States by Reverend Sun Myung Moon, the Unification Church teaches that its founder is the so-called Second Advent Christ. Followers believe salvation can only come through devotion to their leader and to the Unification Church. The philosophy behind this cult is a heretical blend of Christianity and Taoism. Moon teaches that God is both male and female, good and evil, a concept common to Taoist thought.

Zen Buddhism — An anti-authoritarian religion that has as its goal a state of enlightenment known as *satori*. To experience this elusive mental state, Zen monks retire to the monastery to live under the sometimes iron-fisted authority of the Zen master. Meditation on riddles called *koans* is an aid to enlightenment.

Grateful acknowledgement is given to the Spiritual Counterfeits Project of the Berkeley Christian Coalition, Berkeley, California, for their help in providing much of the information for this section.

Summary of Key Issues and Pertinent Scripture

God is distinct from creation	Psalms 102:25-27
Man is sinful	Psalms 51:1-4
	Psalms 53:3
	Isaiah 64:6
Man is accountable to God for his actions	John 5:25-29
	Hebrews 9:27
Faith established on *fact*, not experience	John 5:36, 39, 46
The heart and head must both unite in worship	John 4:24
The mind is important	John 4:24; Isaiah 1:18;
	Acts 17:2-4
Reincarnation not true	I Peter 2:24
	Hebrews 9:27
Karma not true	John 9:1-3;
	II Corinthians 5:17
Christ is only way to God	John 14:6
Christ is the *only* mediator between God and men	I Timothy 2:5
Salvation found in no other	Acts 4: 12 ;
	I John 5:11, 12
Prophecies don't refer to "avatars"	Acts 1:9-11
Christ is permanent Savior	Hebrews 10:10-12
Christ is uniquely qualified Savior	John 3:16
	Acts 4:12
Jesus is atoning Savior	Matthew 20:28
	Hebrews 9:22
Jesus did suffer	Luke 24:26; 9:22
	Mark 8:31
Repeated prayers useless	Matthew 6:7

Biblical meditation based
  on God:
    the works of God   Psalms 77:11
    the Word of God   Psalms 119:11
    the person of God   Psalms 63:6
Kingdom of God is not within   John 3:1-8

SUPPLEMENTARY
RESEARCH SECTION

CHAPTER I
MINING THE EASTERN MIND

A. *Evidence that God is personal.*
The God of the Bible has all the attributes of personality in contrast to the impersonal god of mysticism.

1. He remembers — Isaiah 43:25, Jeremiah 31:20, Hosea 8:13.
2. He speaks — Exodus 3:12, Matthew 3:17, Luke 17:6.
3. He sees — Genesis 6:5, Exodus 2:25.
4. He knows (has mind) — II Timothy 2:19, I John 3:20.
5. He creates — Genesis 1:1.
6. He has a will — Matthew 6:10.
7. He will judge — II Corinthians 5:10.

B. *Further evidence that the eastern god is impersonal.*

According to Bahá'u'lláh, founder of the Bahá'í faith: "It is evident that God, the unknowable Essence, the divine Being, is immensely exalted beyond every human attribute, such as corporeal existence, ascent and descent, egress and regress."

Quoted from the Kitáb-iíqán (Bahá'í Publishing Trust, Wilmette, IL), p. 98.

C. *Further evidence of eastern influence in America.*

1. There is an increasing American desire for "experience."

"Sensation is king in a nation in which it seems the best antidote to pleasurelessness and deadness. How widespread is our joylessness is suggested by a number of products whose advertising appeal is, 'You only go around once in life so you have to search for all the gusto you can.' Or, 'If I have only one life, let me live it as a blond!'

"The cultural trend is toward greater and greater stimulation of appetites. Everyone wants what the other person has. Once the most distinctive form of American envy was the desire for material possessions. But now the most rapacious greed is for experience."

Quoted from Herbert Hendin, *The Age of Sensation*, (WW Norton, NY, 1975), p. 325.

2. Results of the National Religious Beliefs Survey.

Spring/Fall — 1975 — TOTALS
48 U.S. campuses — 9004 respondents
NA — No Answer

a. SEX: Male — 51.5%   Female — 44%   NA 4.5%
TOTAL — 9004

b. What is your belief about God?

I definitely don't believe in God.   7%
I'm not sure if God exists or not.   17.4%
I believe God is in everyone; we're all part of God. 33.9%
I believe God is a distinct supernatural Being, separate from man.   32.7%
Other (specify)   8%   NA 1%

Note: *More than one-third hold an eastern view of God, while less than one-third hold a theistic or Christian view and nearly one-fourth are atheistic or agnostic.*

c. Which is your view of life after death?

I don't believe that there is life after death. 14.4%
I am unsure whether or not there is.   20.5%
I definitely believe there is something beyond death, but have no idea what it is like.   25.5%
There is life after death, but no punishment.   4%
There is life after death, with rewards for some and punishment for others.   26.5%
Other (specify)   2.8%   NA 3.8%

Note: *While many students hold eastern views in other areas, very few believe in reincarnation. More than 60% either don't believe in an afterlife, are uncertain, or believe in an afterlife but don't know what it's like.*

d. What is your belief about truth?

Truth is basically relative; what is right or true for you may not be right or true for me.   50.9%

There are certain absolute truths (i.e., certain actions are right and others are wrong regardless of the circumstances; certain beliefs are ultimately and universally true and others false).   37%

Truth is unknowable and does not concern me.   2.4%

Other 1.6%   Relative/Absolute 3.3%   NA 4.7%

Note: *More than half believe truth is relative, while only about one-third believe in absolutes.*

e. What is your belief about Jesus Christ?

He is a legendary character and probably didn't exist.   2.8%

He was just a man who taught a high standard of life and ethics; a "prophet."   28%

He was a manifestation of God on the same level as Buddha, Krishna, Confucius, Mohammed, etc.   17%

He is God.   32.6%

Other 12.3%   NA 7%

Note: *While less than one-third believe Christ is God, almost half see Him as a "prophet" or "manifestation of God" (an eastern view).*

f. What kind of evidence would most strongly influence you to believe that Christ was God?

A logical, well-reasoned argument would strongly influence me.   12.6%

Historical evidence (such as evidence about His resurrection, His miracles, etc.) would strongly influence me.   22%

Personal testimony of those whose lives have been dramatically affected by Christ would significantly influence me.   13%

Christ would need to appear to me personally and demonstrate His miraculous power.   14.7%

There is no evidence that would strongly in-

fluence me to believe that Christ was God.
18.1%

Other (specify) 11%   NA 7.7%

Note: *Nearly half consider themselves open to the three traditional Christian approaches (rational argument, evidence and testimony). Less than one-fifth consider themselves totally closed to the idea that Christ is God.*

This survey was taken by Campus Crusade for Christ staff on 48 campuses in every section of the U.S. An attempt was made on each campus to obtain the broadest possible sampling of opinions.

CHAPTER II
THE BATTLE FOR THE BRAIN

A. *Further evidence of the dangers of mysticism.*

  1. The danger of mindlessness: gullibility.

  "That Edgar Cayce could diagnose the illnesses of distant patients and predict earthquakes by psychic readings ... that the pyramids were built by ancient astronauts ... that orgone boxes can trap the life energy of the universe ... one does not question these reports, but calmly letting the boundary between fact and fairy-tale blur, one uses them — uses them to stretch one's powers of amazement ... such intellectual permissiveness risks a multitude of sins not the least of which is plain gullibility."

  Quoted from Theodore Roszak, *Unfinished Animal: The Aquarian Frontier and the Evolution of Consciousness* (Harper & Row, NY, 1975), pp. 2, 3.

  2. Another example of eastern antagonism toward the mind.

  "They read the Bible and try to understand it through their minds, right? They can't understand it. Spirituality cannot be described and cannot be understood by the mind. Mind is imperfect. . . .Mind always projects what is false. Mind is a black light."

Guru Maharaj Ji, quoted from R.D. Clements, *God and the Gurus*, (Inter-Varsity Press, Downers Grove, IL, 1975), p. 24.

3. Mysticism redefines the word "logic" as well as other key words.

"A common generally implicit assumption in our society's culture is that there is one true 'logic' and that all intelligent people know what this is. Any logic (and there are many of them) is a set of *assumptions* . . . .The assumptions are to a large or total extent arbitrary. Change the assumptions and the rules for working with these assumptions and you have a different logic."

Quoted from Charles Tart, *Transpersonal Psychologies*, (Harper & Row, NY, 1975), p. 30.

4. The mystics show a lack of concern regarding spiritual deception.

"Start to tune inward to hear the inner voice which is in each of us . . . .Of course there are many inner voices and you'll be led astray many times. That's all right. If you trip and fall just get up, tune in anew and get on with it. Slowly you will come to recognize that inner voice which is free from ego desire."

Ram Dass, The Introduction to *Spiritual Community Guide*, (Spiritual Community Publications, San Rafael, CA, 1974), p. 7.

B. *The modern educational system has contributed to the popular lack of confidence in absolute truth.*

"The wisdom and truth accumulated by previous generations is not a dependable guide to correct thinking and behavior because truth changes with the changing experience of each generation and of each individual."

Charles Coulter, *A Layman's Guide to Educational Theory*.

Coulter had a Ph.D. in sociology, was the former director of Text Research and Education, Inc. and was one of the most respected educators in America until his death.

C. *Evidence for the resurrection of Christ.*

   1. Major theories that attempt to disprove the resurrection and a brief refutation of each.

      a. *The Swoon Theory:* says that Jesus never really died but only fainted on the cross, revived in the coolness of the tomb, escaped the grave and actually appeared alive to His disciples, giving the impression of a resurrection.

      REFUTATION: There are at least four major problems with this theory:

      (1) The evidence all indicated that Jesus was actually dead. Roman soldiers who were trained in the science of killing made certain He was dead by thrusting a sword in His side. (See John 19:33, 34; Mark 15:44, 45.) There was no suggestion in the first century that Jesus might not have really died. Even the enemies of Christianity knew Jesus was dead!

      (2) The cold, clammy confinement of the rock tomb would not have revived the weakened Jesus but would have finished Him off!

      (3) The body of Jesus was embalmed or mummified in approximately 100 pounds of linen wrapping and spices. The idea that any man near death could have escaped that sort of cocoon is ridiculous!

      (4) Jesus' appearances: But even if we swallow the idea that Jesus somehow could have escaped the tomb, we are still left with a problem: how could a man so weak and in need of medical attention ever hope to convince his disciples that God had triumphantly raised Him from the dead? (Notice: This would mean that Jesus, knowing that He had never died, was intentionally deceiving His disciples!)

      b. *The Theft Theory:* says that the disciples stole the body. This theory was spread by the religious authorities of Christ's time. (See Matthew 28:11-15.)

      REFUTATION: The tomb was (and is) empty. Who removed the body? The choices are:

(1) *The disciples*: How could they have overpowered the Roman guard? (See Matthew 27:64-66.) If the guard was asleep (unlikely), it would have been awakened as the disciples attempted to roll away the huge stone. The fact is, however, that the cowardly disciples, who all fled three days earlier at the time of His crucifixion, would hardly have risked their lives simply to recover His dead body!

(2) *The Roman or Jewish authorities*: It was to their advantage for the body to remain in the grave, since they knew that Jesus had predicted His resurrection. (See Matthew 27:63.) If they *had* taken the body, they certainly would have produced it when the disciples began to proclaim the resurrection.

(3) *God Himself*: God removed the body by raising Jesus from the dead. This is the most rational alternative.

c. *The Hallucination Theory*: All of Christ's appearances after His death were hallucinations caused by overworked imaginations.

REFUTATION: Again, this view presents many problems:

(1) Two people almost never have an identical hallucination at the same time. And yet Jesus was repeatedly seen by groups. (See Matthew 28:9; Luke 24:37; John 20:20; John 21:12; Mark 16:14; etc.) At one point He appeared to more than 500 people at once. (See I Corinthians 15:6.)

(2) Normally, only people who are "high-strung," highly imaginative and very nervous would be expected to experience hallucinations. But Jesus appeared to people of widely varying personality types and temperaments (the cowardly Peter, the loving and courageous women, practical fishermen, the trained physician Luke, the skeptic Thomas, etc.).

(3) It is sometimes argued that Jesus' followers wanted so badly for their Lord to be alive that

they began to imagine they had seen Him. But, in reality, most of the followers not only were not *expecting* Jesus to rise from the dead, but did not believe it when they were first told! (See Luke 24:10-11; 22-25; Mark 16:12-13; Matthew 28:17; John 20:9; etc.) The classic example is Thomas, who, when told that Jesus was raised, said, "Unless I put my finger in the nailprint and stick my hand into His side, I won't believe!" It is hard to imagine that this first century rationalist was later the victim of an hallucination!

(4) Hallucinations tend to continue repeatedly over long periods of time. If they end, it is not abruptly, but, rather, they gradually fade away. In contrast, the appearance of Jesus came to an abrupt halt with His Ascension only 40 days later. None of the 500 witnesses ever reported a reoccurrence!

d. *The Wrong Tomb Theory*: The women (and everyone else) went to the wrong tomb: This theory, loosely based on Mark 16:5, 6, says that the women who first reported the resurrection went to an empty tomb by mistake, and when a white-robed gardener tried to redirect them, the women thought he was an angel telling them that Christ had risen.

REFUTATION: But this theory, too, is full of holes:

(1) If the whole story of the resurrection had started only because some women couldn't find the right tomb, the Jewish authorities could (and would) have put a stop to the whole ridiculous story by pointing out the *right* tomb with Jesus' body in it. They certainly knew where it was since they had sent a Roman guard to make it secure!

(2) But even if we say that the women, the disciples, the Jews and the Roman guard went to the wrong tomb, there is still one person who would have corrected them, Joseph of Arimathea. He certainly knew where the tomb was since it was *his* tomb! (See Matthew 27:57-61.) Notice that the two women were actually present when Jesus was buried.

(3) This whole theory rests on an acceptance of the basic events recorded in Mark 16:6. But if we accept one part as true, why not accept the whole account? And if we say some parts are not true, then how do we know the event happened at all? It is terrible scholarship to accept one part of a document and reject another, unless there is a good reason to do so (for example, another independent account or document). The "Wrong Tomb Theory" chooses to ignore the clear statements of the young man: "You are looking for Jesus the Nazarene, who has been crucified. He has risen" (Mark 16:6), and "But go, tell His disciples and Peter, 'He is going before you into Galilee; there you will see Him, just as He said to you' " (Mark 16:7). These are hardly the words of a gardener trying to redirect confused women!

e. Conclusion: The only reasonable explanation for the empty tomb is that God supernaturally raised Christ from the dead. As Simon Greenleaf put it:

"There is enough admissible testimonial evidence to prove in any court of law in the United States or Britain that Jesus Christ arose from the dead."
Simon Greenleaf, *The Testimony of the Evangelists* (Baker Book House, Grand Rapids, MI, 1965).

Professor Greenleaf was a former dean of Harvard Law School and one of the outstanding legal experts in America.

For a more complete study of this topic, see Josh McDowell's excellent treatment in *Evidence That Demands a Verdict*, pp. 185-273.

D. *Evidence that the events of Jesus' life were predicted in the Old Testament.*

1. Commonly raised objections:

a. The Old Testament "prophecies" were written at or after the time of Christ, and therefore are false.
Answer: Though some scholars would argue that the Old Testament was completed later than the date commonly assigned to it (450 B.C.), we do know that

a Greek translation of it (called the Septuagint) was finished during the reign of Ptolemy Philadelpheus (285-246 B.C.). Therefore, the Hebrew Old Testament must have been completed *before* 250 B.C. So we can be certain that *all* of the prophecies were written *at least* 250 years before Christ.

b. Christ knew the prophecies and consciously worked to fulfill them. *Answer*: There are many prophecies concerning Christ which no man (unless He were God) could influence (the events surrounding His birth, His parents flight to Egypt, His betrayal, the soldiers gambling for His clothes, the piercing of His side, etc.).

2. Some examples of prophecies fulfilled by Christ:

a. Messiah would be born of a virgin:
Isaiah 7:14 (Fulfillment: Matthew 1:18, 24, 25; Luke 1:26-35) *Note*: Some argue that the Hebrew word for virgin (almah) could mean merely "a young woman." *Answer*: When the Jewish translators wrote the Septuagint (250 B.C.), they used the word "parthenos" for virgin. This word can *only mean a pure virgin. Obviously these Hebrew scholars felt that Isaiah 7:14 referred to a woman who had not known a man.*

b. The actual date when Messiah would be killed:
Daniel 9:25, 26 says that there will be 69 weeks (of years) from the decree to rebuild Jerusalem until Messiah is cut off. It also says this will happen before Jerusalem is destroyed. From Nehemiah 2:1-8 we know that the decree was issued in 445 B.C. Now 483 years later (by the Jewish calendar) would be about 32 A.D.! In any case, Messiah had to be killed before 70 A.D., and the destruction of the Temple. (See *Evidence That Demands a Verdict*, pp. 176-181.)

c. Messiah's lineage: He would be born of the tribe of Judah (Genesis 49:10; Micah 5:2), the family line of Jesse (Isaiah 11:1, 10) and the house of David (Jeremiah 23:5; II Samuel 7:12-16; Psalms 132:11). Jesus was all of these (Luke 3:23, 31-33).

d. Messiah was to be born in Bethlehem: Micah 5:2

(Fulfillment: Matthew 2:1). Note that the Jewish scribes of Jesus' time were well aware that this prophecy referred to Messiah (Matthew 2:6).

e. Messiah's ministry would begin in Galilee: Isaiah 9:1 (Fulfillment: Matthew 4:12, 13-17).

f. He would enter Jerusalem on a donkey but in a kingly procession: Zechariah 9:9 (Fulfillment: Luke 19:35-37).

g. Betrayal by a friend: Psalms 41:9; Psalms 55:12-14 (Fulfillment: Matthew 10:4).

h. Forsaken by His disciples: Zechariah 13:7 (Fulfillment: Mark 14:50).

i. Hands and feet pierced: Psalms 22:16; Zechariah 12:10 (Fulfillment: Luke 23:33; John 20:25).

j. Garments parted and lots cast: Psalms 22:18 (Fulfillment: John 19:23, 24).

k. Buried in rich man's tomb: Isaiah 53:9 (Fulfillment: Matthew 27:57-60).

Note: For a complete treatment of the Messianic prophecies, see Evidence That Demands a Verdict, pp. 147-183.

E. *Evidence of the biblical view of man's mind.*

1. Man was made in the "image" and "likeness" of God (Genesis 1:26, 27). That likeness includes our rational faculty. Isaiah 1:18: " 'Come now, and let us reason together,' says the Lord" is one of many examples of the infinite supra-rational God condoning rationality.

2. Man's rationality separates him from the animals. Psalms 32:9 says, "Do not be as the horse or mule which have no understanding." The Christian disagrees with the mechanistic rationalist who sees man as just another animal with a slightly larger brain. God crowned man with a special faculty: rational "understanding."

3. Man's mind has been affected by the Fall. Ephesians 4:17, 18 describes the unregenerate mind as "futile" and "darkened" in its understanding. The same adjectives "futile" and "darkened" are used in Romans 1:21 to describe the reasoning processes of the natural man apart from Christ. Here's where the Christians part

company forever with the rationalists. The effects of the Fall have "darkened man's mind." Reason unaided by God's Spirit is no longer able to arrive at the truth. What is needed is for man to be "renewed in the spirit of (his) mind" (Ephesians 4:23). Does this mean it's useless to present rational evidence to the non-Christian? No.

4. Christians can still appeal to man's mind. It has been affected by the Fall, but it's not totally useless. In Luke 12:56, 57, Jesus appeals to the unbelieving multitudes to look at the "signs" (fulfilled prophecies) and to "judge what is right." Paul, in Acts 17:2-4, "reasoned" with the unbelieving Jews, "explaining and giving evidence" with the result that some were "persuaded." And of course the incarnation — the act of God revealing Himself in a human body within the time-space universe — is an example of God offering physical "evidence" for man to rationally analyze.

F. *The proper balance between intellect and intuition.*

"To speak more directly, and without metaphor, of the true relationship between intuition and intellect, intuition is the creative advance toward reality. Intellect needs, first, to perform the valuable and necessary function of interpreting, i.e., of translating, verbalizing in acceptable mental terms, the results of the intuition; second, to check its validity; and third, to coordinate and to include it into the body of already accepted knowledge. These functions are the rightful activity of the intellect, without its trying to assume functions which are not its province. A really fine and harmonious interplay between the two can work perfectly in successive rhythm: intuitional insight, interpretation, further insight and its interpretation, and so on."

Italian psychiatrist Roberto Assagioli, *Psychosynthesis,* (Viking Press, NY, 1971), pp. 217-224, quoted in Robert Ornstein, *The Psychology of Consciousness* (Viking Press, NY, 1972), p. 69.

CHAPTER III
DIAGNOSING THE DISEASE

A. *Further evidence of self-effort in mysticism.*

"If you want to know the past (cause),
Look at your present life (effect). If
you want to know the future (effect),
look at your present (cause)."

—Buddha

"We ourselves are responsible for our own happiness and misery. We create our own heavens. We create our own hells. We are the architects of our fate."

—Narada Mahathera

Quoted from Philip Kapleau, *The Wheel of Death* (Harper & Row, NY, 1971), p. 17.

B. *Further evidence that man is God in eastern religion.*

"God entranced himself and forgot the way back so that now he feels himself to be man, playing — guiltily — at being god."

Alan Watts, *Beyond Theology: The Art of Godmanship.* (Meridian Books, NY, 1967), p. 68, quoted in Os Guinness, *The East, No Exit* (Inter-Varsity Press, Downers Grove, IL, 1974), p. 34.

C. *Evidence of the amorality of the mystic view.*

  1. Another example of the eastern view of good and evil being the same thing.

    Q. "Are God and Satan the same thing?"

    A. "God is in Satan also. God is everywhere. You know, what is God? God is this holy Word; 'In the beginning was the Word and the Word was with God and the Word was God.' That is the Word, that is God . . . and this Word exists everywhere, in you, in every human being."

    Q. "How does suffering exist, do you know?"

    A. "Evil is nothing. Evil is the ignorance of our mind."

Guru Maharaj Ji, quoted from R.D. Clements, *God and the Gurus* (Inter-Varsity Press, Downers Grove, IL, 1975), p. 23.

2. Vedantic de-emphasis of sin problem.

   Vedantists say that "... if we think of ourselves as sinners and miserable, we forget the Godhead within us and lapse into that mood of doubt, despondence and weakness which is the greatest obstacle of all."

   From the booklet "Vedanta in America " (Vedanta Society of Southern California.)

3. Note the parallel between the mystic view of morality and that expressed in this passage from Dostoevsky's *The Possessed*.

   "Kirilov argues with Stavrogin. 'Everything is good.'

   "'Everything?'

   "'Everything. Man is unhappy because he doesn't know he's happy. That's the only reason. The man who discovers that will become happy that very minute. That stepdaughter will die, the little girl will remain, and everything is good. I suddenly discovered that.'

   "'So it's good, too, that people die of hunger and also that someone may abuse or rape that little girl?'

   "'It's good. And if someone breaks open that man's skull for the girl, that's good, too. And if someone doesn't break his skull it's equally good. Everything's good.' "

   Fyodor Dostoevsky, *The Possessed*, p. 224, quoted in Os Guinness, *The East, No Exit* (Inter-Varsity Press, Downers Grove, IL, 1974), p. 41.

4. "Every idea of 'guilt' or 'sin' had to be surmounted on the way to the life of a guru. Since all expressions of the life force were equally holy, all beings and things were 'members of a single mystic family.' "

   "Karma is the master law of the universe but there is no lawgiver."

   Quoted from Nancy Ross, *Three Ways of Asian Wisdom* (Simon & Schuster, NY, 1966), p. 59.

D. *Evidence of self-deception in eastern cults.*

Quote from former Zen enthusiast and eastern mystic Allen Ginsberg:

"I feel as if I am at a dead end and so I am finished . . . . I never escape the feeling of being closed in and the sordidness of self, the futility of all that I have seen and done and said."

Quoted from William Petersen, *Those Curious New Cults*, p. 270.

E. *Evidence of the social impact of the gospel in modern India.*

"But its (Christianity's) greatest impact was made during the modern period. Christian missionary influence has left a permanent mark on the development of literature in all the major vernacular languages of India. It has been responsible for a new orientation in thought and a new spirit in religion. *Every significant movement for social reform in Hinduism in recent times has received an impetus in some measure from the Christian religion.* Evidence of this motivation is found in the lives of the great modern Hindu reformers such as Ram Mohan Roy, Keshab Chandra Sen, Dayananda, Ramakrishna, Vivekenanda, and Gandhi. Sometimes the reforms were carried through in imitation, open or concealed, but often they were forced upon the Hindus by the unfavorable light in which their own social and religious concepts and practices stood in contrast to the Christian ideal."

Quoted from Benjamin Walker, *The Hindu World; An Encyclopedic Survey of Hinduism* Vol. I (Frederick A. Praeger, Inc., NY), p. 241.

Note: This position is agreed upon by the well-known oriental scholar William Jones and eastern scholar Dr. R. G. Bhandarkar, and others.

CHAPTER IV
JESUS: GOD OR GURU?

A. *Further explanation of the source of* The Aquarian Gospel of Jesus the Christ.

"It required many years for Levi to learn the Law of Differentiation, and to come in rapport with the tones and rhythms of Jesus of Nazareth, Enoch and Melchizedec and their co-laborers. But under the direction of the Spirit of Supreme Intelligence, he has attained unto this accomplishment, and now he instantly feels in all his being the slightest vibrations that come from any of these great centres, and of course, all of his transcriptions are true to the letter."

Levi Dowling, *The Aquarian Gospel of Jesus the Christ* (De Vorss Press, 1969), p. 17.

B. *Hindu doctrine of the* avatar.

"The Hindu doctrine of the *Avatars* or saviors of mankind developed relatively late in the history of eastern religion. The theory appeared during the empire of Kanishka, an Indian ruler from about 120 A.D. to 162, who converted to Buddhism. Its justification is found in the *Bhagavad-Gita*, a late scripture of the first century which teaches new doctrines of devotion and love for a personal God. In this scripture, the Lord Krishna says 'in every age I come back to deliver the holy, to destroy the sins of the sinner, and to establish righteousness.' "

Jerry Exel, "The Search for a Genuine Guru," *Right On*, November, 1972, p. 7 (Berkeley Christian Coalition, Berkeley, CA 94704).

C. *Buddhist doctrine of the* Bodhisattva.

"The idea of the *Avatars* was adopted by a new school of Buddhism which arose during the first century A.D., called the Mahayana. In Mahayana the *Avatar* became the *Bodhisattva*, the exalted being who has reached Buddhahood but who refuses to enter Nirvana in order to devote himself to saving mankind. 'I shall become a savior to all those beings, I shall release them from all their sufferings!' says the *Bodhisattva* in Buddhist scripture. 'I take upon myself the burden of all suffering . . . . All beings I must set free. The whole world of living things I must rescue, from the terrors of birth, of old age, of sickness, of death and rebirth . . . . And why? Because it is surely better that I alone should be in pain than that all these things should fall into the states of woe. Therefore I must give myself away as a pawn through which the whole world is redeemed.' "

Right On, ibid.

D. Avatar *idea borrowed from Christianity*.

   1. Evidence that Krishna stories were copied from New Testament gospels.

   "Some scholars believe that, except for the name, the Krishna cycle of stories has borrowed extensively from Christian sources especially in relation to the birth, childhood and divinity of Jesus Christ. The great orientalist, Sir William Jones, held that the spurious Gospels which abounded in the first years of Christianity found their way to India and were known to the Hindus. According to others, Krishna's victory over Kaliya is a travestied version of Christ's victory over Satan, the Serpent. The German writer, Weber, held that Krishnaism was indebted to Christianity on the grounds that the worship of Krishna as the sole deity was a post-Christian phase in Hinduism, and the legend of his birth and the celebration of his birthdays, the honor paid to his mother Devaki, and his life as a herdsman, all showed Christian influence.

   "It is further contended that incidents like the visit of Nanda, foster-father of Krishna, with his pregnant wife Yasodi to Mathura to pay taxes; the birth of Krishna in a shepherd's hut; the adoration of Akura (like that of Simeon); the persecution of Kamsa; the massacre of the innocents; the flight into Braj (like the flight into Egypt); and the various miracle stories; the anointing of Krishna's body with ointment provided by the maiden Kubja are actually taken from Christianity. Summing up the data Hopkins says, 'Considering how late are these Krishna legends in India there can be no doubt that the Hindus borrowed the tales, but not the name.'

"The scholar Lassen held that certain brahmins became acquainted with Christianity in some country to the north of India and returned to India with selected Christian doctrines.

"The final step is taken by Dr. Lorinser. From the premise that there were several Christian communities in India at least in the third century A.D., and there was also an Indian translation of the New Testament, a fact of which we have positive proof in the writings of St. Chrysostom, he arrives at the conclusion that the author of the *Bhagavad-Gita* knew and was inspired by the Gospels and the Christian fathers. He produces parallel passages from the *Gita* and the Gospels to support his statement. Though parts of the *Gita* were written before the third century, a large portion of it was added after that date and some authorities believe that the work received its finishing touches at the hands of Sankara, the ninth century Hindu philosopher.

"Inconclusive as all these separate theories may appear to be, the cumulative proof as it has been adduced by the experts in their respective fields leaves little room for doubt that Christian influence on Hinduism during the early and medieval period was both deep and wide spread. The parallels between certain aspects of the two religions, as close and exact at times, cannot be dismissed as coincidence."

Benjamin Walker, *The Hindu World; An Encyclopedic Survey of Hinduism* Vol. I (Frederick A. Praeger Inc., NY), pp. 240, 241.

2. *Avatar* concept ultimately incompatible with traditional eastern thought.

"The ideal of the *avatar* or *Bodhisattva* seems to be modeled after the Christian proclamation . . . and it is most likely because the Eastern ideal grew out of Christian influence. What makes this plausible is that interaction between East and West was great during the Roman Empire. St. Thomas himself is said to have established a Christian church in southern India in 52 A.D., which still exists as possibly the world's oldest living Christian tradition. What makes it probable is that the doctrine of the Savior, so suddenly introduced, is basically incompatible with Indian metaphysics. For example, one Vedantist writes that 'God himself assumes personal form for the welfare of his devotees.' But how much sense does it make to say that God assumes personal form for the salvation of his devotees when God is his devotees? Is it meaningful to say that God can come as the Savior of the world? Does he have compassion on himself? For according to the oriental metaphysics, the very creation of the world is an infinite impersonal god assuming personal form. But if this Infinite Being must assume personal form to save the world from the illusion of finite personality we might wonder why It created a personal finite world in the first place."

Right On, op. cit., p. 7.

E. *Eckankar's view of Jesus.*

"According to the gospels, Jesus said, 'Come, follow me.' But few knew what He was saying, that He wanted them to go with Him into the worlds beyond. They were not prepared to take the journey, so He turned away from them, leaving an eternal message: 'In my Father's house are many mansions . . . I go to prepare a place for you . . . I will come again, and receive you unto myself.' This means He is always prepared to help us ascend to the heavenly world where dwells the Father of All Things."

Paul Twitchell, *Eckankar the Key to Secret Worlds*, p. 12.

F. *Jews' understanding of Christ's claims.*

"If Jesus had spoken as he did to Indians and not Jews, everyone would have smiled, tossed him some flowers or a garland and passed on down the street. His claims to deity would not have been unique. . . . But Jesus spoke deliberately and plainly to the Jews, the one nation on earth which was historically and theologically predisposed to reject categorically any idea of God becoming incarnate in human flesh. There was no misunderstanding. In fact the Jews understood so well that their reply was the logic of crucifixion. Jesus was no misunderstood *Mahatma* nor an *avatar* unaware."

Os Guinness, *The East, No Exit* (Inter-Varsity Press, Downers Grove, IL, 1974), p. 50.

G. *Incompatibility of Christianity and other systems of truth.*

Even mystic Alan Watts finally admitted this while still remaining critical of Christianity's "narrowness."

"Any attempt to marry the Vedanta to Christianity must take full account of the fact that Christianity is a contentious faith which requires an all-or-nothing commitment .... My previous discussions did not take proper account of that whole aspect of Christianity which is uncompromising, ornery, militant, rigorous, imperious, and invincibly self-righteous."

Alan Watts, *Beyond Theology*, p. XII, quoted in Os Guinness, *The East, No Exit* (Inter-Varsity Press, Downers Grove, IL, 1974), p. 51.

CHAPTER V
REINCARNATION AND OTHER QUESTIONS

A. *Evidence of the reincarnationist's low view of Jesus Christ.*

1. His role.

"Christ is not a man! Jesus was the man! Christ was the messenger! ... Christ in all ages! Jesus is only one!"

Edgar Cayce, quoted in Noel Langley, *Edgar Cayce on Reincarnation* (Castle Books, NY, 1967), p. 157.

"Jesus was simply the first perfected entity rather than the perfect man. The 'Christ Spirit' which is that part of God first created (it may perhaps be thought of as a first emanation from God with souls being a second order of emanation), spoke through Jesus but was not identical with him .... Jesus became the Christ in that the Christ Spirit became perfectly manifested in him."

Quoted in Phillip Swihart, *Reincarnation, Edgar Cayce and the Bible,* (Inter-Varsity Press, Downers Grove, IL., 1975), p. 18.

"In summary, according to the Cayce readings, the Bible is neither accurate nor authoritative. Jesus was only one manifestation of Christ; there were many others. Jesus Christ was not God incarnate but an entity as are you and I."   Quoted from Swihart, p. 19.

2. De-emphasis of the crucifixion.

"Surely Christ's logical purpose in submitting to the crucifixion was to show His followers not only the ease with which earthly ties of flesh can be discarded, but the total unimportance of the body after it ceases to house the soul."

Quoted from Noel Langley, *Edgar Cayce on Reincarnation* (Castle Books, NY, 1967), p. 158. Taken from Swihart, p. 35.

B. *"High" view of man.*

"For almost 20 centuries the moral sense of the Western World has been blunted by a theology which teaches the vicarious atonement of sin through Christ, the Son of God....All men and women are the sons of God ....Christ's giving of his life ... is no unique event in history....To build these two statements, therefore — that Christ was the Son of God and that he died for man's salvation — into a dogma, and then to make salvation depend upon believing that dogma, has been the great psychological crime because it places responsibility for redemption on something external to the self; it makes salvation dependent on belief in the divinity of another person rather than on self-transformation through belief in one's own intrinsic divinity."

Gina Cerminara, reincarnationist and Cayce devotee, quoted in William Petersen, *Those Curious New Cults* (Keats Publishing, New Canaan, CT, 1973), pp. 43, 44. Also quoted in Swihart, pp. 27, 28.

C. *Reincarnation rooted in a view of God without holiness and justice.*

1. Salvation.

" 'We would have to believe that Christ was demanding of His followers an almost superhuman exercise in blind faith,' one Cayce writer states. 'He was offering a hit-or-miss, one-chance-only hope of survival . . . . Only if we sin no more may we enter heaven. Is it so easy to conceive of Him as such an impractical perfectionist?' "

Noel Langley, *Edgar Cayce on Reincarnation*, p. 155 (Castle Books, NY, 1967). Quoted in Swihart, p. 28.

2. Judgment.

"God can neither denounce, sit in judgment, condemn, mete out punishment, be cajoled by lip-service, nor award special dispensations to a favored few."

Edgar Cayce, quoted in Langley, *Edgar Cayce on Reincarnation*, p. 125. Also quoted in Swihart, p. 31.

CHAPTER VI
TRANSCENDENTAL MEDITATION

A. *Scientific evidence against TM and TM "testing."*

1. TM makes no discernible change in personality.

"The degree to which people who stay in TM derive benefits from its practice appears to remain an open question. TM had no discernible effect in changing self-image over the year's test period for those people who continued in the Stanford Research Institute experiment."

Dr. Leon Otis of Stanford Research Institute, quoted in John White, *Everything You Want to Know About TM* (Pocket Books, NY, 1976), p. 54.

2. TM is dangerous for those with psychological problems.

"It would seem that those with insufficient controls to prevent the release of *massive uncontrollable anxiety* represent a potentially high-risk population for training in TM . . . without close supervision."

Ibid., p. 55.

3. SIMS misuses test data to promote TM.

"In Boston at the 1972 Biofeedback Research Society

some of his data in a booklet of charts showing the results of various TM research programs. . . .The chart based on Dr. Otis' data showed that the longer people meditate, the more likely they are to give up drugs. This is true. However, SIMS *didn't* report that Dr. Otis had found that the data on discontinuation of drug use came from a group of people *predisposed to stop in the first place. . . .*"

Ibid., p. 56.

4. TM benefits have nothing to do with the TM *mantra.*

Dr. Jonathan Smith of the psychology department of Roosevelt University in Chicago compared the results after six months between three supervised groups: Group I practiced TM, Group II simply sat with eyes closed for 20 minutes twice daily, and Group III, the "anti-meditation group," sat daily with eyes closed "actively generating as many positive thoughts as possible."

All seemed to be *equally* effective in reducing tension. TM held no edge at all. Why did they all work? Dr. Smith's conclusion:

"I propose (that) the critical aspects may be (1) expectation of relief, and (2) a daily regimen of sitting with eyes closed."

Ibid., p. 56.

5. Some TM "tests" are merely "solicited testimonials."

"One group of TM studies that (Dr. Smith) feels are virtually meaningless was done by mailing out questionnaires. The studies consistently yielded results favorable to meditation. However, Dr. Smith notes: "The major weakness of these studies is that they relied on data resembling solicited testimonials. A meditator asked to participate in a study investigating the beneficial effects of meditation might view this as an opportunity to 'step forth for meditation . . . . ' We cannot conclude from such studies that the practice of (transcendental) meditation is therapeutic."

Ibid., p. 59.

6. Randomly comparing meditators with non-meditators is invalid.

"Studies that compare changes experienced by meditators and non-meditators are faulted because the two populations may not be comparable." In other words, there may be other factors that motivated the meditators to change, other than TM. There are at least six studies of TM that use this approach, and Dr. Smith discredits all of them.

Ibid., p. 59.

B. *Further evidence that TM/SCI is a religion.*

1. The testimony of secular authorities.

a. John White, author.

John White has written an objective, secular analysis of TM. Here are his insights on the religious question:

"Thus you can hear them insisting, as I did on a radio show recently, that TM is not a religion and that it requires you to believe nothing.

"In reality, however, the rich variety of Hindu and Vedantic tradition plays an important part in TM. Maharishi's entire cosmology, with its levels of consciousness and theistic summit, are part of a belief system that you must tentatively accept if you are to operate within the TM framework."

John White, *Everything You Want To Know About TM* — (Pocket Books, NY, 1976), p. 69.

b. T. George Harris, Editor-in-Chief, *Psychology Today.*

"All the Eastern exercises grew out of religious roots, and all are designed to evoke specific religious experiences. The word *yoga* literally means yoked with God. Though TM salesmen deny that their technique has any religious meaning, all TMers go through an ancient Hindu ritual. It is, I'm convinced, more than window dressing."

Psychology Today, December 1975, quoted in John E. Patton, *Religion Maharishi Style: The Camouflage Technique*, 1976, p. 52, 53.

2. The initiation ceremony and the employment contract.

   a. Overview of the initiation ceremony.

   "After a series of preliminary orientation sessions, a prospective candidate for Maharishi's system of transcendental deep meditation was required to undergo and participate in a religious initiation ceremony which was conducted by the teacher or initiator around an altar bearing a picture of Guru Dev. The central focus of the initiation ceremony was the chanting by the teacher of a hymn of praise, adoration, worship and sacrifice, popularly referred to as the *Puja*. Twenty-six times the phrase 'I bow down' is intoned in the *Puja* to the various Hindu deities including by name *Brahma, Vishnu, Shiva, Krishna, Shankara* and Guru Dev. Four times the name 'Lord' is invoked. In the *Puja*, spiritual tribute is paid to the Hindu sacred scriptures including by name *Shrutis, Smritis, Puranas* and *Brahma Sutras*. Finally, the *Puja* refers to traditional Hindu sacrificial offerings including by name a seat, cloth, sandal paste, rice, flour, incense, light, water, fruit, betel leaf and coconut."

   John E. Patton, *Religion Maharishi Style: The Camouflage Technique*, 1976, p. 26.

   b. Complete English translation of initiatory *puja* invocation.

   Invocation.

   Whether pure or impure, whether purity or impurity is permeating everywhere, whoever opens himself to the expanded vision of unbounded awareness gains inner and outer purity.

   Invocation.

   To LORD NARAYANA, to lotus-born BRAHMA the Creator, to VASHISHTHA, to SHAKTI and his son PARASHAR,

   To VYASA, to SHUKADEVA, to the great GAUDAPADA, to GOVINDA, ruler among the yogis, to his disciple,

   SHRI SHANKARACHARYA, to his disciples PADMA PADA and HASTA MALAKA,

And TROTAKACHARYA and VARTIKA-KARA, to others, to the tradition of our Masters, I bow down. To the abode of the wisdom of the SHRUTIS, SMRITIS and PURANAS, to the abode of kindness to the personified glory of the LORD, to SHANKARA, emancipator of the world, I bow down. To SHANKARACHARYA the redeemer, hailed as KRISHNA and BADARAYANA, to the commentator of the BRAHMA SUTRAS, I bow down.

To the glory of the Lord I bow down again and again, at whose door the whole galaxy of gods pray for perfection day and night.

Adorned with immeasurable glory, preceptor of the whole world, having bowed down to Him we gain fulfillment.

Skilled in dispelling the cloud of ignorance of the people, the gentle emancipator, BRAHMANANDA SARASVATI, the supreme teacher, full of brilliance, Him I bring to my awareness.

Offering the invocation to the lotus feet
  of SHRI GURU DEV, I bow down.
Offering a seat to the lotus feet
  of SHRI GURU DEV, I bow down.
Offering an ablution to the lotus feet
  of SHRI GURU DEV, I bow down.
Offering cloth to the lotus feet
  of SHRI GURU DEV, I bow down.
Offering sandalpaste to the lotus feet
  of SHRI GURU DEV, I bow down.
Offering full rice to the lotus feet
  of SHRI GURU DEV, I bow down.
Offering a flower to the lotus feet
  of SHRI GURU DEV, I bow down.
Offering incense to the lotus feet
  of SHRI GURU DEV, I bow down.
Offering light to the lotus feet
  of SHRI GURU DEV, I bow down.
Offering water to the lotus feet
  of SHRI GURU DEV, I bow down.
Offering fruit to the lotus feet
  of SHRI GURU DEV, I bow down.

Offering water to the lotus feet
  of SHRI GURU DEV, I bow down.
Offering a betel leaf to the lotus feet
  of SHRI GURU DEV, I bow down.
Offering a coconut to the lotus feet
  of SHRI GURU DEV, I bow down.
Offering camphor light.

White as camphor, kindness incarnate, the essence
of creation garlanded with BRAHMAN,
ever dwelling in the lotus of my heart, the creative
impulse of cosmic life, to That, in the form of GURU
DEV, I bow down.
Offering light to the lotus feet of SHRI GURU DEV, I
bow down.
Offering water to the lotus feet of SHRI GURU DEV,
I bow down.

Offering a handful of flowers.

GURU in the glory of BRAHMA, GURU in the glory
of VISHNU, GURU in the glory of the great LORD
SHIVA, GURU in the glory of the personified tran-
scendental fulness of BRAHMAN, to Him, to SHRI
GURU DEV adorned with glory, I bow down.
The Unbounded, like the endless canopy of the sky,
the omnipresent in all creation, by whom the sign of
That has been revealed, to Him, to SHRI GURU
DEV, I bow down.
GURU DEV, SHRI BRAHMANANDA, bliss of the
Absolute, transcendental joy, the Self-Sufficient, the
embodiment of pure knowledge which is beyond
and above the universe like the sky, the aim of
"Thou art That" and other such expressions which
unfold eternal truth, the One, the Eternal, the Pure,
the Immoveable, the Witness of all intellects, whose
status transcends thought, the Transcendent along
with the three gunas, the true preceptor, to SHRI
GURU DEV, I bow down.
The blinding darkness of ignorance has been
removed by applying the balm of knowledge. The
eye of knowledge has been opened by Him and
therefore, to Him, to SHRI GURU DEV, I bow down.
Offering a handful of flowers to the lotus feet of

SHRI GURU DEV, I bow down.

Note: This translation is from a secret uncopyrighted TM handbook called *The Holy Tradition*, p. 5. It is given only to those who qualify to teach and be initiators for TM training. The initiates hear the *puja* only in Sanskrit and are not told its meaning even if they ask!

c. A prominent scholar explains the idolatrous meaning of the *puja*.

"Worship of a deity in the form of an image by means of *Puja* is a direct expression of popular theistic religion. At its most basic level, its meaning is summed up in Krishna's statement to Arjuna in the *Gita*: 'He who offers me with devotion a leaf, a flower, a fruit or water, that devout offering of a pure minded one I accept....' The image in *Puja* is treated as one would treat the god himself in person, for the image is the god in person: It is his *murti*, his 'form' made manifest for his worshippers. This sense of the deity as a person and the image as his representative form is fundamental to the meaning of *Puja* and is always preserved in *Puja* rituals."

Thomas J. Hopkins, *The Hindu Religious Tradition* (Dickenson Publishing Co., 1971), pp. 110-112.

d. TM teachers employment contract.

"Every teacher (initiator) who performed the *Puja* ceremony was personally trained by Maharishi himself and before being permitted to teach transcendental meditation was required to sign a form employment contract which was also executed by Maharishi. The concluding paragraph of this employment between Maharishi and his initiators is set forth below:

'It is my fortune, Guru Dev, that I have been accepted to serve the Holy Tradition and spread the light of God to all those who need it. It is my joy to undertake the responsibility of representing the Holy Tradition in all its purity as it has been given to me by Maharishi and I promise on your altar, Guru Dev, that with all my heart and mind I will always work within the framework of the Organizations founded by Maharishi. And to you, Maharishi, I promise that as a Meditation Guide I will be faithful in all ways to the trust that you have placed in me.' "

Patton, op. cit., p. 26.

3. The meaning of the *mantra.*

  a. Number and description.

  The following information is on file in the case of *Malnak vs. Maharishi,* civil action no. 76-341 in New Jersey Federal District Court:

  (1) There are a total of only 16 *mantras.*

  (2) Former TM teacher Greg Randolph has supplied the following complete list of *mantras.* Preceding each *mantra* is the age category of the initiate for which the *mantra* applies.

AGE	MANTRA	AGE	MANTRA
0-11	Eng	26-29	Shirim
12-13	Em	30-34	Shiring
14-15	Enga	35-39	Kirim
16-17	Ema	40-44	Kiring
18-19	Ieng	45-49	Hrim
20-21	Iem	50-54	Hring
22-23	Ienga	55-59	Sham
24-25	Iema	60 up	Shama

  b. *Mantras* represent Hindu deities.

  All of the *mantras* so far identified have traditionally been used to symbolize specific Hindu deities.

  This information comes from a recognized authority in the field, Sir John Woodroffe, in his *The Garland of Letters* (Ganesh and Co., Madras, India, 4th ed., 1963), pp. 4-7 of Chapter XXVI.

  (See also the testimony of Richard Scott below, 3.e.)

  c. The purpose of *mantras.*

  "A *mantra* is not a mere formula or a magic spell or a prayer; it is an embodiment in sound of a particular deity. It is the deity itself. And so, when a *mantra* is repeated a hundred times, or a thousand times, or even more, and the worshiper makes an effort to identify himself with the worshiped, the power of the deity comes to his help. Human power is thus supplemented by divine power."

From essays by Hindu scholars in "The Religion of the Hindus" (edited by K. Morgan), in essay by D. S. Sharma, "The Nature and History of Hinduism," p. 24.

d. Selection of mantras.

According to information obtained through the Spiritual Counterfeits Project of the Berkeley Christian Coalition, mantras are not "individually matched with an initiate's personality." They are picked simply according to the initiate's age. The mantras are given out according to age, with one mantra for all children under 12.

Compare these facts with the following claim by Maharishi:

Maharishi deceptively claims there are thousands of individually suited mantras.

"But one thing is important to know, and that is that there are thousands of mantras and all have their specific values, specific qualities and are suitable for specific types of people.

"We know that each man is a different individual. . . . Similarly, each man has his own type of energy impulses which constitute his personality. Therefore, if the qualities of the energy impulses created by the sound of the mantra rightly correspond to the energy impulses of the man, only then will it be of real value. Any wrong choice of the mantra is sure to create unbalance in the harmony of the man's life."

Maharishi Mahesh Yogi, Meditations of Maharishi Mahesh Yogi (Bantam Books, Inc., New York, NY, 1968), pp. 185, 186.

e. On file in the civil action referred to above in 3.a are 98 pages of testimony from Richard D. Scott, a TM teacher for four years, who initiated more than 400 people into the practice of TM. He also was instrumental in setting up the early scientific experiments at the Institute of Living in Hartford, Connecticut, and worked closely with Dr. Bernard Glueck testing the effects of TM on psychiatric patients.

When Scott was first initiated in 1968, he was given the *mantra Aaing*. (*Aaing* is a variant spelling of *mantra* #5, *Ieng*. In Sanskrit the emphasis is on the sound of the word, and not the spelling.) He was told at that time that it was a "meaningless sound," an explanation which he (more or less) accepted until the spring of 1971. At that time he helped to teach a weekend residence course for meditators in Litchfield, Connecticut. The following are excerpts from Scott's testimony:

"Another one of the teachers residing in Litchfield had in his possession a book, entitled *Tantra Asana*. Late one evening during the course I was in my room glancing through the book and discovered on the first few pages of the book a dedication. The dedication was to someone named *Aaing*, and the description of this particular individual was very similar to descriptions of a god or a Creator. The remarkable thing about this was that this name happened to be one in the same as my own personal *mantra*, which I had received in April of 1968 and which I had been told at the time was a meaningless sound.

"I didn't really give it all that much thought at the time because I knew, or, at least, had a strong inkling, that my *mantra* and others were not meaningless sounds. At that time, keep in mind, I was a teacher of TM and had completed the teacher training course as given by Maharishi Mahesh Yogi. However, I did find it of interest to see written confirmation in the form of this dedication that my *mantra* was not a meaningless sound but was, indeed, apparently, the name of a deity in the Hindu tradition" (pp. 48, 49).

In June of that same year, Scott attended a one-month residence course at Amherst, Massachusetts.

"Near the end of the course I had been meditating for approximately three years, and, if you remember, I had received my second technique, which was advanced technique, while at Estes Park in Colorado. I was eligible for my third technique and made an appointment to receive it from Maharishi himself.

"On the day of my appointment I went to Maharishi's quarters with fruit, flowers and handkerchief, answered some questions from one of the Maharishi's aides, was told to perform a *puja* by myself in a corner of the room, and then was ushered into Maharishi's suite.

"I knelt down by the side of his bed. He was sitting cross-legged on the middle of a double bed. He bowed his head over close to mine and said, 'What is your *mantra*?' I told him, '*Aaing*.' I also mentioned that I had received night technique from him at Estes Park.

He then said — he asked me a few questions about my experiences with meditation and then said, 'Your *mantra* will now be *aaing namah*.'

"This came as a surprise, for although I knew that my third technique would probably involve an additional sound or word to my *mantra*, *it was interesting to actually receive and to discover that this additional word also had a meaning.*

"Remember that prior to this course I had seen the book *Tantra Asana* and had discovered that *aaing* seemed to have a meaning, and now having learned the word *namah* to mean 'I bow down,' which is used . . . approximately 26 times in the course of the *puja*, it was not difficult to realize that my *mantra* now was a devotional phrase which meant, *Aaing*, whoever he was, I bow down to you.

"At that point I said, 'Maharishi, this is very interesting. It seems that my *mantra* does have a meaning.' I told him about the book *Tantra Asana* and pointed out that *namah* was from the *puja* and meant 'I bow down,' and he said — actually, he didn't say, he acted as if he didn't quite understand my question, indicated he was in a hurry, that there were many people in back of me waiting to come in and see him, and I never really received an answer to that question" (pp. 49, 51).

In the summer of 1972 Scott attended an SCI course in Canada, at which time he received his "fourth technique" from Maharishi.

"At that time I received my fourth technique, which was an additional word in front of *aaing namah*, and this word was *shri*, which also was found in the *puja* and is translated as 'oh, most beautiful.' So at this point in my own personal experience in meditation my *mantra* could be translated as 'oh, most beautiful *Aaing*, I bow down to you.' To my way of thinking, it would be difficult to misconstrue this as anything other than religious and of a devotional nature. . . . From this point on I began to develop increasing doubts as to the integrity of Maharishi's movement" (pp. 80, 81).

"I would like to just point out that the foregoing is to serve the purpose of simply bringing out two issues . . .

1. That the *mantras* do have a meaning and that that meaning is of a religious nature; and,

2. That the *puja* is also a highly religious ceremony and not, as publicly stated by the movement, a secular offering of thanks.

"I base this statement upon my own personal experience totaling some nine months of actual contact, personal contact, with Maharishi Mahesh Yogi and four years of in-the-field experience teaching the technique" (pp. 82, 83).

Quoted in *Spiritual Counterfeits Newsletter*, August, 1976.

C. *Further dangers of TM.*

1. The danger of the demonic.

The TM experience closely parallels the mediumistic state.

"A further possible explanation of the TM experience remains. Roy alluded to it previously. When anyone opens his mind to whatever influence comes along, he must realize that Satan may offer a deceptively pleasurable "religious" experience.

"The purposes of spiritualists at seances is remarkably similar to those of meditators. Raphael Gasson, a former medium, explains that in a student's first sessions he learns 'to relax his body and to keep his mind on one thing until he has reached a state of what could be regarded as self-hypnosis and passivity, which results in his not thinking for himself. He becomes an automaton through which evil spirits work by taking advantage of his passivity.' "

Gordon R. Lewis, *What Everyone Should Know About Transcendental Meditation* (Regal Books Division, G/L Publications, Glendale, CA, 1975), pp. 66-67, who quotes from *The Challenging Counterfeit* by Raphael Gasson (Logos Books, NJ, 1966), p. 83.

2. The danger of "pantheistic programming."

The TM *mantra* affects you by "vibrations."

"More than the content of the thought is at work in TM, for thoughts are said to have vibrations. Thinking is considered to be a subtle form of speech, and thought a subtle form of sound. Since the ultimate Reality is beyond thought, it is reasoned, the clue to transcendence may be the vibrations rather than the content."

Ibid., p. 52.

"The influence of a spoken word that is carried by the waves of vibrations in the atmosphere does not depend upon the meaning of the word. It lies in the quality of the vibrations that are set forth . . . ."

Ibid., p. 52. Quote taken from Maharishi Mahesh Yogi, *Transcendental Meditation* (Original title: *The Science of Being and Art of Living*) (New American Library, NY, 1968), p. 51.

D. *Further evidence of deception within TM.*

1. Maharishi encourages keeping the truth from the "unenlightened."

". . . If the enlightened man wants to bless one who is ignorant, he should meet him on the level of his ignorance and try to lift him up from there by giving him the key to transcending, so that he may gain bliss-consciousness and experience the Reality of life. He should not tell him about the level of the realized, because it would only confuse him."

John E. Patton, *Religion Maharishi Style: The Camouflage Technique*, 1976, p. 29. Quote taken from *Commentary on the Bhagavad-Gita*, p. 224 by Maharishi Mahesh Yogi.

2. Opportunism motivates TM's non-religious image.

". . . Here comes a process which attracts the modern man because, not in the name of God-Realization can we call a man to meditate in the world of today, but in the name of enjoying the world better, sleeping well at night, being wide awake during the day. If something makes the practical life of man better from day to day, then everyone is for it. This is the technique being adopted for the spiritual regeneration of the world and this is just suitable for these times."

Maharishi Mahesh Yogi, *Meditations of Maharishi Yogi* (Bantam Books, Inc., New York, 1968), pp. 168, 169.

E. *Maharishi's view of those who refuse to meditate.*

"There has not been, and there will not be, a place for the unfit. The fit will lead, and if the unfit are not coming along, there is no place for them. In the place where light dominates, there is no place for darkness; in the Age of Enlightenment, there is no place for ignorant people."

Maharishi Mahesh Yogi, *In a Generation of the Age of Enlightenment*, p. 47.

F. *Miscellaneous.*

1. TM creates a lack of compassion.

"The answer to every problem is that there is no problem. Let a man perceive this truth and then he is without problems."

Maharishi Mahesh Yogi, *Maharishi Mahesh Yogi on the Bhagavad-Gita* (Penguin Books, 1969), p. 66.

2. In India every "science" has a spiritual purpose.

Thus, when Indians like Maharishi Mahesh Yogi use

the word "science," they mean something entirely different by it. The following quote is from one of the most respected Hindu leaders in India, the Sankara-charya of Kanchi Kamakoti Peetam:

"Indian Science, far from being opposed to religion, had a spiritual origin and a religious orientation. *It is significant that every science in India is called a Sastra — a system of thought with a spiritual purpose.* In our temples, for instance, all sciences and arts are pressed into the service of religion. Architecture, music, dance, mathematics, astronomy, all have a spiritual and religious significance."

Quoted in Arthur Koestler, *The Lotus and the Robot* (Harper & Row, NY, 1960), p. 59.

CHAPTER VII
HARE KRISHNA: A GOD IN SAFFRON

A. *Further evidence of the Hare Krishna's view of Jesus.*

"Jesus is a pure *devotee*, or a *shakti-vaish* avatar (a living entity like ourselves who was empowered by Krishna to teach and descend to earth). He is not God. He was sent from a planetary system that had pure devotees who had compassion for earthlings. Jesus spoke a limited set of religious principles that were appropriate for the limited intellects of the people at that time. The complete set of principles is given in the *Bhagavad-Gita*. One who sincerely desires to be a true follower of Jesus will read the *Bhagavad-Gita* and follow Krishna. Jesus said to believe in Him. To believe is to follow his teachings. Both Krishna and Jesus taught God's teachings, therefore, to follow Krishna is to follow Jesus."

Interview with George Levinton (also known as "Guna Grahita Das") President of San Diego chapter, ISKCON.

B. *Further evidence of Hare Krishnas' extreme lifestyle.*

1. *White body markings.* For sanctification and protection, "tilaka" (a paste made with water and a special clay flown in from India) is applied every morning after a cold shower to 13 different spots on the body while at the same time saying the 13 different names of Krishna. The tilaka is applied in the shape of a "V," the

sign of those who worship Vishnu, one of the gods in the Hindu "Brahma-Siva-Vishnu" trinity. Since Vishnu is believed by devotees to be an "expansion" of Krishna, the sign is Krishna's sign also. It is applied to the forehead, belly, chest, throat, between the collarbones, both arms, both sides of the waist, the upper and lower back and the top of the head.

2. Four regulative principles:

No gambling, sports, conversations not associated with Krishna.

No alcohol, drugs, tobacco, tea, coffee.

No meat, fish or eggs.

No illicit sex (which includes most sex within marriage — see below).

3. Sex Life:

Sex for married devotees only at time of the full moon by permission of spiritual master for having a child only. Pleasure is forbidden, and in order to escape it, the husband must prepare his mind by reciting the Hare Krishna chant 5,000 times, and perform the act while listening to a tape of the 77-year-old stroke victim founder, A.C. Bhaktivedanta Prabhupada, chanting. Emotions, hand holding, kissing by married couples is discouraged in order to avoid sense gratification.

4. Daily Schedule:

3 a.m.	rise, shower, tilaka
4 a.m.	worship idols
5 a.m.	japa chanting
7:30 a.m.	chores, meals, solicit
12:30 p.m.	return for lunch
1-5 p.m.	to the streets, solicit
4 p.m.	idol worshipping in temple
5 p.m.	shower
9 p.m.	bed

— Adapted from J. Stillson Judah, *Hare Krishna and the Counter Culture.*

C. *Evidence of Hare Krishna deception.*

1. According to the founder of Hare Krishna in America: "Refusal to give to charity is lamentable." — Quoted from A.C. Bhaktivedanta Prabhupada, "Teaching of Lord Chaitanya," 1968, p. 23.

In San Diego last year, devotees collected more than a quarter of a million dollars under the guise of helping suffering and starving people around the world, including India.

According to the *San Diego Union Newspaper*, less than 3% of the collected funds were sent to India. The rest went for local expenses and books.
San Diego Union, November 14, 15, 1975, p. B-1.

In an interview, the local Hare Krishna president, George Levinton said, "Starvation is an illusionary concept!"

2. Founder Prabhupada has also written: "Philanthropists who build educational institutions, hospitals and churches are 'wasting their time' when they could be building Krishna temples instead."

"If anyone is charitably disposed, it will be very good for him to give in charity *only* to Krishna."
Quoted from A.C. Bhaktivedanta Prabhupada, "Krishna," Vol. 3, 1970, pp. 189.

3. In contradiction to their universal practice of collecting money from anyone who will give it, Prabhupada says, "As far as material necessities are concerned ... a devotee should never approach a materialistic person for any kind of help."
Quoted from "Teaching of Lord Chaitanya," 1968, p. 127.

D. *Evidence of Hare Krishna view of women.*
 1. Says founder Prabhupada:
 "A man's life is better than a woman's" (p. 7).
 "What to speak of persons who are less intelligent persons like woman, the laborer class and the birds and the beasts" (p. 144).
 "Engage whatever money and women you have in your possession in the service of Krishna" (p. 249).
 Quoted from A.C. Bhaktivedanta Prabhupada, "Krishna," Vol. 3, 1970.

 2. According to *San Francisco Magazine*, Hare Krishnas believe that the natural state for a woman is servant to man. Also that women are robbing men of semen

which is meant to go to the brain to nourish intelligence, to assist the Krishna devotee in answering all questions.

San Francisco Magazine, November 1975, p. 102.

E. *Evidence of Hare Krishna's attitude toward devotee's parents and family.*

   1. Founder Prabhupada says:

   "When a person realizes the effect of association with the Supreme Lord, he naturally hates the association of so-called society, friendship and love" (p. 219).

   "If I (Krishna) especially favor a devotee and especially wish to care for him, the first thing I do is take away his riches. When the devotee becomes a penniless pauper or is put into a comparatively poverty-stricken position, his relatives and family members no longer take interest in him, and in most cases give up their connection with him. The devotee then becomes doubly unhappy .... This arrangement is made by Krishna to make the devotee dependent upon him" (p. 203).

   "There cannot be any happiness within this material world" (p. 29).

   "Take it from me that a person who considers his family and relatives as his own is an ass" (p. 102).

   Quoted from "Krishna" Vol. 3, 1970.

   2. What are the practical results of this "anti-family" attitude?

   a. A.C. Bhaktivedanta Prabhupada himself renounced and left his wife and five children to bring the movement to America.

   b. A Los Angeles man is suing ISKCON for $7.6 million on charges they beat him and took his 12-year-old son.

   Los Angeles Times, November 21, 1975.

F. *Evidence of Hare Krishna's intolerance of other faiths.*

   1. "Abandon all varieties of religions and just surrender unto me."

   Krishna quoted in the *Bhagavad-Gita As It Is*, Chapter 18, Text 66, p. 835.

Chapter VIII
NICHIREN SHOSHU/SŌKA GAKKAI

A. *Evidence of NSA's low view of Christ.*

"If Sakyamuni, Christ and Marx should meet Nichiren," Toda once proclaimed, "they would surely bow and beg for instruction."

Quoted from *New Yorker*, November 26, 1966, p. 154.

B. *Evidence of NSA's appeal to selfish motivation.*

1. ". . . It may be that the strongest pull of the new religions lies in their assertion that, one way or another, temporal benefits are bound to accrue to the believer, whatever rewards the afterlife may also bring. Another, perhaps corollary, attraction is that the new religions rule out sin as an inherent part of man's nature."

   Quoted from *New Yorker*, November 26, 1966, p. 149.

2. "In NSA's unorthodox theology 'happiness' is not defined in terms of the hereafter but the here-and-now. 'The most important thing about it,' enthuses Tom Warner, a one-time fundamentalist preacher, 'is that I've now almost doubled my salary. I have two cars. And I chanted for a house on top of a hill and got that too.' Housewife Joyce Montes who lives near NSA's national headquarter's building in Santa Monica, California,' candidly acknowledges that one thing she definitely was not seeking when she took up chanting was spiritual enlightenment. 'I wanted money to buy food,' she says. 'I wanted my husband to find work and I wanted my son to be healthy.' All three wishes, she says, were promptly granted."

   Quoted from "Happy Talk," *Newsweek*, June 5, 1972, p. 68.

3. The following is an excerpt from an NSA glossary:

   "Bon' No Soku Bodai — Worldly desires equal enlightenment. This means that as we pursue our desires based on the practices of Buddhism, we accumulate fortune and acquire wisdom that ultimately will lead to our enlightenment. This is diametrically opposed to traditional beliefs that the only way to find truth is

through self-denial."
Quoted from NSA Quarterly, Summer 1976, p. 143.

C. *Evidence of NSA's extreme tactics and view of other beliefs.*
(Note: Nichiren Shoshu/Sōka Gakkai is the correct full name of this sect. It means, "True Teaching, Value Creation.")

1. William P. Woodward of Tokyo's International Institute for the study of Religions comments: "Sōka Gakkai does not respect the rights of others. It threatens reprisals to all who oppose it. Followers are obliged to engage in forced conversions, and in doing so, they force themselves into private homes and refuse to leave when asked. They disrupt public meetings and threaten nonbelievers. Leaders encourage violence.

   "Sōka Gakkai has developed in such a sinister manner," Woodward contends, "that most people in positions of public responsibility are afraid to take objective stands against it. They are literally afraid; they never know what form reprisal will take. Its insidious nature makes it a definite threat to a free, democratic society. It creates a kind of private terrorism, something akin to prewar rightist activities here or McCarthyism in the States."
   Quoted from LOOK, September 10, 1963, p. 24.

2. "The Toda-Nichiren doctrine calls for the marriage of church (Sōka Gakkai) and state, a ferocious intolerance of any other teaching and destruction of all other religions as false, baseless or obsolete."
   Quoted from LOOK, September 10, 1963, p. 21.

3. "At a rehearsal for the Japanese adaptation of Bertolt Brecht's The Threepenny Opera, in Tokyo's dimly lit Haiyuza Theater, actress Tetsuko Kobayashi said, 'Yes, Christianity is dominant in the world today, and there will be "discrimination" and "cold war" as long as people believe in this false religion. In order to gain world peace, people everywhere must be taught to believe in Sōka Gakkai.'"
   Quoted from LOOK, September 10, 1963, p. 18.

D. *Evidence that NSA is not "True Buddhism."*

   1. "Daisetz Suzuki, world-renowned Zen Buddhist scholar, told *LOOK*: 'If Sōka Gakkai's so-called True Buddhism practices intolerance and aggressiveness — and it does — it cannot be Buddhism because Buddhism is the continuous striving toward absolute love and absolute wisdom. These are its two vital features. There is no room for intolerance and aggressiveness. When Sōka Gakkai people claim theirs is the only religion with value, they contradict the basic tenets of Buddhism. Sōka Gakkai is not Buddhism at all.' " Quoted from *LOOK*, September 10, 1963, pp. 23, 24.

CHAPTER IX
SUN MOON: THE MILITANT MESSIAH

A. *Evidence of Moon's distorted view of God.*
Although Reverend Moon affirms that God is "the first cause" (The Divine Principle, p. 37), he repeatedly ascribes human attributes to God.

   1. "God and man are one. Man is incarnate God."
      Reverend Moon in *Christianity in Crisis*, p. 5.

   2. "A man who has fulfilled the purpose of creation (the establishment of the Kingdom of Heaven on Earth) becomes one body with God, possessing deity."
      Reverend Moon in *Divine Principle*, p. 176.

   3. "He (God) lost His love, His happiness, His peace and His whole creation because of the human fall."
      Reverend Moon in *New Hope*, p. 73.

   4. "And you can even pray this: 'Father, I'll be responsible to restore the world, and I can do it, believe me. You don't have to come to help me. I don't want you to come to this world of suffering to help me. You stay there and watch me.' With that kind of prayer, you can console God's heart."
      Reverend Moon in *New Hope*, p. 69.

   5. "God's heart is very sad when He looks at conditions of the world. God is crying. We're working to help the heavenly Father, to make God happy. When God feels pleasure, I feel pleasure."

Michiko Miyamura, quoted by George Cornell, AP religion writer, in *Herald Statesman*, Yonkers, NY, October 13, 1973. See also *Divine Principle*, pp. 122, 130, 132, 134, 147, 630, etc.

B. *Evidence of Moon's distorted view of Jesus and His work on the cross.*

Reverend Moon not only categorically and repeatedly denies the divinity of Jesus, but he goes so far as to say that Jesus Christ was possessed ("invaded") by Satan! The death of Jesus on the cross, says Moon, was not the Will of God or of Jesus. Moon denies any redemptive value for sin through Jesus' death on the cross.

1. "Jesus is the man of this value. However great his value may be, he cannot assume any value greater than that of a man . . . ."
Reverend Moon in *Divine Principle*, p. 255.

2. "It is plain that Jesus is not God Himself."
Reverend Moon in *Divine Principle*, p. 258.

3. "But after his crucifixion, Christianity made Jesus into God. This is why a gap between God and man has never been bridged. Jesus is a man in whom God is incarnate. But he is not God Himself."
Reverend Moon in *Christianity in Crisis*, pp. 12, 13.

4. "It is equally true that the cross has been unable to establish the Kingdom of Heaven on Earth by removing our original sin."
Reverend Moon in *Divine Principle*, p. 178.

5. "We, therefore, must realize that Jesus did not come to die on the cross."
Reverend Moon in *Divine Principle*, p. 435.

6. "Satan thus attained what he had intended through the 4,000-year course of history, by crucifying Jesus, with the exercise of his maximum power."
Reverend Moon in *Divine Principle*, p. 435.

7. ". . . The physical body of Jesus was invaded by Satan through the cross."
Reverend Moon in *Divine Principle*, p. 438.

C. *Evidence of Moon's claim of superior knowledge.*

1. "The New Testament was a textbook given for the

teaching of the truth to the people of 2,000 years ago, people whose spiritual and intellectual standards were then very low compared to today . . . . In consequence, today the truth must appear with higher standards . . . we call this the New Truth."
Reverend Moon in *Divine Principle*, pp. 167, 168.

2. "The words Jesus left unuttered will not forever remain a secret, but rather are supposed to be revealed some day as a New Truth through the Holy Spirit."
Reverend Moon in *Divine Principle*, p. 169.

3. "You may again want to ask me, 'With what authority do you weigh these things?' I spoke with Jesus Christ in the spirit world. And I spoke also with John the Baptist. This is my authority. If you cannot at this time determine that my words are the truth, you will surely discover that they are in the course of time. These are hidden truths presented to you as a new revelation. You have heard me speak the Bible. If you believe the Bible, you must believe what I am saying."
Reverend Moon in *Christianity in Crisis*, p. 98.

4. "We are the only people who truly understand the heart of Jesus, the anguish of Jesus, and the hope of Jesus."
Reverend Moon in *The Way of the World*, p. 20

D. *Evidence that Moon views himself as divine.*

1. "Another man must come who sheds tears not for himself but for God and his lost brother; they will be tears of hope. With the coming of that man among mankind, there can be the hope of salvation."
Reverend Moon in *New Hope*, p. 46.

2. "If the world is to be unified, someone must destroy all the problems that were caused by evil. . . .The most important thing is to find one person who has become one with God, who has a mind and a body which do not struggle with each other, centered on God. . . . Therefore, through the course of history, God designed in His providence to call one such person from among mankind."
Reverend Moon in *New Hope*, p. 60.

3. "How sad God's heart has been! If there were a single

man, who in the place of all mankind would sacrifice himself to save the world, to erase the sin of other people, desiring to be a victim for the sake of God, would God be pleased with him or not? . . . So God would be grateful to have found that kind of man, and He would ask that man to do certain things for Him."
Reverend Moon in *New Hope*, p. 60.

4. "There must be a person with a central mission as the agent of God's love, around whom all these relationships will be restored to their desired form. He must become the mediator between God and man to make that relationship a oneness between Father and son."
Reverend Moon in *New Hope*, pp. 25, 26.

5. "He (God) is living in me and I am in the incarnation of Him."
Reverend Moon in *New Hope*, p. 36.

6. "Thus He (God) is a Being to be pitied. . . .I'd tell Him not to worry about anything. I am in His place to work for Him until the last one of all humanity has been turned back to Him."
Reverend Moon in *New Hope*, p. 39.

7. "We will erect the heavenly kingdom on earth with our own hands."
Reverend Moon in *New Hope*, p. 41.

APPENDIX A

HAVE YOU HEARD
OF THE
FOUR SPIRITUAL LAWS?

Just as there are physical laws that govern the physical universe, so are there spiritual laws which govern your relationship with God.

LAW ONE

GOD **LOVES** YOU, AND OFFERS A WONDERFUL **PLAN** FOR YOUR LIFE.

(References should be read in context from the Bible wherever possible.)

God's Love

"For God so loved the world, that He gave His only begotten Son, that whoever believes in Him should not perish, but have eternal life" (John 3:16).

God's Plan

(Christ speaking) "I came that they might have life, and might have it abundantly" (that it might be full and meaningful) (John 10:10).

Why is it that most people are not experiencing the abundant life?

Because . . .

LAW TWO

MAN IS **SINFUL** and **SEPARATED** FROM GOD. THEREFORE, HE CANNOT KNOW AND EXPERIENCE GOD'S LOVE AND PLAN FOR HIS LIFE.

Man Is Sinful

"For all have sinned and fall short of the glory of God" (Romans 3:23).

Man was created to have fellowship with God; but, because of his stubborn self-will, he chose to go his own independent way and fellowship with God was broken. This self-will, characterized by an attitude of active rebellion or passive indifference, is evidence of what the Bible calls sin.

Man Is Separated

"For the wages of sin is death" (spiritual separation from God) (Romans 6:23).

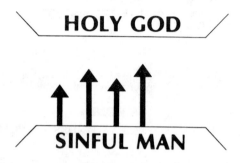

This diagram illustrates that God is holy and man is sinful. A great gulf separates the two. The arrows illustrate that man is continually trying to reach God and the abundant life through his own efforts, such as a good life, philosophy or religion.

The third law explains the only way to bridge this gulf . . .

LAW THREE

JESUS CHRIST IS GOD'S **ONLY** PROVISION FOR MAN'S SIN. THROUGH HIM YOU CAN KNOW AND EXPERIENCE GOD'S LOVE AND PLAN FOR YOUR LIFE.

He Died in Our Place

"But God demonstrates His own love toward us, in that while we were yet sinners, Christ died for us" (Romans 5:8).

He Rose from the Dead

"Christ died for our sins . . . He was buried . . . He was raised on the third day, according to the Scriptures . . . He appeared to Peter, then to the twelve. After that He appeared to more than five hundred . . ." (I Corinthians 15:3-6).

He Is the Only Way to God

"Jesus said to him, 'I am the way, and the truth, and the life; no one comes to the Father, but through Me' " (John 14:6).

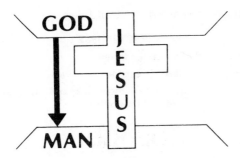

This diagram illustrates that God has bridged the gulf which separates us from God by sending His Son, Jesus Christ, to die on the cross in our place to pay the penalty for our sins.

It is not enough just to know these three laws ...

LAW FOUR

WE MUST INDIVIDUALLY **RECEIVE** JESUS CHRIST AS SAVIOR AND LORD; THEN WE CAN KNOW AND EXPERIENCE GOD'S LOVE AND PLAN FOR OUR LIVES.

We Must Receive Christ

"But as many as received Him, to them He gave the right to become children of God, even to those who believe in His name" (John 1:12).

We Receive Christ through Faith

"For by grace you have been saved through faith; and that not of yourselves, it is the gift of God; not as a result of works, that no one should boast" (Ephesians 2:8, 9).

When We Receive Christ, We Experience a New Birth

(Read John 3:1-8).

We Receive Christ by Personal Invitation

(Christ is speaking) "Behold, I stand at the door and knock; if any one hears My voice and opens the door, I will come in to him" (Revelation 3:20).

Receiving Christ involves turning from self to God (repentance) and trusting Christ to come into our lives to forgive our sins and to make us the kind of person He wants us to be. Just to agree intellectually that Jesus Christ is the Son of God and that He died on the cross for our sins is not enough. Nor is it enough to have an emotional experience. We receive Jesus Christ by faith, as an act of the will.

268

These two circles represent two kinds of lives:

SELF-DIRECTED LIFE

S—Self on the throne

†—Christ is outside the life

•—Interests are directed by self, often resulting in discord and frustration

CHRIST-DIRECTED LIFE

†—Christ is in the life

S—Self is yielding to Christ

•—Interests are directed by Christ, resulting in harmony with God's plan.

Which circle best represents your life?

Which circle would you like to have represent your life?

The following explains how you can receive Christ:

YOU CAN RECEIVE CHRIST RIGHT NOW BY FAITH THROUGH PRAYER

(Prayer is talking with God)

God knows your heart and is not so concerned with your words as He is with the attitude of your heart. The following is a suggested prayer:

"Lord Jesus, I need You. Thank You for dying on the cross for my sins. I open the door of my life and receive You as my Savior and Lord. Thank You for forgiving my sins and giving me eternal life. Make me the kind of person You want me to be."

Does this prayer express the desire of your heart?

If it does, pray this prayer right now, and Christ will come into your life, as He promised.

APPENDIX B

HAVE YOU MADE
THE WONDERFUL DISCOVERY
OF THE SPIRIT-FILLED LIFE?

EVERY DAY CAN BE AN EXCITING ADVENTURE FOR THE CHRISTIAN who knows the reality of being filled with the Holy Spirit and who lives constantly, moment by moment, under His gracious control.

The Bible tells us that there are three kinds of people:

1. NATURAL MAN
(One who has not received Christ)

"But a natural man does not accept the things of the Spirit of God; for they are foolishness to him, and he cannot understand them, because they are spiritually appraised" (I Corinthians 2:14).

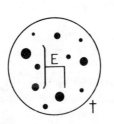

SELF-CONTROLLED LIFE

E—Ego or finite self on the throne

†—Christ outside the life

•—Interests controlled by self, often resulting in discord and frustration

2. SPIRITUAL MAN

(One who is controlled and enpowered by the Holy Spirit)

"But he who is spiritual appraises all things ..." (I Corinthians 2:15).

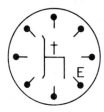

CHRIST-CONTROLLED LIFE

†—Christ on the throne of the life

E—Ego—self dethroned

•—Interests under control of infinite God, resulting in harmony with God's plan

3. CARNAL MAN

(One who has received Christ, but who lives in defeat because he trusts in his own efforts to live the Christian life)

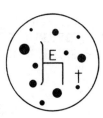

SELF-CONTROLLED LIFE

E—Ego or finite self on the throne

†—Christ dethroned

•—Interests controlled by self, often resulting in discord and frustration

"And I, brethren, could not speak to you as to spiritual men, but as to carnal men, as to babes in Christ. I gave you milk to drink, not solid food; for you were not yet able to receive it. Indeed, even now you are not yet able, for you are still carnal. For since there is jealousy and strife among you, are you not fleshly, and are you not walking like mere men?" (I Corinthians 3:1-3).

1. GOD HAS PROVIDED FOR US AN ABUNDANT AND FRUITFUL CHRISTIAN LIFE.

Jesus said, "I came that they might have life, and might have it abundantly" (John 10:10).

"I am the vine, you are the branches; he who abides in Me, and I in him, he bears much fruit; for apart from Me you can do nothing" (John 15:5).

"But the fruit of the Spirit is love, joy, peace, patience, kindness, goodness, faithfulness, gentleness, self-control; against such things there is no law" (Galatians 5:22, 23).

"But you shall receive power when the Holy Spirit has come upon you; and you shall be My witnesses both in Jerusalem, and in all Judea and Samaria, and even to the remotest part of the earth" (Acts 1:8).

THE SPIRITUAL MAN—Some personal traits which result from trusting God:

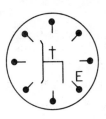

Christ-centered
Empowered by the Holy Spirit
Introduces others to Christ
Effective prayer life
Understands God's Word
Trusts God
Obeys God
Love
Joy
Peace
Patience
Kindness
Faithfulness
Goodness

The degree to which these traits are manifested in the life depends upon the extent to which the Christian trusts the Lord with every detail of his life, and upon his maturity in Christ. One who is only beginning to understand the ministry of the Holy Spirit should not be discouraged if he is not as fruitful as more mature Christians who have known and experienced this truth for a longer period.

Why is it that most Christians are not experiencing the abundant life?

2. CARNAL CHRISTIANS CANNOT EXPERIENCE THE ABUNDANT AND FRUITFUL CHRISTIAN LIFE.

The carnal man trusts in his own efforts to live the Christian life:

A. He is either uninformed about, or has forgotten, God's love, forgiveness, and power (Romans 5:8-10; Hebrews 10:1-25; I John 1; 2:1-3; II Peter 1:9; Acts 1:8).

B. He has an up-and-down spiritual experience.

C. He cannot understand himself—he wants to do what is right, but cannot.

D. He fails to draw upon the power of the Holy Spirit to live the Christian life.

(I Corinthians 3:1-3; Romans 7:15-24; 8:7; Galatians 5:16-18)

THE CARNAL MAN—Some or all of the following traits may characterize the Christian who does not fully trust God:

Ignorance of his spiritual heritage	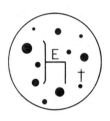	Legalistic attitude
Unbelief		Impure thoughts
Disobedience		Jealousy
Loss of love for God and for others		Guilt
Poor prayer life		Worry
No desire for Bible study		Discouragement
		Critical spirit
		Frustration
		Aimlessness

(The individual who professes to be a Christian but who continues to practice sin should realize that he may not be a Christian at all, according to I John 2:3; 3:6, 9; Ephesians 5:5).

The third truth gives us the only solution to this problem . . .

3. JESUS PROMISED THE ABUNDANT AND FRUITFUL LIFE AS THE RESULT OF BEING FILLED (CONTROLLED AND EMPOWERED) BY THE HOLY SPIRIT.

The Spirit-filled life is the Christ-controlled life by which Christ lives His life in and through us in the power of the Holy Spirit (John 15).

    A. One becomes a Christian through the ministry of the Holy Spirit, according to John 3:1-8. From the moment of spiritual birth, the Christian is indwelt by the Holy Spirit at all times (John 1:12; Colossians 2:9, 10; John 14:16, 17). **Though all Christians are indwelt by the Holy Spirit, not all Christians are filled (controlled and empowered) by the Holy Spirit.**

    B. The Holy Spirit is the source of the overflowing life (John 7:37-39).

    C. The Holy Spirit came to glorify Christ (John 16:1-15). When one is filled with the Holy Spirit, he is a true disciple of Christ.

    D. In His last command before His ascension, Christ promised the power of the Holy Spirit to enable us to be witnesses for Him (Acts 1:1-9).

How, then, can one be filled with the Holy Spirit?

4. WE ARE FILLED (CONTROLLED AND EMPOWERED) BY THE HOLY SPIRIT BY FAITH; THEN WE CAN EXPERIENCE THE ABUNDANT AND FRUITFUL LIFE WHICH CHRIST PROMISED TO EACH CHRISTIAN.

You can appropriate the filling of the Holy Spirit **right now** if you:

    A. Sincerely desire to be controlled and empowered by the Holy Spirit (Matthew 5:6; John 7:37-39).

    B. Confess your sins.

       By **faith** thank God that He **has** forgiven all of your sins—past, present, and future—because Christ died for you (Colossians 2:13-15; I John 1; 2:1-3; Hebrews 10:1-17).

    C. By **faith** claim the fullness of the Holy Spirit, according to:

    1. HIS COMMAND—Be filled with the Spirit. "And do not get drunk with wine, for that is dissipation, but be filled with the Spirit" (Ephesians 5:18).

    2. HIS PROMISE—He will always answer when we pray according to His will. "And this is the confidence which we have before Him, that, if we ask anything according to His will, He hears us. And if we know that He hears us in whatever we ask, we know that we have the requests which we have asked from Him" (I John 5:14, 15).

Faith can be expressed through prayer . . .

HOW TO PRAY IN FAITH TO BE FILLED WITH THE HOLY SPIRIT

We are filled with the Holy Spirit by **faith** alone. However, true prayer is one way of expressing your faith. The following is a suggested prayer:

"Dear Father, I need You. I acknowledge that I have been in control of my life; and that, as a result, I have sinned against You. I thank You that You have forgiven my sins through Christ's death on the cross for me. I now invite Christ to again take control of the throne of my life. Fill me with the Holy Spirit as You **commanded** me to be filled, and as You **promised** in your Word that You would do if I asked in faith. I pray this in the name of Jesus. As an expression of my faith, I now thank You for taking control of my life and for filling me with the Holy Spirit."

Does this prayer express the desire of your heart? If so, bow in prayer and trust God to fill you with the Holy Spirit **right now**.

HOW TO KNOW THAT YOU ARE FILLED (CONTROLLED AND EMPOWERED) BY THE HOLY SPIRIT

Did you ask God to fill you with the Holy Spirit? Do you know that you are now filled with the Holy Spirit? On what authority? (On the trustworthiness of God Himself and His Word: Hebrews 11:6; Romans 14:22, 23).

Do not depend upon feelings. The promise of God's Word, not our feelings, is our authority. The Christian lives by faith (trust) in the trustworthiness of God Himself and His Word. This train diagram illustrates the relationship between **fact** (God and His Word), **faith** (our trust in God and His Word), and **feeling** (the result of our faith and obedience) (John 14:21).

The train will run with or without the caboose. However, it would be futile to attempt to pull the train by the caboose. In the same way, we, as Christians, do not depend upon feelings or emotions, but we place our faith (trust) in the trustworthiness of God and the promises of His Word.

HOW TO WALK IN THE SPIRIT

Faith (trust in God and in His promises) is the only means by which a Christian can live the Spirit-controlled life. As you continue to trust Christ moment by moment:

A. Your life will demonstrate more and more of the fruit of the Spirit (Galatians 5:22, 23); and will be more and more conformed to the image of Christ (Romans 12:2; II Corinthians 3:18).

B. Your prayer life and study of God's Word will become more meaningful.

C. You will experience His power in witnessing (Acts 1:8).

D. You will be prepared for spiritual conflict against the world (I John 2:15-17); against the flesh (Galatians 5:16, 17); and against Satan (I Peter 5:7-9; Ephesians 6:10-13).

E. You will experience His power to resist temptation and sin (I Corinthians 10:13; Philippians 4:13; Ephesians 1:19-23; 6:10; II Timothy 1:7; Romans 6:1-16).

SPIRITUAL BREATHING

By faith you can continue to experience God's love and forgiveness.

If you become aware of an area of your life (an attitude or an action) that is displeasing to the Lord, even though you are walking with Him and sincerely desiring to serve Him, simply thank God that He has forgiven your sins— past, present and future—on the basis of Christ's death on the cross. Claim His love and forgiveness by faith and continue to have fellowship with Him.

If you retake the throne of your life through sin—a definite act of disobedience—breathe spiritually.

Spiritual breathing (exhaling the impure and inhaling the pure) is an exercise in faith and enables you to continue to experience God's love and forgiveness.

1. **Exhale**—confess your sin—agree with God concerning your sin and thank Him for His forgiveness of it, according to I John 1:9 and Hebrews 10:1-25. Confession involves repentance—a change in attitude and action.

2. **Inhale**—surrender the control of your life to Christ, and appropriate (receive) the fullness of the Holy Spirit by faith. Trust that He now controls and empowers you, according to the **command** of Ephesians 5:18 and the **promise** of I John 5:14, 15.